*"Thou hast formed us for Thyself*
*and our hearts are restless*
*until they find their rest in Thee."*
—AUGUSTINE

# Rest Assured

## BILL EWING
with DONNA WALLACE and TODD HILLARD

**Real Life Press**
P.O. Box 9466, Rapid City, SD 57709

www.reallifepress.com

Published by Real Life Press
P.O. Box 9466, Rapid City, SD 57709
www.reallifepress.com

Printed in the United States of America

Library of Congress Cataloging-in-Publication Data

Ewing, Bill
Rest Assured/Bill Ewing with Donna Wallace and Todd Hillard
ISBN 978-0-9747308-6-8
[Suggested data searches: include Wallace, Donna K.]

# DEDICATION

This book is dedicated to
my wife, Nancy, my lifelong partner
and companion of my heart.
*Oh, how blessed I am!*

# Contents

# ACKNOWLEDGEMENTS

What a remarkable journey this book has been! I've found that the process of writing a book is a rich and courageous one involving more people than I can count. I am deeply grateful for the team that worked together so diligently to make this happen. Since my gifts lie in speaking rather than writing, this project would have never happened without the help of others offering their gifts as a part of the body of Christ. I would like to thank all those named, as well as all those who, behind the scenes, believed in and participated in the writing of this book.

With appreciation I extend my heartfelt thanks to:

-Donna K. Wallace, my collaborator who guided me with care and kindness in writing and amazed me every time she made sense of my thoughts on paper. Thank you, Donna, for your flexibility, commitment, and meticulous attention to detail. And to your family, I express my gratitude for sharing you with me.

-Todd Hillard, my comrade in bringing the vision of this message to the page. My friend, not only have you made my stories come alive, you've reminded me of God's humor and have kept me smiling. Thank you not only for your amazing gift of writing, but also for hanging in there with me through it all. And to Mo and the kids, a special thanks for sharing you with me.

-Dale Stradinger, thanks for the artwork and creativity you added and the confidence you instilled into my life to believe this was a good project. Your selfless commitment in the home stretch of the project made this book a reality.

-Perhaps one of the most profound influences on my life and ministry, Jim Craddock. His continued faithful dedication to Abba and His Word have led me and taught me with wisdom and insight.

-To all who have had the courage to speak and write about the

Grace message so I could learn and experience this intimate walk with our Lord: SCOPE Ministries, Gillhams, Neues Laben, and many others. The Life-giving gospel goes forth!

-My board of directors who are some of my dearest friends and share incredible bits of wisdom at exactly the right moment. Thanks for believing in me and giving me the freedom to work this project into my schedule.

-My staff who deserve more than a special word of gratitude for invaluable input and for allowing me to take time away while continuing to liberate so many with these truths.

-Pat and Connie Karn who labored with us many long and late hours while putting much of this in handout form for our classes, and made the grueling process fun!

-Dave and Carol Greenhood for careful editing and contributions to the law chapters, a welcomed source of wisdom and discernment.

-To Sharon Smith, your attention to detail in the proofreads and your concern for uprightness raised the book to a higher level in all ways. Any remaining errors are ours, not your's!

-Ray, Tom, Paul, and their wives, as well as others whose loving and generous support encouraged me and made this book financially possible.

-My parents, Fuzz and Elaine Ewing, and mother-in-law, Donna Woodle, for showing Nancy and me through your love a glimpse of what our Heavenly Father's love looks like. Thank you mom, dad, and Donna for continuing to encourage me.

-My brothers, Joe and Dick, and my sisters, Marci and Mary who have supported me and shown me a clear picture of hungering after God's presence.

- My three sons: Jess, Nic, and Kyle, and my new daughters, Janie and Sherri, who have taught me about the magnitude of my Father's love for me as His child, because of the passionate love you, as my children, draw out of me.

- And especially my wife, Nancy, whose contribution to this book and my life can never be measured. Not only have you inspired me, Nanc, your godly discernment and prayer underscores all that I've said and done. Your dedication to stay beside me line-by-line through the sometimes exhausting process of producing a manuscript has been a pure and lovely gift of grace. You make coming home the highlight of my day.

- Finally, thank you Abba for your gracious Life gently leading us through this journey. Rest assured, any good that comes from these writings is for Your glory alone!

# INTRODUCTION TO A
# CHANGED LIFE

"You shall know the truth, and the truth will set you free."
—JESUS CHRIST

J ust this morning, it happened again. You would think that after a quarter of a century, I would be used to it, but it always takes me a little by surprise, particularly when it involves a friend, as it did this morning. He is a good friend, and he is also a good man. He is a devoted father, faithful husband, committed church attendee, and a successful businessman. But this morning, he came into my office at our counseling center and collapsed in a chair, holding his face in his hands. Tears welled up in his eyes as he began to tell his story.

Physically, he is exhausted, his body depleted from nights with little sleep. Mentally, his thoughts whirl like a tornado as he faces challenges that he doesn't feel he can handle. Emotionally, he is frustrated, discouraged, and depressed. He feels empty, with nothing left to give; yet the world around him continues to demand more and more. Worse yet, a cold, dense fog has set in around my friend's spirit. While the pressure around him builds and his problems become more and more vivid, God seems more and more distant, silent and uncaring. He has lost all hope, doubting that there is anything or anyone that can help.

Over the last twenty-four years I've dealt with thousands of clients in similar situations. They come from different backgrounds. Some are rich, some poor. Some are from shattered pasts and some from solid families. They come from different professions. Some are athletes, teachers, pastors, mothers, students, lawyers, and missionaries. The issues they deal with are as unique as they are. Some are struggling with relationships, some dealing with anxiety attacks. Some are bored, apathetic, and just don't care about anything anymore. Others are trying to salvage a broken marriage or save a failing business or control a rebellious teen. There is often a lingering loneliness that echoes in the chambers of a broken heart. They feel many different emotions and the intensity of their feelings varies as well. All are dealing with some degree of discouragement and confusion. More than a few are suicidal. Different as they are, pain and disillusionment are common to all.

The details vary, yes, but the story is the same. With sincere effort, they have tried to live life as best as they know how. They have tried to be who they thought they should be. They believe that what they have been doing should lead them to significance, peace, and fulfillment. But instead the road they are on has led them to disillusionment, discouragement, exhaustion, and emptiness.

Hannah Whitall Smith, a writer from the 1800s, talking with an intelligent agnostic, hears this comment, "Well, madam, all I have to say is this. If you Christians want to make us agnostics inclined to look into your religion, you must try to be more comfortable in the possession of it yourselves. The Christians I meet seem to me to be the very most uncomfortable people anywhere around. They seem to carry their religion as a man carries a headache. He does not want to get rid of his head, but at the same time it is very uncomfortable to have it. And I for one do not care to have that sort of religion."[1]

Deep down inside all of us begin asking the same questions. Does God even care? Is there any chance that things can change? Is there any way out?

I'm familiar with all these questions because I've desperately wrestled with them myself. The first season of my Christian life was filled with devotion, dedication, service, Bible study, and prayer. On the outside, I lived a model life, one that earned me self-respect and respect in my church and community. It was not to last, however. While things appeared to be going very well on the outside, my

Christian life had been built on a twisted understanding of God, an incomplete awareness of who I am, and deceptive lies about how to live life. Little did I know, a slow drain was taking place on my body and my soul. I was never designed to be giving and living the way I was. I was living in my own strength, my energy was running very, very low, and I had no gauge to tell me so. I thought I was doing great, but instead I was headed for a major breakdown. When my life came apart, it did so with a crash. I was the one with my head in my hands in the counselor's office. I was the one who was disillusioned, frustrated, and in despair. I was the one who could barely get out of bed in the morning. I was the one who was confused and depleted. I had given my all. But my all just wasn't enough. I felt I had nothing left, and I felt terribly and completely alone in what I was experiencing.

*... my Christian life had been built on a twisted understanding of God, an incomplete awareness of who I am, and lies about how to live life.*

But I wasn't alone. Most of us start with the expectation of an "abundant life" that promises so much. At first we live our lives for God with excitement and eagerness. But over time (or sometimes more rapidly through a traumatic event), our concepts about God, ourselves, and life are eroded and shaken. Some of us give up fairly soon. Some try harder and harder, hoping to find the life we think we should have. We do our best, but time after time, God doesn't seem to hold up His end of the deal. In the end, the most we can do is try to ignore the haunting, persistent longing for the fulfillment, adventure, and purpose we desire so much.

Can I ask how you are today? What is your story?

Like many people, you could be doing "okay." You could be coping, managing, and making it through the days, but finding it all rather directionless and tiring. You might be wondering if this is really as good as it gets in the Christian life.

It could very well be that you feel stuck in an unending cycle of temptation and sin. Battles with lust, desire, and addiction show up regularly. The harder you fight, the worse it seems to get. Maybe you are thinking about giving up the fight and giving in. Maybe you already have.

Perhaps you've taken some hard shots lately, or perhaps there are deep wounds still festering in your past. You know now that the Christian life isn't an insulator against hardship and pain, but you don't know what to expect from God anymore. Maybe the pain and the hardship have been more intense than that, and you've become skeptical about expecting anything good from God at all.

It is also possible that your only desire today is to help change the lives of others. Your life is going just fine and you've come to this book looking for insights that you can use to help someone else. Even if you a "fixer" and are reading only to help others, keep your heart open. You might get more than you bargained for.

Or maybe you are the "fixee." Possibly someone has given you this book to help you get your life on track. Maybe, you've ended up where my friend is and where I was. You've given the Christian life 110 percent and now there is nothing left. You can't think of a single thing you know for sure… except that you are worn out, exhausted, confused, and without hope.

Ken Gire recorded the following in his journal after writing for two years and selling nothing. "I don't know who is wrestling against me, God or Satan, but whoever it is, I surrender… I have done everything in my power to serve Him (God) in the way I feel most qualified and effective. I have depleted all my material resources, my prayers, my energies, my heart. I don't know what else I can do. I've given all I can give. And now I give up. . . He has stripped me of all my self-worth, my self-respect, and now I stand naked, impotent, and ashamed before Him… Today, someone has won a victory. I don't know if it is God or Satan—but I know who lost—me."[2]

If you were my counselor back then, or if you were trying to help my friend today, what would you suggest we do? Take a break to get rejuvenated so we can try again? Do we need to quit being so selfish and start thinking about others more? Maybe we need to read the Bible more faithfully or memorize more verses? Should we go to a good conference or the latest retreat? Perhaps we should pray or pray harder. Or maybe we should just "suck it up," keep doing what we are doing and get on with life because maybe this is just the way it is when you try to live life God's way.

But that just isn't true! I've found over and over again that while most of us think we are living our lives God's way, the vast majority of us don't realize that we are still living by deeply ingrained beliefs that aren't from God at all. These old beliefs reinforce old habits as we attempt to find what we are looking for in all the same old places using the same old strategies to reach the same old goals. When it comes down to it, most of us are pursuing life just like everyone else in the world. We have just dressed it all up with Christian words and Christian activities and Christian appearances. We are trying to build our lives on a foundation of half-truths, lies, and twisted deception. The power of this deception lies in its ability to look so right. It seems to work okay, but in the end, the very things we thought would lead us to freedom and fulfillment end up leading us into bondage and frustration.

*If we keep doing more of the same, it is likely to make things even worse.*

No, just trying harder or trying the same thing over and over will not work. How do you think we got in such a mess in the first place? If we keep doing more of the same, it is likely to make things even worse. We don't need more of the same. We don't need more church. We don't need more Bible studies. We don't need more concerts, conferences, books, or CDs. We don't need to try harder. What we do need is to begin a total transformation in the way we think, believe, and choose to act.

We need so much more than a little inspiration and a few hints to help us on our way. We need to dig down into the foundations of our lives and begin to rebuild from way below the surface. As we dig, we may need to totally destroy old beliefs (we will call them "mental maps" and "grids") we hold about God and ourselves and the way life works. I don't mean the things we say we believe, I mean the things we really believe, the beliefs that direct our decisions and our actions every moment of every day.

Somewhere in the course of our Christian lives, we need to break away from the lies that entangle us, the traditions and legalism that shackle us, and the assumptions about God that cause us to doubt Him. Our faith needs to enter an entirely new dimension, one free from the rules and constraints of the world and our past.

When we do, and begin our Christian lives again, this time on a new, fresh Biblical foundation, we will be able to survive the worst that comes our way. But even more than just survive, we will able to thrive. The Truth will set us free. Free to be who we were recreated to be. Free to do what we were recreated to do. Free to love, to really love God, and those He places around us.

As a counselor, I've seen hundreds of people set free in this way. My prayer and my passion is that in the pages that follow, your life will be set free as well, rather than simply knowing the right words, the right terms, and even memorizing all the right verses.

For without the Truth of God's Word as our primary and final authority for living, the only system to live by is a devious system of legalism that is sometimes subtle, sometimes obvious, and always oppressive. It's the system of the world and it's everywhere we look. It's in the church, in our workplace, on the TV and, yes, deep in our hearts. It turns us into people who must "do" and "try," often striving to be something we already are. But under this system we can never rest from our efforts. Left alone, it kills us, ever so slowly, robbing us of ever experiencing the supernatural grace of God.

Why are we writing this book? Because the Lord longs to be gracious to His people, and so few know it. Because Jesus' prayer before going to the cross was that we would be one with Him and the Father, and so few experience it. Because the presence of the Creator living in the creature is essential to living life, and so few live it.

And that's where I desire the words on these pages to lead us, into the supernatural grace of God, into a rest from our self-efforts and into an assurance of God's presence in our spirits. There, in that place, we can rest assured in the midst of a powerful, peaceful, and practical experience of God's promises. There we can see ourselves as we really are and taste the pure love that God offers...

the pure love that He actually is. We can get beyond words and terms and begin turning our theology into our biography. Imagine waking each morning in anticipation of a passionate, intimate, unbridled walk with God on this earth. When our doctrines become our reality, we will greet each day with the expectation of a child on his way to an amusement park, a groom on his way to the honeymoon suite, and a newly retired couple on their way to a Caribbean cruise.

It will be a process, for sure, but it is not only a process, for we will discover what He has already accomplished. It will be a journey, for certain, but it is not only a journey, for we will discover that we have already been brought into the very place we long for. A place of intimacy with God that has no earthly equal, where formulas are stripped away and traditions fall by the way. A place where we can walk and play and run with Him as children, reaching toward the future and eternity.

❈ ❈ ❈

My friend left the office today with some hope. There are still difficult days and tough decisions ahead for him, but he now knows that he need not stay in bondage to his pain and his fears. If he allows God to use this trial to do surgery on his soul, he will find that this is not the end at all. God is opening a new door to him, a door that opens into a life of true peace and real rest in the midst of this, or any storm, that comes his way. As he allows the Spirit of God and God's Word to massage his soul, he will find the assurance that God has not left him, that life is not some cruel joke, and that there is a way out of boredom, discouragement, depression, and despair.

I left our meeting this morning with hope as well. Hope for my friend and hope for you. The details of my friend's story revolved around his business. The details of my story revolved around the game of baseball. The details of your story undoubtedly revolve around other things, perhaps your marriage, your health, your job or your addictions. Your details might include painful failures or empty successes, fame or malicious rejection, but remember, the story is the same. A God who is supernaturally accepting, loving, and caring is in pursuit of a real, intimate, passionate relationship with you.

Give Him the chance and He will show you that He has more in store for you than just survival. He has a plan that even goes far beyond healing you from your past and providing for you in the present. He is opening the door to a totally new and different approach to life that has potential beyond anything you can imagine or contemplate. In that you can rest assured.

# PART I

## Let the Search Begin

"One hand full of rest is better than two
fists full of labor and striving after wind."
—Ecclesiastes 4:6

# 1

# "Make Me Seven!"

There is something about a baseball field. It's hard to put my finger on just what that something is, but as far back as I can remember, I wanted to be nowhere else. Was it the smell of fresh cut grass in the early morning? Was it was the oiled leather in my glove, or the feel of a baseball's stitching on my fingertips?

I don't know, but I can't ever recall not wanting to play baseball. It was the favorite pastime of the neighborhood, and I worked hard to be tough and to keep up with the older town kids. As early as I can remember I wanted nothing more than to play on a real team. At five and six years old I almost salivated as I watched my big brother, Dick, play with his team. How I ached to be seven so I could play "for real!"

Forever inched slowly by. It seemed like the day when I would at last be big enough to join the league would never come. Once while I was still only six, I turned to my mom sitting in the bleachers and pleaded, "Please, Mom, please, make me seven!" I figured if anyone had power over such things, she did!

*The long awaited day had finally come. A seven-year-old grinds his tiny cleat into the gravel at home plate like he's seen it done a hundred times before. He wears his miniature uniform boldly, boasting the team name in green iron-on letters across the front: "Squirts." He's up to bat for the very first time, poised with bat on his shoulder, standing tall, eyes squinting forward at the pitcher and he can't help grinning. He's not the*

3

*shy type whose parents have had to nudge him along. No, he's going to be the next Willie Mays! He's dreamed about this moment for as long as he can remember and can't wait to hit the ball over the outfield fence.*

*It doesn't exactly go over the fence, but when the little slugger's bat connects, the ball makes a straight path all the way to the pint-sized outfielder bent over picking dandelions with his mitt. Charging around the bases, he stops breathless on second. Next batter up. After a couple wild swings, the bat miraculously taps the ball and the little guy on second base now sprints as hard as his legs will carry him all the way to third. Can he do it? Can he make it home? Relishing the challenge, he believes that nothing but victory awaits him! With shoulder tucked, he makes a beeline for home plate. The catcher tries with all his might to tag the determined Squirt, but while doing so, the ball drops from his mitt. Making a dramatic slide like the big boys do, our batter is safe! Team fans clap and cheer with delight.*

It was fantastic. Better than I ever dreamed it could be. Exhilaration filled my senses. I was seven and I was alive and I was a Squirt hero. Not only did I score the first run for the Squirts that game, I also hit the first home run of the season! I was rewarded with a six pack of Squirt Soda, which came in bottles back then, and I got the whole pack all to myself. Popping off the first cap, I guzzled down the fizzy drink. Bubbles burned up my nose, but I wasn't the least bit fazed. Aaahhh! Swiping my mouth with my sleeve, I knew victory! Little did it matter that I didn't care much for the taste of Squirt, it was my trophy—the first of the many that would come my way.

My first medal of success, the highly acclaimed Squirt six pack (minus one), now sat on my bookshelf. As I lay in bed that night, grand illusions of running the bases under bright stadium lights played before my eyes. Triumph! I would taste it many more times, feeling a sensation as real as bubbles burning up my nose. Slipping a hand under my pillow, I tucked my ball snug into the mitt safely hidden there. Before my eyes would open the next morning, and the next, and all the mornings after that, I would be dreaming of the place I longed for most, the ball field.

By the time I was eight years old, the entire world began to rotate around home plate and every star in the universe looked on over the outfield fence. Baseball became my filter for reality, sifting out all irrelevant and mundane aspects of day-to-day life, allowing me to focus, laser sharp, on the game.

During summers and weekends, my buddies and I would bound out of bed with the early morning sun. After swallowing a bite or two of cereal, six or seven of us would dash out to the field to play. Like in the movie, *Sandlot*, we'd compete and play all day long. We belonged to a realm outside of time, free of responsibilities and grown-ups, a realm where even appetites were easily forgotten. Lunch was an unnecessary interruption so we would go home only for dinner. Still eager to get back out after dark, we'd rig up our own lights for the field and my

*By my tenth birthday, baseball had become my life.*

sisters would set up a little concession stand at our games. As my mind reels back to those early golden years, I remember feelings of exhilaration beyond description.

With undying passion, I loved the American dream and was in hot pursuit of making it my own. It wasn't long, however, before the roar of the crowd (even when it consisted of only a handful of neighborhood kids) became almost as important to me as the game itself. All too soon playing was not only about going out to have fun with my buddies. It started to feed a gnawing hunger—filling an empty void inside. By my tenth birthday, baseball had become my life.

Since peak performance comes through practice, ball and glove became my constant companions. Parents and other boys admired how disciplined I had become. Long after other kids had hit the "rack," I would stay up for hours, throwing a ball against the brick wall of our house, practicing dive catches and honing my fielding techniques, imagining myself in the World Series. In fact, my friends' mom from the house next door would get so frustrated with the continual "thud, thud, thud" of the ball that she'd holler at me from her bedroom window. I'd just shake my head feeling sorry for the sheltered woman. How could she think about sleep while I was engaged in "matters of life and death?"

*Cracks off the bat were heard above rowdy cheering. With goals set high, my many late nights of throwing the ball against the house and buckets of rocks thrown one-by-one up into the sky and hit with precision began to pay off. The season was packed with wins and I walked tall and proud.*

*My team was going to the playoffs and I was "there" for them. Needing one run, I was up to bat with runners on second and third. This was the part I loved most—the heat of the moment. Pressure mounted. The stands grew silent. "Time out." The coach came out of the dug-out to talk over how they were going to pitch to me. The pitch was thrown, a fastball right into my hitting zone. "It doesn't get any better than this," I thought.*

*I swung. I connected. But I just missed the "sweet spot." The ball popped up, the pitcher caught it, and the umpire screamed, "YOU'RE OUT!"*

*My world stopped. I couldn't breathe. For a moment everyone sat stunned. Ewing had blown it. For the first time in my life something I thought was mine, was lost. I'd never known the devastation of not winning. Wiping away a threatening tear, I turned back to the dug out. My dreamy world had collided with the harsh reality that I wasn't worth all I believed I was. I was just an ordinary kid. Nothing special.*

It was a defining moment. A new reality began to take the place of my innocent optimism. I was playing by the world's rules now and I began to understand something very, very important: "If I perform I will be praised, honored, and respected. But if I blow it, I will be a nobody." You see, team victory was just a friendly veneer. During a game where another teammate hit in the winning run, something would be missing for me. The cheering crowd would gather around him, leaving me alone and empty.

After a great game teammates and fans would pat me on the back and extol my abilities. In those moments I had worth. I knew who I was. And if I got three hits in a game, my emotions would reel into ecstasy. But a game with no hits dealt a deathblow. I would be miserable until the next game—my next chance to prove myself and reclaim my spot "in the sun."

As I excelled and grew physically so did my belief that performance was the way to acceptance. The team, my friends, the whole world seemed to support the subtle message I had come to believe as true: not only did I have to be good, I needed to hit the most home runs and the highest batting average had to be mine.

I had to be the best. My life depended on it.

## Iron Man

For a good long while, I won the game of performance. Breaking through barriers I was at last on my way to the top. The payoff for fifteen years of grit, dirt, and determination would be mine. Only a few steps to go and I would be in "the show" (what players call the major leagues). At age twenty-one I was drafted by the California Angels and each year in the minor leagues my stats looked better than the last: thirty home runs, over one hundred RBIs (runs batted in) and a batting average over .300. Known by my team as the "Iron Man" for never missing a game, I never let up.

But my body could give only so much. I could handle any other player and showed no fear against higher ranked teams, but physical limitations began manifesting themselves, regardless of my determined will. A shoulder dislocation was the first real sign of my weakness.

Then, during spring training of my third season, I was playing left field in a pre-season training game. One of the first hits of the game was a line drive over the shortstop's head. I picked up the ball to "cannon it in" when something suddenly ripped. A burning fire exploded in my shoulder. Something was terribly wrong and I knew it. I knew I was hurt, but I believed I had to continue. I had to perform. I was the Iron Man and this game was my life.

Looking back now, it's hard to imagine what I did next. With my arm dangling uselessly at my side, pain screaming through my arm and back, I dutifully returned to my post in the field. Without question, I had to go back out. Fifteen years of everything I believed in was at stake. I had no choice. Beads of sweat formed across my brow as I pulled my shoulders back one more time. A groan escaped my lips. Still refusing to acknowledge the obvious trauma to my shoulder, I remained in the field.

Next batter up.

*. . . an undeniable spiritual truth began to be revealed—one that I would share to comfort and encourage others for many years to come.*

Another crack off the bat sent the ball directly to me... I made the catch and reached back to throw with everything I had left. But in that defining moment of truth, things seemed to move in slow motion. My shoulders sagged. My throwing arm fell limp. Instinctively I clutched my elbow and fell to my knees. I had given it my all... and the ball had dropped to the ground and rolled a pathetic two feet along the turf.

It was over. I would never play on a professional field again.

◊   ◊   ◊

I quietly left the field and went straight to the locker room, each step bringing me closer to the inevitable collapse of my self-made empire. While handing my uniform over to my coach, my resignation was surreal. But as I walked through the dugout for the last time, an undeniable spiritual truth began to be revealed - one that I would share to comfort and encourage others for many years to come.

In that moment all the demanding voices in my head quieted. Rather than experiencing sheer panic about my future, I felt deep relief. In a very real sense I felt free. For the first time in a very long time, my mind wandered back to my little hometown field. If I'd known how to cry, tears would have streamed down my face.

Remembering my childhood awe for Willie Mays, I now realized how unlike my hero I'd become. Willie played with passion and only for the love of the game. In fact, he would often run out of the locker room right after a record-breaking pro game without taking time for any acclaim or even showering. One day, curiosity piqued, his coach followed him to discover that Mays had run back to the streets of his inner city neighborhood to continue playing stickball with his friends, the young neighbor kids. He knew who he was. And because of this, nothing compromised his childlike love for his friends and the thrill of the game.

In marked contrast, the unrelenting drive to be "the best" defined me. The belief that I had to hold a certain position in order to be valued stripped me of all I loved most. How my heart ached to wake up again with the first rays of sunlight with nothing on my mind but my buddies and the field.

How I longed to be seven, again.

◊   ◊   ◊

*There is something about a baseball field. It's hard to put my finger on just what that something is, but as far back as I can remember, I wanted to be no where else. Was it the smell of fresh cut grass in the early morning? Was it the freshly oiled leather in my glove, or the feel of a baseball's stitching on my fingertips?*

Or is there much, much more to baseball than grass and leather and stitching? For me, at least, I'm now certain there is. There is something about those days that still draws me back where I find something pure, something simple, something desirable, and something childlike. In baseball I see a surface expression of an inner yearning. A yearning that reaches far beyond the baseball diamond and into the heart of every man and woman.

*Rekindle the dream and rest assured. Your desires may be closer to reality than you think.*

Maybe for you it was feeling the wind on your face while riding your bike through wooded trails or dancing barefoot on soft grass or perhaps writing poetry hidden way up in the branches of your tree house. For some, maybe for you, childhood wasn't dreamy at all, but something deep inside your heart knows that it should have been, and you find yourself yearning for days that never were.

Do you still dream about those carefree days? Days when you could dance and play throughout the seasons, "out on the edge" of exploration and expression, living as you were fashioned to live, freely and fully?

Rekindle the dream and rest assured. Your desires may be closer to reality than you think.

## Reflection ~

· Do you remember a time in your life when you were carefree and joyful?

· If not, what would a carefree, childlike life look like to you?

· Can you identify some things that robbed you of that carefree living?

## God's Desire ~~

"For you have not received a spirit of slavery leading to fear again, but you have received a spirit of adoption as sons by which we cry out, "Abba Father! The Spirit Himself bears witness with our spirit that we are children of God."
—ROMANS 8:15 & 16

"I will welcome you and I will be a Father to you, and you shall be sons and daughters to Me..."
—2 CORINTHIANS 6:17B-18

## Your Response ~~

*Father, please begin to show me the kind of relationship You want to have with me. I want to enter the childlike, carefree rest that You offer Your children. Thank you Father for coming alongside me to lead me into a new and better way of living in tenderness and love.*

# 2

# *The Quest*

"Every man seeks his own good, and this is without exception...
even the man who kills himself."
—Pascal

A pastor's wife has come to my office during the quiet hours of the evening when she won't be accidentally recognized. Confused about her relationship with her husband and her children, she sobs, "I don't know what happened!" She went into this marriage anticipating happiness and a shared life with her chosen one, for whom she had saved herself all those years. But now there is only loneliness and discord - the fire of love snuffed out. To make the emptiness seem less real, she's become consumed with keeping her house spotless and exquisitely decorated. Her life is now merely a showcase.

A CEO makes an appointment out of sheer desperation. Overwhelmed with work, he has grown deeply depressed with no hope in sight as the piles on his desk stack higher every day, threatening to topple over—much like his life in general. With no energy left, he tries to read the Bible more often in an attempt to battle his dilemma but seems to be gaining no ground.

A young Christian seeks freedom from sexual addiction. He's battled and battled but fights to no avail. While wanting with all his heart to be pure, he has vowed again and again to stop using pornography, but he succeeds only for short periods of time before falling again.

I've been a full-time counselor for over two decades. Over the years, those of us at our counseling center have seen thousands of struggling, hurting people. When I look into the eyes of those sitting in our waiting room, I recognize the fatigue. I know the yearning for freedom and the powerlessness over belief systems that suck the joy out of the marrow of life.

Especially after a long day at the office I yearn to be like a little child again, running and playing outside of time without inhibition or fear. And I want to take all those I see with me. How I wish for just a day in another time and place where we could all be wild and carefree, where passion fuels the heart and we could dream once more - a place where we could run and laugh without fear of failure or rejection.

Maybe my memory of childhood has become too idealistic. For many, childhood was every bit as brutal as the competitive world of adults. Memories of teams being chosen during recess on the elementary playground or dance partners being paired up for gym class is enough to make anyone break out in a cold sweat! We had to learn survival skills early on. For some it meant pushing hard to win, for others it meant rebelling and making a statement that they didn't need society's values. For you it might have meant disappearing into the crowd, simply hoping to survive without getting hurt.

Whatever path we choose, we do so anticipating that we might live life to its fullest, or at least with the hope of avoiding pain. Our methods differ and the results may vary, but the pursuit is the same—to find the kind of life that will give us the sense of love and acceptance we most need and desire. But all too often we come up empty-handed.

I'm reminded of a movie starring Jack Nicholson in the role of a foul-mouthed, obsessive-compulsive. After having barged into his therapist's office and being told to make an appointment, he turns and charges back into the crowded room full of people waiting for their appointment time. Stopping mid-stride he exclaims, "What if this is as good as it gets?"

*"What if this is as good as it gets?"*

Nobody wants to believe that being "stuck on survive" is all God has to offer. We may feel safe with matters concerning life after death, trusting that our eternity rests secure, but dare we ask, "What about life now?" Every Christian embraces the liberating truth of our forgiveness through Christ. But life on earth is more complex than being forgiven. The wife whose Christian husband mistreats her or forgets to come home finds no comfort in knowing that he's forgiven![1] What about the woman who faces deep emptiness within her family, or the executive who can't face his job? What does a young man imprisoned by his secret sexual addiction actually hope for?

We're not alone, you and I. Have you ever considered the search of all humanity for lasting purpose and meaning throughout the course of history? Whether through keeping with family, religious, and cultural traditions or selling out for the promise of upward mobility and recognition, every man, woman, and child has sought after lasting significance on this quest called "life." No matter how simple or complex, rural or urban, we all, by God's design, have an inner ache for lasting purpose and worth. In his book, The Journey of Desire, John Eldridge suggests, ". . .We all share the same dilemma – we long for life and we're not sure of where to find it. We wonder if we ever do find it, can we make it last?"[2] And deep down we ask the question, is this really "as good as it gets?"

*. . . we all, by God's design, have an inner ache for lasting purpose and worth.*

## The Quest

Humanity is on a quest. "The drive to live is strong even in the most tiny of human beings," says Rachel Naomi Remen, author of Kitchen Table Wisdom. "I remember as a medical student seeing one of my teachers put a finger in the mouth of a newborn and, once the baby took hold, gently lift him partway off the bed by the strength of his suck. That tenacity toward life endures in all of us, undiminished until the moment of our death."[3] The desire "to live" is inborn within each of us, and while its source often seems elusive, our pursuit of it permeates our every action.

I must ask you, "What defines the life you live? Why do you do what you do?" I'm amazed at how many people, unbelievers and Christians alike, are unclear about the life they've been given. It's no wonder it's not abundant! If we allow each day to happen by default, we may never realize the potential we've been given. What is it you are searching for?

## Life

The Greeks had two words for the English word "life." The first was the word *bios*, which means "physical life," from which we get our word "biology." It refers to all the cells and chemicals that work together so our bodies don't die. In other words, the physical state of being. Much of our ordinary day is spent focusing on our *bios*.

*If we allow each day to happen by default, we may never realize the potential we've been given.*

Scuba diving has become one of my favorite hobbies. It is one of the few things I do that truly helps me leave the rest of the world behind for a while. When I'm diving near coral reefs, I'm *literally* submerged in a totally new, fantastic part of God's creation, full of color, activity, and wonder.

Scuba diving has also brought me to a full appreciation of the simple fact that we need air to live biologically. It seems obvious that when submerged underwater, oxygen is not something to be taken for granted. In fact, special training is required to get past the crucial issues of breathing before one is able to enjoy the world below the depths.

As risky as mountain climbing or sky diving, scuba diving is a dangerous sport and must always be done in pairs. One's diving partner is referred to as his or her "buddy." Each buddy diver has an extra gauge connected to an apparatus called an "octopus," a back up breathing device that will save your partner's life if his or her equipment fails.

Let's say you and I have passed our certification course and now we're down at the Cayman Islands at Eden's Rock diving at a depth of one hundred feet. It's really dark down there and far too deep to make it to the surface if our air should run short. If for some reason I run out of air, the octopus connected to your tank is my only hope. Now let's say my tank malfunctions and after showing you the distress signal, instead of responding immediately to my plight, you start clowning around and don't respond to my signal.

I'll warn you now, I won't be thinking about good protocol or the best way to keep from hurting your feelings. I'm going to get air! You might get seriously hurt in the process, but make no mistake, I'll fight and do whatever is necessary for my body to live. By nature, we are fashioned to fight for *bios* life. When life is threatened, our adrenaline kicks in and we either fight or flee.

The fact that you are reading this book indicates your bios needs are primarily being met. Remember Maslow's Triangle? Only after our basic needs of food, clothing, and shelter are met, can we begin to pursue other more complex issues. When we are confronted with people who spend the majority of their lives seeking food and shelter, we are saddened. Why? None of us wants to consider simply existing; life encompasses so much more than caring for this body, "bios." We are designed for something more. What makes life worth living? Why are we on this planet? *What makes up the element of life that goes beyond survival?*

## Zoe Life

The answer we're looking for is found in the other Greek word for life, *zoe*, a word that carries a much deeper and mystical meaning than *bios*. *Zoe* speaks of life that goes beyond the body and is found *at the core of who we are*. It is the internal motivator that keeps us pushing forward each day. It is what we use to define who we are, why we do what we do, and why we have value. With the same zeal a newborn searches for and clutches to her mother's breast, humanity searches for life. And when threatened, we are capable of responding with the same force as a diver low on air.

*Zoe* life is what makes our biological *bios* life worth living, giving us direction, vision, and purpose. It is the search for this *zoe* that is the central theme in the story of all humanity. Significance, purpose, and inexpressible value are part of God's design for us. But as evidenced in early childhood development books, these traits don't just automatically come packaged with birth. Each of us at some point, (usually early on), experiences a painful awareness that something is missing. Something precious that belongs to us has been lost—*zoe* life. Our *zoe* must be found. We set out on a journey to find, by any means possible, what it is that will fill our ache.

*Each of us... experiences a painful awareness that something is missing, something precious that belongs to us has been lost—zoe life.*

◊    ◊    ◊

At the age of sixteen, I tasted the most extraordinary flavor. For the first time I inhaled the breath of God. Life at last! I gulped it down and wanted to exclaim, "Why isn't everyone celebrating?" I felt like laughing, weeping, running. I'd come home. I was free. Without conditions, pure and perfect love was mine. I'd found it, *zoe*!

On this night I found myself walking down the isle at a David Wilkerson Crusade where I had a powerful encounter with Jesus Christ. Having focused primarily on religious tradition as a young altar boy, I'd never realized I could know the living God personally. Bible verses I'd heard through out my childhood came to life.

Jesus said, "I am the way, and the truth, and... the LIFE!"

The smudge and soot was now scrubbed away from the lens through which I'd been squinting, and the heavens broke open. It was as if I'd been blind and now could see. I was ready to explode with the joy washing over me. Absolutely unable to keep still, I had to get up and dance!

Why hadn't someone shown this to me before? I figured no one on earth could have possibly experienced what was now pulsing through my spirit or surely I would have heard about it! Heady with love, I said, "I do" to God. I felt more love than I could contain in those early days of my salvation and I had to express it. True and selfless affection spilled over on everyone close by. But my ecstasy would be short-lived.

Overcome with passion, I'd approach other Christians and exclaim, "Have you experienced Him too?" You can imagine my disillusion when they'd respond with dull expressions akin to, "Of course." I soon discovered how few shared my new excitement. Life for them seemed routine and muted. Where was their joy? This was *zoe* life! Young teens fitfully attended church only because their parents forced them; old men dozed in the same pew week after week; women gossiped and fussed if anything changed in the course of the service. Exhausted and preoccupied with trying not to sin, they had lost their passion and zeal for life. I walked away from these encounters baffled and disheartened. In my naiveté, I was determined I could help them.

I refused to fall in line with the status quo Christian. I memorized hundreds of Scripture verses. With impressive diligence, I trained in discipleship, hard pressed to share the Good News with those who didn't know the salvation message. Awed by the holy and righteous nature of God, above all else I wanted to do right. I wanted to please my Lord! I led Bible studies and learned firsthand about the power of prayer. My leaders marveled at the remarkable progress I was making.

I could think of nothing I'd rather do than sell out for God. With an unrelenting drive for holiness and perfection, I invested everything I had with uncompromised fervor into my Christian walk. I had Satan by the tail, or so I believed.

Each year I set tangible goals while resolving to try harder than ever to live for my new Master. But it was never enough. If I memorized five verses one day, I'd believe it should have been six. If I shared my faith with two people, I'd lay down at night apologizing to the Lord for having not shared with three. Daily I prayed, asking for an added measure of power and strength.

◊ ◊ ◊

One morning I awoke to a day seeming like any other. Little did I know that what lay ahead would forever change the way I'd live my life. While pressing on toward "the goal of my high calling," not looking to the right or the left, and measuring up to all my "shoulds" and "should-nots," suddenly out of nowhere, I got slammed. The wind was knocked out of me. And because I was so weary from fighting "the battle," I didn't have the inner strength to get back up. Exhausted from a religious regimen too heavy to bear, my belief systems could no longer shoulder my burden. I collapsed under the weight of mounting anxiety and all the self-imposed principles under which I'd been living. Literally, my faith shattered. "God help me!" I cried out.

*Exhausted from a religious regimen too heavy to bear, my belief systems could no longer shoulder my burden.*

If there was any answer at all, it was cloaked in silence.

Losing all sense of time and location, I felt lost out in space, as if my life cord had become disconnected from the mother ship and I was left alone to float in utter darkness.

Was it all wrong? Was my belief in God and His Son futile? How could I know what was true? Why would He let me come to this place of utter brokenness? Why didn't He help me? The gospel I thought I understood so well and loved so dearly now lay useless at my exhausted feet. I wondered if I'd ever pick it up again. I had surrendered all, but my all apparently wasn't enough.

❀ ❀ ❀

## With God's Help?

Have you embraced the idea that "with God's help" you will find deep meaning and purpose in a life marked by victory and freedom? Each one of us at some point has cried out, "God, help me!" Has He answered your prayer? Are you living in victory? For those who aren't, it means either God isn't responding or we are mistaken.

Riddled with disbelief and disillusionment, those who darken the doorways of our counseling center now turn to us, hoping we can help them because it seems God has chosen to remain silent to their pleas.

I can't tell you how many Christians have secretly admitted to me through their personal story that the "abundant life" Jesus spoke of seems to be a joke. His promise of "making our burdens light" is a bitter disappointment to those who come seeking my counsel. "Help me!" they cry. "Help me change my rebellious child." "Help stop my abusive husband." "Help me save my marriage." "Help me overcome my addiction."

If Christians are supposed to have a monopoly on the riches of God, why do our lives look so similar to those who don't believe? Philip Yancey admits he has to face "the honest fact that Christians live in poverty, get sick, lose their hair and teeth, and wear eyeglasses at approximately the same rate as everyone else. Christians even die at exactly the same rate: one hundred percent."[4] When Christian statistics are similar to the rest of the world, don't you wonder? I have.

How pure and simple the gospel message appears when preached from our pulpits. "Jesus Saves!" And for those who are "lost and dying in sin," it is the obvious answer. But what about those who diligently study Scripture, pray, attend conferences and marriage seminars, yet are still (most often in secret) miserable? "Has God promised more than He can [or will] supply?"[5] What does the gospel—the good news—mean for those who've done all they know to seek God yet still continue to battle against their sinful patterns? Burdens certainly don't grow lighter throughout the course of life and the steps of a believer rarely seem to become any easier. Too often we find only more responsibility, more commitments, more rules, and a whole lot more guilt than those who never try Christianity.

This couldn't possibly be the life we hoped for.

Am I being too raw here? Unbelievers enjoy their success while Christians seem to make unwanted and unproductive sacrifice. Even the psalmist cried out: "I was envious of the arrogant, as I saw the

prosperity of the wicked... their body is fat, they are not in trouble...
always at ease, they have increased in wealth. Surely in vain I have
kept my heart pure, and washed my hands in innocence..." (Psalm
73:3-4, 12-13). Our neighbors spend time out on the lake and we
sign up for another church committee. "Who hasn't at one time
or other wondered if this is really what God had in mind. For the
most part our religious lives are the most uncomfortable part of our
existence."[5]

Instead of being the most free, we remain all bound up. Rather
than being the most risky people in the world, the least confined by
the opinions of others, and the most free to love unconditionally, we
Christians have become stiff, unbending, unloving and judgmental.
Rather than dancing, "most of us are tiptoeing
through life so we can reach death safely," said the
Christian critic, Tony Campolo.[6]

*... we Christians have become stiff, unbending, unloving and judgmental.*

"Why should the children of God lead such
uncomfortable lives when the Lord promises His
yoke is easy and His burden light?" pondered
Hannah Whitall Smith, a woman revered for her
faith. "It seems exceedingly incongruous that a
faith that is meant to bear the fruits of love, joy,
and peace should work out just the opposite...
bearing doubt, and fear, unrest and discomfort,"[7] Like the psalmist,
Christians down through the ages have cried out, "Where does my
help come from?" (Psalm 121:1). If God is my help, when will He
answer?

Our spiritual journeys don't often lead us to an oasis of green meadows
and cool water or to tables set with a feast. Instead our lives are dotted
here and there with fleeting hill top experiences across wide expanses
of desert, and we can be certain that deep, dark valleys are sure to come.
Few of us consider ourselves to have inexpressible value or significance in
our Christian life much of the time. Writes Steve McVey in his book *Grace
Walk*, "From the earliest years of my Christian life, I had a mental picture
of what I thought I should be. In this picture there was always a wide gap
between where I thought I ought to be and where I was."[8]

❦ ❦ ❦

In the hours that followed my breakdown, my wife Nancy quickly sent me away to get help. Her rock-solid mate, who had always kept everything in control, could no longer hold it together. I had come unhinged. After seventeen years of never shedding a tear, I cried for days and nights without eating or sleeping.

Ten days of extreme anxiety and twenty years of bottled emotions broke lose, leaving me a spiritual quadriplegic. Everything within me crumbled and broke: my goals, my motives, my intentions— everything that seemed good. I couldn't seem to make sense of the past, present, or future.

In times of utter brokenness and vulnerability, when we cannot do one more thing to help ourselves, we feel as though both our physical life and our *zoe* life is literally being snuffed out. This was true for me too… at first. But many days later I began to discover I was experiencing the best thing that had ever happened to me. My carefully built structure had cracked and was falling away. Slowly I was relinquishing control of all that I feared, all that I felt I must conquer.

And in the stillness I began to hear the steady rhythm of God's heartbeat. In my extreme brokenness, God was setting me free—free from the burden of *having* to rise in the early morning for prayer watches and Bible study, free from the inner *obligation* I felt toward church growth and evangelistic campaigns.

He had never left me. He just needed me to come to the realization that He didn't want me to perform harder. *He wanted me. God didn't want better service. He wanted me.*

It was the beginning of an entirely new journey on a brand new road.

## The Lie Exposed

Those of us who've been in church much of our lives know the truth about God's forgiveness. Some of us have begun to experience His relentless love for us. Therefore most of us believe that we are to let God *help* us through life, not only with our troubles, but also in loving others and ourselves. But the fact is, we've been deceived.

Many Christians understand about grace as it relates to our salvation from hell. We know there is nothing we can do to bridge the gap between God's holiness and our sin. After all, it is purely by God's grace that we will enter heaven. What an incredible day that will be, when we enter eternity as God's forgiven children.

But what about now? More often than not, shortly after we give our life to Christ, we get bombarded with a list of religious standards for righteous living. This list of "do's" and "don'ts" is clamped securely around our neck. As new believers, our hearts are open and vulnerable to anything we feel we are supposed to do. As we try to do it all, we will most likely spend the first few years *and perhaps the rest of our lives* shackled in a prison of standards that we must live up to "or else." We pray for help, but after expending every bit of will power we can muster, we still fall short. We feel guilty, and begin to get disillusioned. We pray for help, but usually our joy and peace evaporate in the same mist as our sweat of self-effort.

God did promise to be our help in time of trouble (Psalm 46:1). But perhaps we haven't understood the *way* of His help. There is more to the good news than the eternal salvation of our souls in the future and God helping out as needed in our daily dilemmas. That's only half of the gospel.

One of my good friends, Lee LeFebre, describes the common path of Christianity. "We've been taught that the greatest thing God has done for us was to forgive our sins so we can get to heaven. Now we should be thankful all the rest of our lives and serve the Lord. We are expected to now live "the Christian life" *with God's help* and practice the principles we learn at the Christian seminars."[9]

It was not until the writing of this book that I recognized the striking parallel between my baseball story and my early Christianity. My strategy for finding fulfillment and value had not changed. I had simply traded baseball for religious activity. And I too believed what LeFebre calls "the pervasive lie"—that Christ was in me to be my *helper*, rather than to be *my Life*. I was among the thousands who have been led to believe that dependence on Christ means trusting Him to help, strengthen, and guide us as we live out of our own resources. I too had become "the casualty of a half-gospel; serving as powerful witnesses to the world that Christianity doesn't work, and Christ is not enough."[10]

◊  ◊  ◊

Held securely in a place where God could begin exposing the choking half-gospel I had come to believe, I realized anew how the demands of those around me had permeated my thoughts and formed my beliefs. I had read and understood Scripture through grids formed by my culture that limited my understanding of God's character.

I had been defrauded and I was defrauding others.

I had mistakenly traded my freedom in exchange for a ticket freeing me from the penalty of my sins. Just as my love of baseball had been squelched by my desire for a professional contract, I had allowed the mechanics of ministry to rob me of the sweet fragrance of the indwelling presence of Christ. The enemy had wielded his classic weapon against me—enticing me to focus more on "*doing* the Christian life" than being *changed* and captured by the radical love of Christ Himself. I sincerely loved Jesus, but the counterfeit life I had created felt so real that I let the genuine and intimate union with Christ slip away.

I fully trusted the powerful gift of grace for my salvation, but I had come to believe the lie that I must somehow prove myself to Christ in order to be victorious over my sin and shortcomings and be a "good Christian." The deceit is that we can be self-sufficient, relying on God's help and values to be the winners we set out to be.

I'd expected to keep everything intact from my old life while wearing the Holy Spirit like a heavy shield to help me through life's trials. I was like the young boy, David, who would one day be Israel's king. Like him, the little shepherd boy trying on Saul's armor before going out to meet Goliath, I'd heave on iron armor that looked like it belonged to God. Hunched over from the overbearing weight, I stumbled out toward the battlefield to meet my giants. I anticipated that God would stand along side me and wait until I cried out for help.

Little did I understand that David in his childlike innocence knew the presence and protection of God from *within*, not from *without*. Instead of hoisting on more standards of righteousness, I needed only to breathe deeply the presence of God already in my spirit so I might be made fully alive again with His Spirit.

The *zoe* life we yearn for most is the very desire of God's heart. Like the boy, David, wide-eyed and reckless, I finally threw off the heavy coat of virtuous responsibilities and started to become naive and carefree again. Finally, I could live fully, freely, and boldly in God's strength and I began sharing my journey and newfound exhilaration with others.

"Jesus makes two offers to everyone," stated the well-respected evangelist of the early 1900s, Charles G. Trumbull. "He offers to set us free from the *penalty* of our sin. And He offers to set us free from the *power* of our sin. Both these offers are made on exactly the same terms: we can accept them only by *letting Him do it all*."[11]

As God's truth began to release me of all the chains I had wound around my spiritual freedom, it was as if I was being awakened. I could remember again a world fresh as the morning air after a spring rain. Although I wasn't sure where the journey would lead, I wanted no other. Like Philip Yancey, who refused to settle for a God defined by a debilitating church past, "I wanted to identify for myself how a relationship with God really works, not how it's supposed to work."[12]

I sensed for the first time in many years the freedom I'd first discovered on that exhilarating night as a teenager. I began to rediscover His love and acceptance in new and powerful ways. I began to learn that "victory" was not in my future, but was actually in my past. I began to experience that my true value lay not in what I did, but in who I was and Who's I was.

And then I found I could rest. I could rest assured that the most important thing I had been searching for in my quest was already in my possession.

## Reflection 〰

• How have you gone about getting acceptance in life? How much of your time and energy is spent trying to keep that acceptance? If you have to perform to keep it, is it really acceptance?

• Do you feel you are stuck in "survival mode"? If so, describe.

• What do you think Christ meant when He said, "I came so they can have real and eternal life, more and better life than they ever dreamed of"?
—John 10:10b *The Message*

## God's Desire 〰

"Are you tired? Worn out? Burned out on religion? Come to Me. Get away with Me and you'll recover your life. I'll show you how to take a real rest. Walk with Me and work with Me—watch how I do it. Learn the unforced rhythms of grace. I won't lay anything heavy or ill fitting on you. Keep company with Me and you'll learn to live freely and lightly."
—Matthew 11:28-30 *The Message*

## Your Response 〰

*Father, please show me the things that have become burdens, things I feel I must do, or ways I feel I must be, or things I feel I must have in order to be acceptable to myself, others, or You. Thank You for offering me a restful life. Continue to help me discover how I can enter Your rest.*

# ☀ 3 ☀

# Gridlocked

"There is a way that seems right to a man,
but its end is the way of death."—Proverbs 16:25

Blue smoke belched into the dew-laden grasses as the
engines coughed to life and the propellers chopped through
humid air. Checklists were covered, doors locked, and seat
belts fastened. Crowds cheered as the engines roared; the pilot and
navigator took a deep breath. Brakes released and the wheels began
to turn faster and faster until they cleared the grass. They lifted into
the air and with a turn to the west, the little plane began to climb
into the tropical sky... and into history, never to be seen again.

The year was 1937. With the best equipment and the prayers and
support of thousands of people, Amelia Earhart and her navigator
had just taken off for their next destination on what was expected to
be the first round-the-world trip in an airplane. The destination?
Howard Island. A small stretch of sand and trees would become
a makeshift runway in the Pacific Ocean. The evening would find
them in the company of sailors from a signal ship waiting off the
coast of the island. Amelia headed for open water with confidence,
limited fuel, a few hours of daylight and, in order to save weight, no
life raft.

Tragically, the journey would not end as planned. The maps
they used for navigation were not fully accurate and winds that were
stronger than forecasted sent the plane off its intended course.
Increasingly desperate transmissions were made as the plane
drew near, but the signal ship was experiencing communication

difficulties. Huge billows of smoke released from the ship to help the plane find its way went unnoticed. The young pilot and her navigator would never see land again.

## Navigational Systems

We want to believe that Christianity works—that Christ is enough. But even after accepting Jesus, the true Source of Life, we can still feel lost and unable to make sense of our surroundings. Which path is the right one? Even if we no longer want to live the pervasive lie of self-effort, how do we know if we're heading in the right direction? What if we want to turn around, but don't know how?

Everyone tries to navigate through life using what I call a "grid" or a "mental map." Your personal mental map is made up of all your experiences and everything you've ever learned. All of this information has been assembled in your mind into a complex belief system that you constantly use to figure out what is true and what to do. Your map is constantly being updated and modified as you experience and learn new things.

*What if we want to turn around, but don't know how?*

Navigational maps help us figure out three important facts: first, where we are; second, where we want to be; and finally, what is the best way to get there. Our personal life maps offer us these three guidelines as well as helping us determine:

- Who we are
- Who we can trust
- What is good and bad
- What is right and wrong
- What we are worth
- What we can expect from others
- What is our purpose in life
- What God is like

I asked the question early in the book if you've ever dreamed of going back to a carefree existence, where innocence rules and spontaneity reigns supreme . . . living outside "the lines" without ever violating God's plan. But often that seems too good to be true because our lives are so carefully defined by the lines that hem us in. Do you ever wonder how these lines got drawn in the first place?

What does your personal map really look like and how did it get that way? Is it truly guiding you in the direction you want to go?

Have you ever had a really fantastic map, say a laminated Thomas Guide atlas (that costs almost as much as the trip itself), and still gotten confused or turned around? You may say that your ultimate "map for life" is the Bible and that it is your guide in all you do. But is that really true? Is it possible that your personal mental map has distorted your perception and interpretation of God's written Word?

*I find that in nearly all of the counseling I do, it's an individual's personal mental maps, made up of faulty belief systems, that lead them astray,...*

Just the idea may raise the hair on the back of your neck because you may boast that the Bible is your only guide and as such, you couldn't possibly be off course. Be that as it may, you feel confident you know exactly where to look in the "map of life" to find your answers. Yet I find it fascinating how varied and unique each of our lives play out and how many different answers people find for the questions listed above. Are you sure that your understanding of Scripture is full and complete?

When lifelong believers come to me for counseling, they often release intimate details of their deep guilt and shame, soaked in tears of remorse and repentance. Then they often start choking out Scriptures that they believe relate to God's response to each one of their "sins." When a sex addict comes in, confesses his sin, and then quotes his own rendition of Matthew 18:8, "If it offends you, cut it off," his plight is enough to make any grown man weep!

Is this really what God would have him do? Why does he struggle so with his addictive bondage if he is fully repentant and believes the Bible as truth? This can't possibly be the only way he'll be free. But believe me, he is so desperate he's seriously considered it. He's losing everything most precious to him: his family, his job, and his respect. Genuinely sorry, he desires nothing more than lasting change. But is this the truly Biblical way to approach his struggles, or is his personal mental map leading him astray?

I find that in nearly all of the counseling I do, it's an individual's personal mental maps, made up of faulty belief systems, that lead them astray, and sometimes with results as devastating as they were for Amelia Earhart.

I recently heard about a humorous navigational nightmare that just about ended in a relational disaster for a guy and his girlfriend from my church. While visiting Minneapolis, the couple was attempting to visit the Mall of America. She read the map while he was at the wheel. Love was in the air and they each held secret thoughts about a future life together. Onward they drove through the city full of optimism.

Soon the city started to look like suburbs, and then the "burbs" began to look a little like cornfields. Was she sure they were going in the right direction? "Yes, I'm positive," she said. "But we're not seeing any signs or indications that we're close," he noted semi-politely.

"We're heading right toward it. It's right here, plain as day!" she insisted.

"Well, these are definitely cornfields!" came the icy response. As the tension grew and Cupid dove for cover, he grabbed the map and tears welled up in her eyes.

"See, the map says we should be right here," she says with a shaky voice.

Indeed it looked that way. There in the corner of the map was the mall. The only problem was one small detail. The map had an enlarged portion of the mall area in a boxed portion at the bottom right hand corner of the city map and the girlfriend thought it represented the actual *physical* location of the mall.

In reality the Mall of America was, and still is, located in the south central part of the city. The story is kind of fun to tell now. Tears and anger soon gave way to laughter. Cupid showed his head again and today they are happily married and living in Seattle where she drives and he holds the map.

Have you ever been there, thinking you are headed in one direction only to rudely discover you're on the wrong path? Maybe you are in a bit of denial and those cornstalks do still look a lot like buildings. Regardless, we need to backtrack a little and take a look at some of the major influences that impact and form our maps and the belief systems that guide our thinking every day.

## Major Mind Influences

Pain and pleasures, victories and defeats, love and rejection, life and death. These are a few of the experiences that teach us what "works" and what doesn't in our quest for love, our pursuit for belonging, and our desire to avoid pain. How we deal with these experiences and how we store them away in our mind will make a remarkable difference when it comes time to answer real questions in real life.

### FAMILY

When I was growing up, there was a narrow strip of grass that separated our house from the neighbors' next door. We shared so much of our lives, that for all practical purposes our houses might as well have been connected. We had ten kids between our two families, and we were never entirely certain who belonged to whom. I don't think our parents even gave it much thought.

Every once in a while our moms would make a collective head count. As long as there were somewhere between five and ten youngsters showing up at one dinner table or the other, they didn't bother to sort us out. My early programming taught me that my house belonged to everyone, their fridge belonged to me, and the world was just one big happy family. Why would anyone be upset if I walked into his or her house and went straight for some milk?

*... the presence (or absence) of our family is perhaps the greatest of all influences on our view of life.*

You might imagine how this part of my mental map got me into trouble when I decided to graciously mow the new neighbors' lawn two houses down. Wow! You can imagine my shock and dismay when the dad of that house went ballistic. Not only was I trespassing, but also, according to him, I had my mower set a little too low and had "damaged his property."

As we learn about love and life, fighting and making up, and what's normal or weird, the presence (or absence) of our family is perhaps the greatest of all influences on our view of life.

FRIENDS

Soon friends begin to take over the lead influence on our lives. Values of the group to which we belong make a major impact on the direction and ideas we take with us on our journey. If only we outgrew peer pressure after junior high! In our current circle of friends, all sorts of unspoken rules remain about what we drive, what we wear, how we decorate our homes, what to say, what not to say, and what our kids should or should not be doing. This programming proves to be complicated. Since trends change constantly, we can never be quite sure that we're doing it right.

CULTURE

Our culture and environment have such influence on what we think is normal, abnormal, right, wrong, good, bad, helpful, or harmful that we can't separate ourselves from it. Many influences are obvious, such as promotions in the media. But there are also a lot of ideas and pressures around us that affect our thinking in more subtle ways as well. These things are harder to put a finger on. For example, what influences the way we vote? How do we tell if an idea is right or wrong?

Preston is a friend of mine who often travels overseas and has been met with some radically different convictions about alcohol consumption among Christians while visiting other countries. When in a third world country recently, one of his hosts asked Preston if he would be offended if the host had a drink with his meal, noting that Americans have "funny ideas" about this sort of thing.

Preston was caught a bit off guard. He assured the host that he would not be offended, but he had to think for a while about the host's comment. What his host said was true. Many American Christians not only abstain from all alcohol, but their mental grid tells them that drinking is wrong and sinful. Where does that belief come from? Since Scripture doesn't forbid drinking alcohol in moderation, the belief most likely comes from our American Christian culture.

## EDUCATION

In addition to all we learn on the streets, we can include all the messages we learn from books or in classrooms, and the rewards that are received for our accomplishments. The impact of preachers, teachers, or professors, and the "glasses" they wear cannot be underestimated in the direction of many lives.

Major influences make your map what it is. Some of these things you may have asked for and many of them you didn't. A few of them you might be readily aware of, but most of them are hidden like the foundation of a house. They may be out of sight, but they support everything we see.

*Did you know that even if you've never stepped foot in a church or a synagogue, every-where you go you find "rules about God" intended to help you find your way in this life and on into the next?*

## RELIGION

Did you know that even if you've never stepped foot in a church or a synagogue, everywhere you go you find "rules about God" intended to help you find your way in this life and on into the next? There is an abundance of religious people who are going way out of their way to tell you how to dress, what movies you can and can't see, what music you should listen to, how to be a godly husband or wife, how you should worship, and so on. Some of it is blatant and some of it is very subtle, but it all adds up to one thing: man-made religious traditions. But what is God really like on a practical level? What is expected of someone who is striving to follow God? What does it mean to "worship," and how do you do that? What is truly "good" and what is "bad"?

For example, let's consider "giving thanks in all things." How and when do you pray? In the American Christian tradition, there

34

are two things you can do that will universally indicate you are prayerful: if you close your eyes and fold your hands, we will know what you are up to. We all know godly families are those who even in public places bow their heads to give thanks for their meals. But how often do you see the dad bowing his head at the gas pump before getting gas? Why doesn't Mom close her eyes and thank God for the abundant gift of heat before turning up the thermostat? Could it be that our way of praying has been influenced more by religious traditions than by Scripture? Traditions are not good or bad in and of themselves, but they are not to be confused with doctrine.

On both superficial and profound levels, the presence of man-made religion becomes an important factor in navigating through life. Whether you reject religion entirely or embrace it wholeheartedly, it's influences are so significant we could devote a whole book to this topic alone. If you've been hanging around religious folks very much, or if you are one, you may be shocked to realize just how far man-made traditions can distract, distort, and pollute one's view of God.

*. . . you may be shocked to realize just how far man-made traditions can distract, distort, and pollute one's view of God.*

Sure, Christians claim Scripture is their "map for life." Even when pressed on the issue, most firmly deny that they still rely very heavily on other sources for guidance, such as self-help books, movies, classic literature, philosophy, habits of highly effective people, psychology, sermons and their own religious traditions as the real map that guides their life.

But these things do have significant influences on our belief systems. The influences of family, friends, culture, education, and religion on our personal mental maps can only be ignored at great expense.

## We Have a Problem

Remember the famous words from the Apollo 13 flight: "Houston, we have a problem?" We too have a problem. Sometimes it may not seem like the problem is that serious. We can often go long periods of time without concern, but our concern should be great. The problem is this: Our belief systems, our personal mental maps, are in very, very bad shape.

Have you ever been given a hand-drawn map to a party but find it's nearly impossible to follow because the dimensions are skewed? The person who drew it might have forgotten to tell you that between the second stop light and the next left hand turn is a stretch of ten miles. Maybe she forgot to mention the right turn that comes before the next left. You've got problems because the hand-drawn map you are holding will not bring you to your desired location, no matter how much you believe in it.

*You've got problems because the hand-drawn map you are holding will not bring you to your desired location, no matter how much you believe in it.*

This may not be the best analogy because we aren't trying to get to something as trivial as a party. We are on a quest for *zoe* life, and if we miss that, we miss everything important to our earthly existence. If you are really going to find this life, you need to be honest about several things about your mental maps and belief systems.

First, you must realize that your map is incomplete and your understanding of God isn't altogether accurate. No matter how many places you've been, how many degrees you hold, or how successful you've become, just the narrow scope of our human understanding means we can anticipate significant limitations in the way we all think about God and the world. We can be certain our perspective has a shortage of facts. There is an undeniable gap between what we humans can know and what God knows. In his book, *What Good is God?* Doug Herman describes what he calls "the illogical gap."

"If God is omniscient, meaning he knows all, then we must admit that we are not. Few of us would argue that though we have been given great mental abilities, we would never be equal to God in intelligence. Therefore, we must accept that in this lifetime, we will never fully understand the mind or purposes of God. We get truths and revelation—the best being through Scriptures and Jesus' living example for us—but the rest will seem, well, senseless. Logic as we perceive it ceases to exist when we step into the realm of divine thought... We must learn to trust God regardless of how we think or feel."[1]

Second, you must admit that your beliefs are distorted. Certain events, both positive and negative, can smear your mental map or put a fold or tear right where we need it to be whole.

Consider for a moment the unthinkable. You are a young woman who has just been raped. Imagine how that single event could forever change the way you see your world. In a moment, every part of life has become polluted and twisted. The way you see men, what it means to be touched, the way you see God, the way you see yourself. Every man could now be a predator. A God who once seemed close and caring could now seem distant and cruel. And even the way you see yourself can be tragically marred.

Finally, in many cases, we must admit that our perceptions of reality are twisted by false or incomplete information. Recently, my wife Nancy, our son Kyle, and I decided to make a quick stop for lunch at a Pizza Hut downtown. We found a table and then I immediately excused myself to the rest room.

I appreciate the service of gracious waitresses and enjoy rewarding good service. But on this particular day when I came back to our table, what I experienced made me angrily pare down the waitress's tip to mere pennies. Not only was the waitress serving water to other tables who were seated after us, entire meals were being served while we were being completely ignored! Time continued to tick past. By the time I had the entire menu memorized, I began to seethe in a quiet rage. We didn't have all day. How could someone be trained so poorly? Finally, I couldn't remain quiet a minute longer. Furiously, I exclaimed to my wife, how inept the waitress was.

Surprised at my outburst, she filled me in on an important detail. Unbeknown to me, Kyle was expecting a friend to meet us, and while I was in the rest room he had asked the waitress to postpone our order until his friend arrived.

I was stunned by the impact of knowing only a portion of the facts. I had misjudged, I had gotten angry, and I had slandered someone I didn't even know because I had missed just one fact and assumed the worst. Assumptions like these can lead us astray as we make our way through the most important stages of our journey.

How would I have viewed the waitress for the rest of my life if I'd left the restaurant before learning the whole truth?

*I had gotten angry and I had slandered someone I didn't even know because I had missed just one fact and assumed the worst.*

◊ ◊ ◊

The rest of this book will largely be *a journey out of the bondage, depression, and death that results from living our lives out of belief systems that are incomplete, distorted, and based on lies.* Be encouraged. It is possible to get things turned around, and get back on the course that God created us to walk. But there is one more major barrier that could short circuit your journey right here.

**Noise**

"The Desert Fathers praise silence as the safest way to God."
—Henri J.M. Nouwen [2]

A TV special several years back documented the excursion of four men descending a river on the same day. The first two were a team of experienced kayakers, seasoned in the ways of the water. The other two were "weekend warriors," strong and energetic in a newly purchased inflatable raft.

The day started much the same for all four. There was plenty of anticipation for the adventure that awaited them. But as the calm waters gave way to the roaring of rapids, it became immediately clear that their days would end very differently.

Indeed, as the sun dipped below the mountains, the two

kayakers pulled themselves from the water. Tired, but refreshed, they reflected on the adventure with a sense of accomplishment. But only one of the other two was able to drag himself to the shore that evening. Battered, bloodied, broken, and alone, what had started as a promising excursion had turned into an uncontrollable nightmare.

The same river, the same currents, the same day. The difference? The first team had the knowledge and ability to pick their path through the violent waves to small patches of quiet water hidden behind the large rocks in the middle of the foaming currents. During the easy sections of the river, these quiet places offered a comfortable place to relax, reflect, and soak in the scenery. On the toughest sections, the protection of the rocks offered a few precious moments to catch their breath, rest their bodies, and plan the next step before re-entering the roar of the rapids.

I observed this for the first time while my wife, Nancy, and I were dining on the deck of a remote restaurant high in the Colorado Rockies. As we took a break from our first cross-country motorcycle trip, a kayaker in the raging river below was doing what seemed impossible. He was taking a break too, but he was resting quietly right in the middle of violent rapids. It was a different story for the second team in the TV documentary who found themselves swept mercilessly by the currents and constantly tossed about by the waves. With their strength soon exhausted, the waters smashed them against the rocks time and time again. They got pounded like pieces of metal between an anvil and the hammer of an uncaring blacksmith.

*. . . noise is actually a major obstruction to being aware of God's presence and direction in our lives.*

More than just an influence, noise is actually a major obstruction to being aware of God's presence and direction in our lives. In our modern world we are plagued by it and our spiritual life is terribly stunted as a result. Real noise from traffic, TVs, and telephones hammer us. We live in rivers full of thoughts, concerns and stress that leave us in a steady current of mental noise, and often we are inundated by waves of emotional noise that seem to flood every dry corner of our life. How can we possibly hear the directive of the "still, small voice" of the Holy Spirit speaking to ours?

It is my hope that in the middle of the waters that swirl around you, you will gain the knowledge, the desire, and the ability to find a place for quiet reflection, free from noise, where you can begin to rest with the Lord. I'm not simply speaking of a private place where you are not bothered by other people and can express your own thoughts and complaints. And it's not a place where you can recharge your batteries and gain new strength to continue living a busy life.

*It may be what He has intended to be your destination all along.*

I'm speaking of the kind of place where you can meet with yourself and your thoughts with God.

A place where you can ask Him to open your eyes afresh to His truth, where you can meditate on His Word, search your mind for lies and become vulnerable and dependent. Letting His Spirit speak to you, guide you, and live through you, charting out a new course in your life where the new man emerges.

But I just don't think this can happen out there in the noise. Find a place; find a time to be with Him. It may turn out to be more than an important part of your journey. It may be what He has intended to be your destination all along.

❀   ❀   ❀

Family, friends, culture, education, religion . . . is it possible that your mental map is incomplete, distorted and full of lies? Real noise, mental noise, emotional noise . . . is it possible that noise is blocking you from hearing the fullness of God's heart?

Though many of us have accepted Christ's death as our salvation from sin, we have yet to allow God's Spirit to make us fully alive. Why? Because we have become engrained in religious traditions, philosophies and teachings that have little to do with Biblical truth.

The Gospel of Mark records how the Pharisees and scribes

gathered around Jesus one day, trying to catch Him breaking the religious law. "Why do Your disciples not walk according to the tradition of the elders, but eat their bread with impure hands?" And He said to them, "Rightly did Isaiah prophesy of you hypocrites, as it is written, 'This people honors me with their lips, but their heart is far away from Me. But in vain do they worship Me, teaching as doctrines the precepts of men.' Neglecting the commandment of God, you hold to the tradition of men" (Mark 7:5-8).

Few Christians would argue the fact that it is through the reading and understanding of God's Word that we come to know truth. But would you now admit that there is at least a chance that you hear the Message through preset grids rather than realizing the living, breathing Spirit of God within His message?

My friend, there is a reason we get so far off track, our quest ending in frustration, exhaustion or devastation. Our search for *zoe* Life is navigated through our own faulty mental maps. But by understanding the grids through which we hear and understand God, we can become aware of the false influences in our lives. Then we can ask God to lift the lies that have kept us boxed in and proceed in purer, more accurate truth toward our goal.

This process is rarely easy and sometimes unpleasant, but the stakes could hardly be higher. You can choose to continue on the path you are on, ending up with only a fake, empty façade of the life you seek, or you begin to dismantle the grid of lies and discover ways towards truth, freedom and true *zoe* life.

"Whoever loves discipline loves knowledge,
but he who hates reproof is stupid."
—Proverbs 12:1

# *Reflection* ~~

Remember the Pizza Hut example? Identify a situation in your own life where incorrect information led to a misunderstanding.

From the list below choose those that had a positive affect on your life and explain how. Choose those that affected you negatively and explain.

- *Family*
- *Friends*
- *Culture*
- *Education*
- *Religion*

Schedule a time and place to meet with God regularly and keep that appointment! Become accountable to another person by informing them of your daily, weekly, and monthly appointments with the Lord and enlist their help in keeping these dates. Find a place free of distractions (Phone, music, people, etc.). This will be different for different people, and may be very uncomfortable at first, but well worth it!

# *God's Desire* ~~

"Many are the plans in a man's heart, but the counsel of the Lord, it will stand."
—Proverbs 19:21

"My soul, wait in silence for God only, for my hope is from Him."
—Psalm 62:5

"The Lord your God is in your midst, a victorious warrior. He will exult over you with joy, He will be quiet in His love, He will rejoice over you with shouts of joy."
—Zephaniah 3:17

## *Your Response* ～

*Father, I realize that all too often the "noise" in my life has distracted me from the most important things, most of all, time alone with You. Help me begin to identity the noises that keep me from hearing Your voice. Please give me the wisdom and will to make time to be with You.*

# 4

# Genuine Zoe Life

"I came that you might have life..." —John 10:10

**B**eau and Melody McCleary had everything going for them. The cosmopolitan couple and their three beautiful, well-behaved girls lived in a quiet, historical neighborhood. A modest inheritance allowed Beau the freedom to work in full-time ministry and lives were being changed. Not only was Melody complementary to all her husband did, she was upbeat and stunning in her appearance. When the McCleary's pulled up in their shiny SUV on Sunday mornings, they looked picture perfect—even enviable.

What most onlookers wouldn't recognize, however, was the crack forming in the veneer of their happy lives. Three pregnancies had taken a toll on Melody's once slim and shapely body, and she now needed more hours in a day to keep up her appearance. For starters, she was spending the first two-and-a-half hours of every day showering, doing her make-up, fixing her hair, and getting dressed. The hours to get herself and the girls ready didn't include the time she needed for her workout schedule and shopping. Cosmetic surgery, several of them actually, seemed to be just the ticket to provide some permanent fixes, which would allow her more time for the children and ministry, she reasoned.

The beautiful woman recovered in private and no one seemed to notice her subtle alterations. She felt great, but having invested so much on her public image, Melody couldn't justify not wearing the latest fashion. Being married to a minister had its dark moments and when Melody needed a little "pick-me-up," she went shopping.

Beau knew of his wife's love for shopping, but never thought much about it until the afternoon he was called into the police station to pick up a woman caught for shoplifting. You can imagine his shock when he found his wife handcuffed and detained for multiple counts of theft. Filled with shame and disgrace, Melody knew she couldn't explain how this innocent hobby had grown into an insatiable need for more. Random theft soon developed into an uncontrollable addiction.

*The desire to be attractive, time pressures, financial stress, and ministry demands weigh heavy on many of us.*

She hated herself for it, but she stole again and again, and couldn't stop. By the time Beau and Melody came to me for counseling, they weren't sure their relationship could be repaired. When the mask of a beautiful life lifted, a disfigured face full of contempt and rage emerged.

Most of us can relate to the pressures faced by the McCleary's. The desire to be attractive, time pressures, financial stress, and ministry demands weigh heavy on many of us. But when an escape like shopping turns to compulsive addiction like shoplifting, the behavior seems extreme. Why would a person—a pastor's wife—who seems to "have it all" behave like that?

Let me first ask, "Why do you act the way you do?" How far from an extreme or addictive behavior are you? What influences the choices you make each day? Do certain actions seem to take control over your will in certain circumstances? How can we possibly be conquerors over temptation and sin?

Most of us believe we must conquer destructive tendencies on our own so we privately bear not only the weight of sin, but we also fight back waves of panic, guilt, and shame alone. With tear-stained faces, ordinary Christians come to me every day exhausted and pleading for help. We've come to believe that the strategies of the world can somehow meet deep spiritual needs. Without questioning these patterns of self-effort, we anticipate God will come along and help our strategies work. However, our desire for *zoe* (that deepest longing for inner meaning, love, and security) can never be fulfilled from the outside in. Since birth something precious and internal is missing, and we desperately need to find it.

**Born with a Birth Defect**

From their day of birth our children cry out searching for satisfaction of their physical and relational needs. "Mine!" rings loud and clear. Isn't it fascinating to watch how little children develop various strategies to manipulate getting their perceived needs met? Whatever they want or need is most important in their little world and they will do whatever they find necessary to get it. We were no different when we were children, and we do the same now, just in more "mature" ways.

Before being told, how many of our children know that it was God who formed them and fashioned them for a relationship with him? None, right? The Bible says "Behold, I was brought forth in iniquity, and in sin my mother conceived me." (Psalms 51:5) We don't have to teach our kids to be sneaky or to lie. Parents don't school their children in self-centeredness; they just come out that way! Our offspring are precious, but like us, they are focused on "self" right from the start. Something went wrong at the beginning of humanity; we are all born with a birth defect.

*Something went wrong at the beginning of humanity; we are all born with a birth defect.*

From day one, we are left wanting. Why? Our totally self-centered approach to living doesn't jive with our true design. In other words, it's just not normal. The irony of the human condition is that for all the selfishness and the pain it brings, we weren't designed to worry about self.

**Created with a Purpose**

Humanity was created expressly to have an intimate relationship with God. Our purpose in life is to worship and enjoy our Creator forever. Do you believe that? We understand the worship part because it is something we do, but how many of us fully realize the extent of enjoyment God hopes to share with us?

Have you ever stopped to ponder the reason we long for relationship? Why is our need to be liked and accepted so strong? Simply, according to our design, we are built to be loved infinitely and to dwell together in peace. God desires intimacy with us! (John 17:22). Our Creator is Love and as the Imago Dei, made in His image, we are fashioned expressly to know Love and to love without reserve. Because this is our created purpose and God's original plan, the deepest, most profound level of *zoe* is found only while fulfilling that plan. That's why we're here. And even though we live in a distorted and fallen world, being fully alive to God is still the plan—our purpose. This is what's normal.

These next bits and pieces of poetic excerpt from Gene Edward's, Divine Romance, take us to the scene of our genesis and beautifully describe us, the apex of God's creation.

〇　〇　〇

The first tick of time had never sounded. There were neither things created nor things uncreated to share space with Him. He dwelt in an age before the eternals, where all there was... was God.

He was *love*.

Passionate, emotional, expressive. . . love.

A love so vast, so powerful, yet, there was no "other than."

Until one day He said, "I. . . the living God. . . shall have a counterpart!"

And so he spoke. "Let there be..."

The words, "Let there be. . . " sounded across the sphere of nothingness, and there came a blinding flash that filled that hollow void. Light!

He then created living creatures, calling them messengers.

Speaking aloud once more, the Lord called out to the abyss

of nothingness, and a visible realm now burst forth from His word... As he labored, he filled the little ball with things never before imagined.

His audience, the accompanying angels, watched him create a wholly different life from them—visible life that could hear, that could fly, that could run, that could even cry aloud.

. . . The sixth day of creation was drawing to a close. Therefore, the angels were quite surprised to see God plunge into a final act of creation.

He paused, reached down, and scooped up a small handful of earth. He stared at the soil for a moment, then spoke again.

"From this red dirt I will create the highest form of life within the realm of things visible. The creature I am about to bring forth will rule over the material universe just as I rule over the spiritual universe."

The Lord God began to shape, mold, and model the red dirt.

With the last sculpting stroke, he stepped back from the moist sod, allowing the angels to have a full view of his completed work. They gasped in amazement and cried together,

*His image! Visible!*

Once more the Lord God bent gently over the sculptured clay. For a moment the face of the Living God and the face carved upon the lifeless clay almost touched.

The Lord God breathed.

Clay nostrils quivered and flared. The wet clay fleshed, stiffened, stirred, and began quietly breathing.

The Lord approached the model. Again their two faces almost touched, while angels whispered their approval.

"Of all the innumerable creatures fashioned by his poetic hand, there was but one of whom it could be said, 'The Lord God was thinking of Himself when he created this one.'" [1]

{} {} {}

We were fashioned by His own hand from the clay and then unlike any other creature made before, God bent down close to what would soon be His own personal counterpart and gently breathed life into the nostrils of man.

The word "breathe" here literally means "movement of spirit." In so doing, God imparted His own spiritual life to the man! His Spirit inhabited man's human spirit-giving life to mankind. Together God and man now shared the same tent (Adam's body) in intimate relationship, inhabiting the same temple. Woman was then fashioned from man's side and she too knew Life because she also shared the breath of God. This is what God intended for us—what He considered "normal."[2] God fashioned us—a body, a vessel in which man and God would live together in intimate spiritual relationship.

*"Of all the innumerable creatures fashioned by His poetic hand, there was but one of whom it could be said, 'The Lord God was thinking of Himself when He created this one.'"*

This was genuine Life—pure, undiluted, one hundred percent *zoe*. There at the dawn of humanity, the man and his wife experienced Life as full as it was created to be—without want, emptiness, or frustration. Oblivious of any need, they knew no loneliness, fear, or pain. Born fully awake to God, man and woman were filled with Life.

Created for unlimited wonder and play-filled days, their innocent sense of admiration and awe beckoned them as they walked hand-in-hand with their Creator. Each new day was filled with new discoveries under a canopy of radiant color. How God must have delighted in them! Sharing a life of unfathomable riches, without inhibition, they were absolutely free to revel in the world around them.

## The Right to Choose

Together, man and woman would discover all that had been lavishly created for them. God would show them His display of glory in how the world worked and how they would reign over it. Sharing in deep, dynamic relationships of love requires communication, commitment, and *choice*, but somehow we miss this simple truth when reading the Genesis passage. That's why there was a tree in the garden. Everything man and woman chose to do would be an expression of love to God.

Can you force anyone to choose you? You may manipulate him or her, but you can't make another love you. When a person is forced, is that a valid expression of love? Never. Love is a choice—always. It is an exchange that goes two ways.

What one word is most descriptive of God? Love. How does God sum up His being? Love. God is the source of pure, perfect love. In fact the Scriptures say that God isn't just full of love, He actually is love (1 John 4:8). He doesn't just *have* what we are looking for, He *is* what we are looking for. He could have chosen the angels or any other heavenly or earthly being to draw to Himself, but instead He chose humanity.

*He doesn't just have what we are looking for, He is what we are looking for.*

Every motive, every choice made would reveal Adam and Eve's intention of loving God. In fact, I believe the Tree of Good and Evil was placed right in the middle of the garden so Adam and his wife couldn't miss it. There was no confusion. Their God, Creator, Friend, and the One who is perfect love, said, "Do not eat."

What would happen if they did? Would there be harsh punishment? No, but spiritual consequences would follow. They would surely die. They would make a choice, which carried heavy consequences according to a divine spiritual nature. What did God mean? To die means "to lose life." What was Life to man and his wife? God! Death then, would most certainly be separation from God—mere existence after a broken relationship with Him. Theirs was not an innocent mistake. Eating the fruit of the tree was a devastating choice that would forever mar the future of the human race.

Just as the snake set out to deceive the first two, we can be assured that Satan is still in the business of setting himself against God. When the talking serpent came and presented man and woman with an alternative choice, his sneaky battle plan was initiated. And his every intent on this earth since then has been to take us out of relationship with God and each other—to bring spiritual death and to break down the glorious reflection of God.

Satan tempted man and woman by saying, "You will be like Him." But they were already created in God's image; they were already like Him! The snake went on to promise they would know good from evil. But everything was good. There was only one obvious evil—the tree. *What the man and woman didn't have was independence.*

Satan's true scheme was getting God's children to believe He was holding out on them. Why? Satan was actually after God's throne. Satan no longer had access to God's heavenly throne because the rebel angel had been cast out of heaven and had been confined to earth. What would be the enemy's next target? God's earthly throne... located in mankind.

Unrelenting, Satan had one goal in mind, to get Adam and his wife to surrender the throne, God's dwelling place. Mesmerized by the idea that they could become their own masters, Adam and Eve mistrusted the heart of their Creator while embracing the possibility that there *might* be something else, something better that God had kept from them. Satan's scheme was dark but ravishing, exciting, alluring, and extremely subtle.

*What was Life to man and his wife? God! Death then, would most certainly be separation from God—mere existence after a broken relationship with Him.*

The sly voice of twisted logic challenged the one boundary God erected. And then the lie, from the Father of Lies, was spoken—the lie that reverberates throughout human history, the lie we now live with every day, woven into the fabric of our world and our being. "Die? Ha! You won't die! God is holding out on you! He knows that if you eat, your eyes will be opened; you will know both good and evil, *and you can become like Him*!" (Genesis 3:5, paraphrase)

The Father of Lies deceived them and they bought into it. By eating of the tree's fruit, man and woman declared the choice of no longer wanting to be in perfect unity with each other and with God.

What a day of despair it must have been. Anyone who's grieved the turning away of a child, friend, or lover has a notion of what God experienced that day.

God honored the choice of His children and made His quiet exit. God's Spirit, the Source of *zoe*, departed from mankind and spiritually they died. Breathing in the noxious fumes of deceit, their eyes were opened and shame descended upon their childlike innocence. They would now be separated, walled off from God by the sin of their own choosing.

*... at the center of his being he was left with an aching void wherein every child born after him would begin a continual, but fruitless, search for significance through success and the approval of others.*

One of the tragic implications of the fall is that Adam lost his secure status with God. In his letter to the Romans, the apostle Paul solemnly wrote: "Therefore, just as through one man sin entered into the world, and death through sin, and so death [the loss of life] spread to all men because all sinned" (Romans 5:12, brackets mine).

Adam and Eve were deceived into thinking they could be more whole apart from God. The deception continues. We too strive to be fully human apart from His presence. The serpent has been hard at work and humanity has been entranced ever since by the corrupt message that robs us of our true self-worth. Adam gave up his life source—perfect love—his spirit died that day and at the center of his being he was left with an aching void wherein every child born after him would begin a continual, but fruitless, search for significance through success and the approval of others. This is the spiritual heritage passed on to us. We are now born into the image of Adam, a man without *zoe* (Genesis 5).

Why do we choose to do the things we do? John Eldridge, in *The Journey of Desire*, explains it this way:

"Adam and Eve set in motion a process in our hearts, a desperate grasping that can only be described as addiction. We are forever and ever grasping for life and exchanging our freedom for bondage."[2]

Since Adam and Eve, all of humanity is born without the living spirit of God within us. Our *zoe* life source is missing. We are born without the knowledge of God and soon we learn to make it on our own in the very best way we know how. Believing we must perform until we get it right, we try to figure it out. Accepting the pervasive lie of self-strategy, we become frustrated, believing we'll never be full and life might never get any better. Because self-centeredness doesn't work we don't experience lasting contentment from all we strive to accomplish. Instead, we are left feeling anxious. In the dark caverns of our mind, we find echoes of the lie that has plagued all of humanity, "God is holding out on you. You are not deserving of His love and favor. You better compete for something more, something better or you'll never get it."

*Eden is reenacted every day as we strive for the very things that enslave and destroy us.*

So we continue on the long search to find strategies for things to fill us up. Even when we are looking for life in God, we still have one eye looking to the world to find it. What makes me feel good? How can I experience contentment? Love? Acceptance? Significance? Security? Perhaps, we think, we will find it here—while performing for others. *Not here.* Maybe we will find it in acquiring possessions. *Not there.* Most certainly in the adventure of travel or the arms of another. *Nope, disappointed again.* The story of a Lost Eden has not ended. Eden is reenacted every day as we strive for the very things that enslave and destroy us. And the quest goes on.

## Our True Destination

Our original design is to know *zoe* life. But like Beau and Melody, we've been trying to piece together the puzzle of life as best we know how, namely by finding acceptance and avoiding pain and disappointment. Those needs are temporarily relieved through our efforts, and the ability to produce things such as money, power, status, possessions, education, looks, talent, relationships, spouse, and kids. The list goes on. Obviously, there is nothing wrong with this list, but the problem lies in that we turn to these to fill the void rather than turning to God. With the twisted strategies of the world's philosophies, Christians too have taken the search into their own hands rather than acknowledging the deep pulse of God within their spirits.

Perfect love always allows a full and free choice and Adam and Eve made theirs. Still, God did not "slam the door" behind them. Although His perfect holiness could no longer be joined with imperfection, He cared for them, watched over them, and provided a way for them to repair the relationship as best as could be accomplished in the presence of sin. From the beginning, He had a plan for restoration in mind. When the time would be fulfilled, God would send a second "Adam" and through Him, a new covenant of intimacy and *zoe* would again be made available to His beloved creation.

*Christians too have taken the search into their own hands rather than acknowledging the deep pulse of God within their spirits.*

This second Adam was Jesus, conceived when the Spirit of God came upon Mary, and born of a virgin birth. Once more, God's Spirit was housed in human flesh. God's redemptive plan was set in motion. After thousands of years of separation, perfect *zoe* was once again contained in mankind. Jesus, the model of God's perfect design, would show us who we were intended to be—the image of God reflected—with His Spirit living in us.

When people saw Jesus, they knew exactly what God was like (Hebrews 1:3). Remember when Philip said to Jesus, "It'd be enough if You'd show us the Father." In amazement Jesus asked, "Have I been with you this long. . . ? When you've seen Me you've seen Him." (John 14:9)

And this is how He did it. He showed us normalcy just as humanity was designed to do. The Spirit of the Father dwelt within Him and God communicated purpose, truth, wisdom, and direction to Christ's human spirit. Jesus knew the truth. He knew his Father's voice. He knew God loved him, and never doubted that He could trust Him. From the very beginning He demonstrated love back to His Father by choosing to do all God said. Jesus, in His entirety, revealed the image of God, showing us what we were intended to be.

◊   ◊   ◊

Beside a well, on a dry and dusty road between Judea and Galilee, they talked—a man and a woman. Not just any woman—a Samaritan woman—a stained woman. And not just any man, she stood face to face with the holy Son of God. Witnessed by one of Jesus' closest disciples, John records the encounter for us in John, chapter four.

*"May I have a drink?"* He asks.

She knows right away that something is different. *"How can it be that You would ask of me, a woman and a Samaritan?"* she replies.

*"If you knew who I am, and the gift of God I offer, you would have asked Me, and I would have given you the water of Life,"* He answers. *"Drink from this well and you will thirst again. But if you drink of the water that I offer you, you will never thirst. The water I offer will become a well, springing up to eternal life!"*

But the Samaritan woman doesn't get it. Jesus is offering her all the *zoe* life she can receive and she thinks He is merely discussing H2O.

Jesus, however, is not finished. She has met Him for the first time today, but He has known her forever. He knows her pain, He knows her rejection, and now He reaches deep into the dry desert of her soul and touches her desperate desire to find Life.

*"You have had five husbands,"* He says. *"And the one who shares your bed now is not your own either."*

This is all He says, but it speaks loudly, echoing in her empty heart.

He knows. *He knows.* And He understands. The deep, insatiable longing for love has left only a trail of shattered relationships, giving all she has, night after night, man after man, only to live in fear that tomorrow she will be alone again.

And then a possibility enters her mind. Could it be? She wonders if this is the One that the Prophets of old predicted would

*Jesus, in His entirety, revealed the image of God, showing us what we were intended to be.*

55

one day come.

"I know that the Messiah is coming," she says.

*"I who speak to you am He,"* Jesus answers.

It is not an isolated incident. Incredible as it may seem, Jesus repeated this claim many times to many different people. Those who were close to Him received it and affirmed it. Others who understood it, rejected it, and eventually killed Him for it. Not just claiming to know the way to life, not just offering us help in finding it. No, He linked Himself to life in a way that makes the wisest of theologians shudder and the most foolish dance in celebration.

*He said, "I am Life."*

He said, **"I am Life."**

*"I am the way, the truth and the life"* (John 14:6).

*"In Him was life, and the life was the light of men"* (John 1:4).

*"Jesus said to them, 'I am the bread of life. . .'"* (John 6:35).

*"Jesus said to her, 'I am the resurrection and the life. . .'"* (John 11:25).

*"And this is eternal life, that they may know Thee, the only true God and Jesus Christ whom Thou hast sent"* (John 17:3).

*"When Christ, who is our life, is revealed then you also will be revealed with Him in glory"* (Colossians 3:4).

I AM Life. I AM your *zoe.* I AM the answer to your desperate desire! This is that fabulous mystery the epistles refer to over and over. . . *"Christ in you, the hope of glory"* (Colossians 1:27b). Jesus, the eternal Son of God, came to show us His Father. He who is perfect love knows our deepest longings, and is willing to be our Life. This is not just another claim. Jesus is uniquely qualified to look you in the eye, to touch you at your deepest level of longing, and to offer you Life. And not only that, He passionately desires that you allow Him to do so.

❁   ❁   ❁

"Starting with Adam and Eve, sin spread like an avalanche, damaging not only humanity but even creation itself. Punishment must come; but as God's judgment upon human sin commences, so does His gracious effort to redeem fallen humanity. [In Genesis] the long, sad history of human brokenness begins. Yet the longer, joyous history of God's salvation begins there as well."[3]

*Jesus is uniquely qualified to look you in the eye, to touch you at your deepest level of longing, and to offer you Life.*

God did not just turn away leaving us forever separated from Him. With His perfect plan of redemption, Jesus came as the second Adam, embodying perfect *zoe* life. Not only did He model this life, He came to give us that for which we so desperately search. The coming of the Holy Spirit is God's plan to be united with mankind again! The word "salvation" literally means, "to be made whole again," to put God back into mankind so we can experience again the fullness of Him.

Why do I do what I do? I was born with an ache inside for something better. And though I've accepted His Spirit into mine, I must unlearn Satan's lies and spend the rest of my life hearing afresh God's truth. Jesus taught us to pray, "Thy kingdom come, Thy will be done, on earth as it is in heaven." We catch glimpses of that kingdom. Yet grasping the *zoe* life promised us through Christ is very much like trying to comprehend what it was like in the garden for Adam and Eve, because that's very much what it is. I can't pretend to have a full grasp of it. A feel for it and a taste of it, yes, but it will take a lifetime to discover and an eternity to live out and enjoy.

The great challenge that lies before us now is to listen with clear understanding and to see without blurred vision the truth God has revealed. God created us for intimacy, for adventure, and for unity with Him, as much like life in the garden as is possible in this world. He is absolutely committed to bringing us back to that original design.

## *Reflection* ~~

· Have you ever stopped to ponder the reason we long for relationship? Why is our need to be liked and accepted so strong?

· How does the fact that God was thinking of Himself when He created you affect you? (Gene Edward's *Divine Romance* story, page 48)

· What strategies do you see Americans using to "get life" (find acceptance or avoid pain)? How about you?

## *God's Desire* ~~

"Your old life is dead. Your new life, which is your real life—even though invisible to spectators—is with Christ in God. He is your life."
—Colossians 3:3, *The Message*

"Anyone here who believes what I am saying right now and aligns himself with the Father, who has in fact put me in charge, has at this very moment the real, lasting life and is no longer condemned to be an outsider. This person has taken a giant step from the world of the dead to the world of the living."
—John 5:24 *The Message*

## *Your Response* ~~

*Father, thank You for bringing me real, lasting life in Christ. Teach me to live to the fullest the life that You have so freely given me. Reveal to me when I am using my old strategies to gain "life," showing me the futility of these efforts, and help me to enjoy my new life in intimacy with You.*

# ❧ 5 ❧

# *Why, Why Did I Do That?*

"As in water, face reflects face,
So the heart of man reflects man."
—Proverbs 27:19

S cott Hickey was a great Little League coach and is a friend
of mine. Like the rest of us coaches, he knew that the key to
winning games was getting the right players on your team.
We made a special point of watching all the kids in the league closely,
keeping track of their stats, and making notes of their strengths and
weaknesses in order to identify which key players we would want for
the next season.

To get those players, each year we would go through a draft
process where every coach was given a certain number of points
and the players were then, essentially, auctioned off to the coach
who bid the most points. Now don't get me wrong, it's not like
we were judging little boys' worth as individuals based on their
athletic performance. But I can't exactly deny that we were guilty of

perpetuating the world's system of "winners" and "losers" in order to satisfy our adult male instincts to conquer and maim.

But that's not the point here. The point is that Coach Hickey was a pro at picking kids who could really play . . . which is why I couldn't imagine what he had in mind when he opened with an unusually high bid of 200 points on the Ackerman kid.

Ackerman was a nice enough kid, but it takes more than nice kids to win Little League baseball games. According to my notes he was an average player at best, yet if Hickey wanted him so much, I feared that maybe I had overlooked something. Shuffling through my papers, I glanced over my comments: "Doesn't show well, missed two grounders. . ." My mind raced. Did I have the wrong set of records? I quickly bid 250 just to buy myself a little time and to compare my notes with the other coaches who were scratching their heads as well. On the next round Scott Hickey upped his bid to 300 points without hesitation, and our jaws dropped again. The savvy coach's strategy made no sense to the rest of us. Without being outbid, "Average Ackerman" went to Hickey for 300 precious points.

When the dust settled and the draft was over, my curiosity was killing me. I had to ask my rival why he had bid so high on Ackerman! Breaking into a sly grin he said, "It's the mother option, Bill."

"The 'mother option?'" I asked.

"Ooooh yaaaaa," he answered, "The mother option. Where have you been?"

As it turns out "Average Ackerman" was just average, but Mama Ackerman . . . she was anything but average and, like Coach Hickey, she was also anything but married. Hickey figured that with her kid on his team, he might have a chance to throw a couple of pitches Mama's way after the games, and if she took a swing he might even make it to first base himself. (With a last name like that, we should have known Scott was up to something.)

Has it ever occurred to you that every behavior makes sense? Whether going to parties or standing in the pulpit, man is left to his own efforts to find *zoe* life. Our choices and actions, whether good or bad, don't just appear out of nowhere. Each day's choices are built upon the previous day's choices for strategies to get life and avoid pain. As demonstrated by our drafting methods in Little League, we humans display a tremendous amount of creativity in our quest and there are an infinite number of options. Still, the goal is always the same: to gain life or avoid pain. Behind every behavior, there is a belief promising that what we are doing will "pay off."

Based on these beliefs, we choose behaviors that we depend on to help our strategies succeed: endless curls for bigger biceps, prayer and fasting, longer work hours, fly fishing, newly-leased vehicles, church bus programs, furniture for the new house, building programs, playing the lottery, eating disorders, potlucks, witnessing, new romances, and on and on. We cannot deny the fact that these things make us feel like we're "making it." Without argument, they make us feel full, for a while at least.

You may be a little miffed with the fact that I just threw admired Christian services in with selfish endeavors. How can I possibly claim that both gambling and doing mission work can be done with a motive to gain life? Stay with me.

If I were to wait for a famous professional athlete to return to his Mercedes after a party on a yacht with women, lots of alcohol, and great sex, and told him that he isn't truly being fulfilled, he'd look at me in disbelief and laugh out loud. With his muscular arm wrapped around a beautiful woman, he'd exclaim, "Don't tell me I'm not full!"

You see, my main concern is not whether the Christian society accepts a certain behavior as good or bad. *Behavior reveals our belief and it is the belief we want to get at.*

Jeremiah the prophet warned, "For My people have committed two evils: They have forsaken Me, the fountain of living waters, to hew for themselves cisterns, broken cisterns, that can hold no water" (Jeremiah 2:13). Cisterns are underground "holding tanks" which catch the runoff of rainwater. They are common in the Middle East, where wells are scarce. Unlike natural wells and springs, they were never expected to give an ever-flowing fresh supply of water. When Jeremiah speaks of "broken cisterns," he is referring to holding tanks that can't even retain the water poured into them because the stonework within is broken.

Jeremiah is describing something akin to pouring water into a paper cup with a tiny hole in the bottom. It will fill all the way to the brim of the cup and the cup will remain full for a moment, but in just a matter of time, it will be empty because of its flaw. To keep it full, we have to fill it again and again. In contrast, when we go to God for Life, we go to a spring of living water that never runs dry!

Self-centered reasoning leads each one of us to develop our own strategies to find fulfillment—even when they are as fleeting as a leaking cup. How much do you need to be happy? Isn't the human reply, "Just a little more"? The message we hear is the same one Eve heard in the garden: "All this is fine, but you just need a little more."

The liar (John 8:44), and therefore the lie, is alive and well. Using any means available at his disposal for manipulating our feelings and intellect, Satan "... the enemy of all righteousness, full of all deceit, and fraud ... making crooked the straight paths of the Lord" (see Acts 13:10), tempts us to search for our own fulfillment apart from God. He wants nothing more than for us to become our own gods, and to worship and be controlled by anything other than our true source of Life.

**Good Versus Evil**

Jeff VanVonderan in his book, *Tired of Trying to Measure Up*, does a fine job of revealing the code of Satan's deceit:

"Satan, the liar, offers a counterfeit to those who lack life by promising them life from a source that can't give it. If that doesn't work, he obscures the seriousness of their condition. The great con artist's suggestions go something like this: "What you've done is not that bad. You're not that bad. You're not dead and you're not helpless. You are a part-bad/part-good person. You've got some bad qualities and some good qualities. (Doesn't everyone?) So just work on it. Nurture your good side, and deny, ignore, or starve your bad side. You can do it. Just try harder."[1]

The Deceiver has craftily created an illusion that he is involved in only "bad" stuff like murder, adultery, stealing, fighting, or lying. But did you know Satan doesn't really mind when we do "nice" stuff? Did it concern the evil one whether Beau and Melody were compulsively working out, shoplifting, or attending church functions? No, his plan was to have Melody settle for counterfeit definitions of life, and that is precisely what was taking place. Not only was her marriage falling apart, she was feeling more and more estranged from herself, her community, and from God.

We must recognize the great battle being fought for the soul of humanity. If you're willing to contemplate this, you will find the residue of this toxic reality in the details of your own life and throughout the history of mankind. Satan's aim is to keep you from joining into sweet unity with God. He will attempt to lead you down any path that will lead you away from your Maker.

If drugs, sex, and rock and roll will alienate you from God, if a little internet porn will cause you to hide your face from Him in shame, so be it. But if sitting on church committees or saving the planet from nuclear destruction will distract you, God's rival has accomplished his purpose. You can be sure Satan won't give up. He may use different strategies, but the battle plan is always the same, leading people to first, question God, second, act independently of Him, and third, act like gods as Adam and Eve did in the garden.

If Satan can get us to focus on ourselves, rather than on our Creator, his mission has been accomplished. As is written in *The Mystery of the Gospel*, "The devil isn't necessarily out to get humans to commit as many murders, indecent acts, or thefts as he possibly can. . . . No, his primary aim is to have an alternative society—a rival empire to the kingdom of God."[2]

Generations of men and women acting independently of God, aimless, empty containers following lies and reflecting the god of this world rather than the Holy God who created them . . . this is truly evil. And though it might look like beauty and success on the surface, deep alienating pain and anguish are the hidden reality.

God is good. Goodness is one of His attributes. He cannot be separated from goodness. Therefore, to be separated from Him is to be separated from good and can be only evil. Can you see the critical difference between what is good and evil on a spiritual level? Seeing beyond the surface enables us to begin recognizing the deep ramifications of our actions, whether they appear good or evil.

Satan wants to keep us estranged from God. Do you see why it was so easy for me to become caught up in performing the Christian life so soon after I had trusted Christ as my Savior? The same motive that possessed me to remain on the baseball field also reigned in my Christian life—the drive to be successful by the standards of our culture, family, and church. By focusing only on what seemed good, I was easily convinced that I was living rightly and therefore pleasing God even though I was doing it on my own . . . until I got so tired I collapsed.

The quest, our search for true and lasting change, for victory over the darkness in our lives is not to shun evil by living as good as we can. Our search is to regain our lost relationship with the Source of Life. Just like "mother options," parties, yachts, and bulky muscles make sense; pious Christian standards do too. We easily believe the subtle misconception that if Jesus died for us, the least we can do is live a life pleasing to Him. Setting out to make Him happy, we become entranced by all that we hold worthy, admirable, and righteous. How quickly we become slaves of our own making! Believing Satan's lies, we've slowly traded the genuine source of *zoe* Life for its counterfeit.

Jesus came saying, *"I am the way and the truth and the Life."* When we receive Christ, we know He is our savior, meaning we have received forgiveness and accepted salvation from our obvious past and future sins. But still being so engrained in our belief systems, we've not yet allowed Him to free us from our deepest disappointments, motivations, desires, or strategies.

Melody knew Jesus loved her and had died for her sins. In fact, this knowledge made her truly grieve about her obsessive sin of stealing. She begged God to forgive and help her. Her guilt and secrecy made her feel more alienated, and her need for acceptance became only more desperate. Regardless of how brief, in the moments she felt accepted by others, she felt happy and admired. But over the course of her life a nagging belief developed. She believed that in order to avoid rejection, she must look picture perfect, always. How tiring it became to always protect herself from criticism by presenting herself properly.

As I listened intently during our counseling sessions, I discovered this strangling belief took root one day when Melody's father was taking pictures of her sister, as a photographer would a model. Striking a pose of her own, Melody asked her daddy to take a picture of her too. Without a thought, her dad's response was, "No honey, chubby little girls are to be snuggled, not photographed."

The pain stung deep. Her dad would never know what he triggered in his little girl in that defining moment. Left unattended, this wound inflicted by careless words upon a tender heart would go on to infect many different aspects of Melody's life and the lives of those around her.

She didn't measure up. She looked at herself differently from that day forward. Her body was something to battle rather than to enjoy. Against the backdrop of society's billboard, the pain of a moment's rejection fueled the fire of her new belief, which began to burn hot in Melody's life. "Pretty, thin, girls are desirable... chubby girls get rejected. If I want to be accepted, I must look picture perfect."

From that moment on, Melody determined she would do whatever it took to be pretty enough to be a model. By the time she came to see me, she wasn't even conscious of this belief that was so engrained in her thinking. Although unnoticed, it drastically affected her entire life. This one belief controlled her, being the origin of nearly all her behavior.

"A lie accepted as truth will affect your life as though it is truth, even though it is a lie." —Jim Craddock

This beautiful woman had been deceived. She was completely unaware that her belief was a lie, yet it affected her as if it were true. Never was there a moment that she wasn't aware of her appearance and how others were looking at her. Always being aware of her posture, her makeup and the lay of her outfit, she *could not* let go of her looks; to do so would feel as if she were unplugging her life support system.

*"A lie accepted as truth will affect your life as though it is truth, even though it is a lie."*
*—Jim Craddock*

Melody's belief was extreme and as a result her behavior went beyond the norm, but it works the same way for all of us. By this point, you might be recognizing some of the strategies you use in trying to get life. You can probably even recognize how your behavior is linked to these beliefs and strategies. The goal here is not to pick and choose which behaviors are good or bad. Like my clients, if you long for victory in a particular area of life, you must set out to understand more fully how your behaviors reveal what you believe. If our beliefs do determine the strategies and behaviors we choose, then our actions are an important clue to uncovering what we truly believe. Only then can true change begin.

**It Matters**

A popular motto in our culture today goes something like this, "It doesn't matter what you believe as long as it works for you." Amazing, isn't it, how something that sounds so sensible could be so far off base? It *does* matter what you believe. It matters at work. It matters in the bedroom and at the ball field. It matters for your friends and family. It mattered yesterday and it certainly will tomorrow.

After Melody's story unfolded, it may have been tempting to modify her behavior immediately, however, I didn't tell her to stay out of the shopping malls or cut up her credit cards (all of which might have been necessary). Why? God's light had revealed her pain and wall of defenses, but it had not yet penetrated to her deepest thoughts and beliefs about herself. The process of healing takes time. Therefore, I didn't spend time telling her how to correct her behaviors, rather I allowed her behaviors to lead us to her beliefs so we could begin replacing lies that had enslaved her with the truth that would set her free—truths about her actual identity, security, and significance as one of God's chosen.

My role as a counselor is not to tell clients how to get all the "garbage" out of their life. I attempt to seek God's wisdom in helping to clear a path in order to expose the lie and bring God's truth so healing can take place. God is the only one who has the perspective to make a proper judgment. Proverbs 16:2 says, *"All the ways of a man are clean in his own sight, but the LORD knows the motives."*

I called Melody recently to see how she is doing. It's been several years since she and Beau were in my office, and both are doing well. Though the process of exchanging lies with truth will continue over a lifetime, they have found new freedom, new intimacies, and new peace with each other and with God. Each day they now step toward the lasting change they so desperately seek.

## Opening a Window of Understanding

Getting down to the level of our beliefs is the key to understanding behavior. What brings deep, lasting contentment? At any one time, there will be different beliefs and strategies at work in your mind. Often they can lead to actions that seem totally contradictory. I'm talking about the things you do that you hate and the things you wish you would do, but don't.

*We must not forget that our children are involved in the same quest we are.*

Let me illustrate this very important point. Desperate parents often make appointments for me to meet with their rebellious teenagers, hoping I can somehow make a difference. Their beautiful daughter has gone gothic or a son is partying and not keeping curfew. Few parents, however, stop to ask, "Is this true rebellion or is my teen simply trying to find acceptance and avoid pain?" We must not forget that our children are involved in the same quest we are. Kids don't pursue negative behaviors to make themselves (and their parents) miserable. They choose their method because it promises some success in their quest, even when it makes no sense to any one else.

*. . . sometimes all that has taken place is the kids have learned how to please a different group of people.*

Granted, the "behavior modification" approach will work with teens to a certain extent because kids are sharp enough to figure out that it's not a bad idea to stay in line and get temporary rewards while avoiding the temporary pain of punishment. I learned as the father of three boys that if I wanted to see real, lasting change in one of my son's life, I'd have to help him discover the issues of life and pain, and then lead him to beliefs that would guide him into a deep and practical relationship with his Creator. In the long run, it's the search for *zoe*, not one's current behaviors, that really matters.

"What a waste to attempt changing behavior without truly understanding the driving needs that cause such behavior!" —McGee[3]

**Bad or Good Reflection on Parents?**
FIG. 1

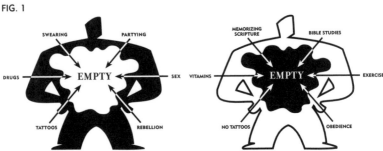

Too often our youth are taught to substitute positive behaviors for negative ones. Pastors and parents come back feeling a sense of relief, but sometimes all that has taken place is the kids have learned how to please a different group of people.

Regardless of the behavior, all the arrows on the diagrams above are pointing from the outside inward. But what has happened to the emptiness on the inside? Nothing. A person's heart can remain relatively unchanged regardless of his or her learned activities. Whether a Bible study or a party, the event still fulfills a purpose—being accepted. The "healthy kid" is the one who is freed from performing for his teachers, parents, and coaches or youth leader because he has seen the truth. He knows his meaning comes from Christ Himself, not whether he does drugs or takes nutritional supplements.

*When we know to consider one's beliefs or needs rather than focusing only on the behavior, not only is the window opened to understanding, but the door is closed to condemnation.*

Children build strategies for living around whatever brings the most hope, what pleases "self" and others most, and whatever appears least painful. These same issues build the foundations of our choices. We all have "me" as the main focus. Left to our own reasoning, the bottom line concern is "What about me?" We are born with a mind-set like Winnie the Pooh. "What purpose is there for a bee," he wonders, "other than to make honey? And what purpose is there for honey other than for me to eat it?" From the beginning of life our reasoning is the same as the "silly, willy old bear." The puzzle pieces of life come together according to our own understanding.

When we are determined to consider one's beliefs rather than focusing only on the behavior, not only is the window opened to understanding, but the door is closed to condemnation. While I'm not talking about condoning or even tolerating harmful behavior, I am referring to a constructive understanding of both our own actions and beliefs as well as those of others. Only then can we begin to understand that actions are a product of our beliefs. Only then are we moved from judging one another's actions to coming alongside to participate in God's healing work.

Instead of seeing only a wrong action, we need to see a declaration, sometimes as bright as a flashing neon sign, that says, "HELP! I'm caught in a lie." Then we can help address the faulty belief systems rather than trying to simply correct the action.

## In Summary

I might *say* that I believe something, and I might even think I believe something, but if my behavior isn't consistent with that belief, I am only fooling myself. Quite simply, life takes on power and purpose only when our beliefs, and consequently our behavior, are founded in truth.

*Whether conscious or subconscious, our beliefs rule our life.*

Counterfeit strategies undoubtedly make us feel full, but like broken cisterns, the fulfillment never lasts for long. What first appears to be *zoe* turns out to be as fulfilling as a leaking cup. Is your way working? Is it possible that you too have been deceived? If so, it's time to reconsider how you got to this place and what misconstrued perceptions may have led you to arrive here. "Lean not on your own understanding," the Bible says. It is faulty! ". . . but in all your ways acknowledge Him and He will direct your path." When we rely on our own thinking we become enslaved to what the Bible calls fortresses, strongholds, or citadels and we become bound by the very things from which we are seeking to gain fulfillment. Whether conscious or subconscious, our beliefs rule our life.

"A plan in the heart of a man is like deep water."
—Proverbs 20:5

Who is able to reveal our deep subtle beliefs that flow through our soul like deep waters? Only God. The One who fashioned us knows exactly how to bring them to the surface for evaluation. It takes place in the safety of His embrace. In His intimate love for us, He begins to reveal how we have wrongly chosen independence and shows us another way—the truth—so that we may be united again with Him and enjoy the purpose for which we were created.

"You shall know the truth and the truth shall make you free"
—John 8:32

## *Reflection* ~~

Think about how Melody's behavior was influenced by her relationship with her father and his remark about her weight. What early criticism or disappointments in your own life may have caused you to believe something about yourself that isn't true? How might this false belief have contributed to frustrating behaviors? How has this belief or behavior been reinforced over the years?

Examine how *beliefs* affect *emotions* and *behavior* in the following individual's lives:

• The ten spies contrasted with Joshua and Caleb in Numbers 13:1&2, 25-33

• Abraham in Hebrews 11:8

## *God's Desire* ~~

"There is a way that seems right to a man but its end is the way of death." —Proverbs 14:12

"As in water face reflects face, so the heart of man reflects man." —Proverbs 27:19

"My people have committed two evils: They have forsaken Me, the fountain of living waters, to hew for themselves cisterns, broken cisterns, that can hold no water." —Jeremiah 2:13

## *Your Response* ~~

*Father, I invite You to shine light into my life and reveal the wrong beliefs that lay behind wrong behaviors and emotions. Thank You for providing truth so that I can recognize lies, set them aside, and embrace truth so my life will be transformed. Thank You for the freedom and rest this will bring.*

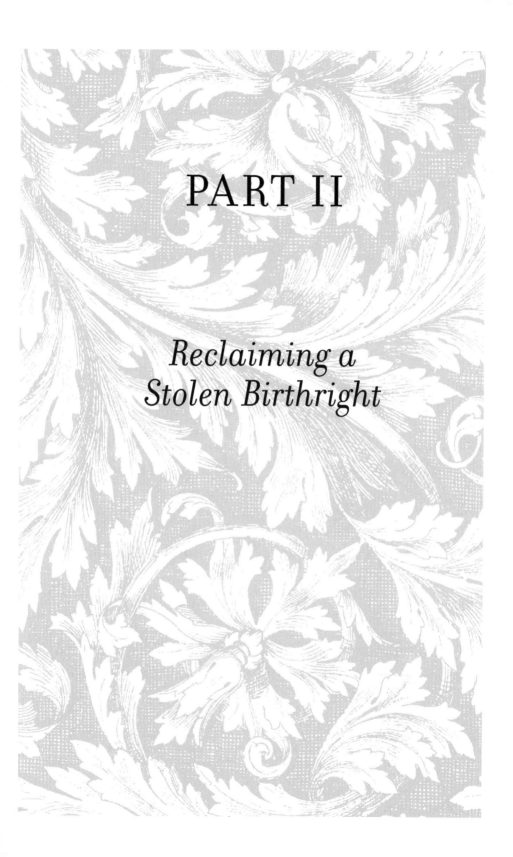

# PART II

*Reclaiming a
Stolen Birthright*

Walking into the waiting room of the counseling office, I glanced around its perimeter to locate my next set of clients – a husband and wife with marriage troubles. Interesting combinations of people come to the center, ranging from the wealthy, high society to rough, hungry-looking people who don't always smell too keen. Differences diminish as they all cram in together with hope of finding answers to life. This particular afternoon we had a colorful variety of people and I smiled to myself, marveling at how we're all welcome in God's kingdom no matter how we look or smell.

Nodding to several I recognized, I scanned the room for the new couple I was about to meet. A godly-looking woman dressed in business attire and holding a Bible securely in her lap looked expectantly into my eyes, and started to rise from her seat. Was this my client and her husband? I glanced to her left where a nice-looking man her approximate age was sitting. Interestingly, he didn't seem to anticipate any interaction just then. In fact, he didn't even glance up from the magazine he was reading. Perhaps I was mistaken.

Looking to the woman's right I couldn't miss the hairy bulk of a man with a long beard concealing most of his face. Seemingly oblivious to any other human being, he stretched out taking more than his fair share of the cramped space. He looked to be snoozing; his heavily tattooed arms folded securely across his chest. As I approached nothing on him moved except a bicep that twitched, animating the naked bust of a sensuous woman etched in blackish-green amidst the other colorful art covering his arms. His relaxed state could hardly be a result of our overtly Christian atmosphere of soothing music and hushed tones. The biker looked as though he'd been "around the block a time or two." I wondered which "lucky" counselor would get the privilege of meeting this character with his cigarette jammed behind one greasy lock of hair that was pulled back into a long braid beneath his skull cap. Stepping over the worn leather boots that stretched out into the middle of the room, I approached the couple sitting nearby.

The attractive man kept reading.

All at once the woman reached out and with her elbow jabbed the snoozing hulk. In response to her icy whisper, he grumbled and shuffled a bit. Annoyed, the man groaned to a hunkered-over position before standing to his full height of 6'3". And there I stood face to face with an obscene picture on the front of the guy's black T-shirt. Stepping back so I could look into his eyes, I reached for a handshake. He diverted his gaze and his hands remained at his side, clenched in uncomfortable fists. "Nice to meet you, Jim and Susan," I said. "Please come on back to my office."

Prior to meeting my clients, I look over information they provide on their intake form so that I have a head start on their unique needs, but the notes on this couple's record did little to prepare me for what lie ahead. My job is sometimes a joy, sometimes heartbreaking, and always unpredictable!

Once inside, I invited the mismatched couple to take a seat. I briefly considered the fact that I'd never encountered two more stubborn-looking people in my life, and was thankful I could rely on tried and true introductory comments to make my guests feel more comfortable. I wasn't sure how they were doing, but I started to relax a little after I began asking specific questions that help counselors gain pertinent information. Soon we'd be well on our way to "a bright new future." As always, I asked leading questions and then clarified what I'd just heard.

"OK, Susan and Jim. Let's see if I've heard you right. Susan, you say that you're a Christian. Is that correct?"

"Yes," came the curt reply. "A born-again believer."

"And you said you are extremely miserable. Is that accurate?"

"Yes!! He watches R-rated movies. He's selfish, he swears, he . . ."

I quickly interrupted. "Now Jim, you don't claim to be a Christian. Is that right?"

"Nope." I was met by a scowling stare.

"And you say you feel happy and your life is going pretty well?"

Straightening up in his chair, Jim answered quickly with his eyes narrowing. "Yeah, ever' thangs good 'cept her. Ha-ell, she's ticked off at me all the time!"

Nodding, I said I understood.

"So," I said, "In summary, Susan, you're a Christian but angry and miserable. Jim, you're not a Christian and fairly happy." I let a brief silence punctuate my findings. "And Susan, you want me to persuade your husband to be a Christian and make his life like yours?!"

She began to nod in agreement, the realization of what I suggested not yet sinking in. Jim jumped in. "That's exactly what I been trying to tell 'er!"

What I said next would have shocked me several years ago, but not now.

"Jim, I see you rode your Harley here today and the weather is gorgeous outside. How would you like to ride for a while? You're free to go."

Jim sat stunned.

Pausing for a moment I then started toward the door to escort him out. "Susan," I said midstride, "I think we have quite a bit to talk about."

Turning toward my huge client who now looked more like a big teddy bear than a threat to society, I again offered my hand, and this time he accepted it.

"Thank you for your time, Jim."

Baffled, he gave a wide grin that made his blue eyes crinkle. "Well, I'll be . . . Thank you!" Without a backward glance he made a skip-like motion out the door.

Turning back to my client, Susan's shocked expression was cold and filled with toxic frustration. She didn't have to say a word. She all but screamed, *"What did you just do? I can't beee-lieve this! After all I went through to get him here, you go and do a thing like that!"*

"I ask you the reader to examine the message. . .
using both your heart and your mind; it is worth the exercise
because it will determine your destiny."
—Ravi Zaccharius[1]

# ❧ 6 ❧

# *The Crux Move*

"Choose for yourselves today whom you will serve. . ."
—Joshua 24:15

This past spring, my youngest son, Kyle, graduated from high school. It's amazing really, how the years have flown. From diapers to bicycles, baseball fields to high school plays – raising three boys has been an adventure all the way. I marvel at the deep joys and sorrows my three sons have brought to their mother and me.

As I turned down the homestretch of this season of our lives, I found myself desperately trying to connect with Kyle in every way possible. He had to find his own set of wings, and I followed him, sharing in the things that interested him most. One day during my recent adventure in parenting, I found myself clinging frantically to the face of a seventy-foot cliff.

I'm always up for a good challenge—as long as it's on the

level grass and sand of a baseball diamond. But when it comes to adventure, my third son has always had something far riskier in mind. While Kyle confidently worked his way up high above carnivorous boulders on jagged ledges like Stallone in the movie *Cliff Hanger*, I too made progress as any good dad would, trying my best to not soil my drawers, all the while wondering why we couldn't have gone snorkeling or started a stamp collection.

Looking back now, however, I find a day forever etched in our memories—though father and son's version assuredly look different. I took hold of valuable lessons up there on the rock. I learned how to follow the lead of a boy who is now a young man. I grasped new things about confidence and faith, or the lack of them. I acquired new skills in the school of fear, accomplishment, and trust. But perhaps the most important thing discovered was the "crux move."

To most people, a cliff looks like a big chunk of rock. But if you know what you are looking for on the face of that big rock you will find cracks, indentations, and little ledges. Sometimes they are so tiny that you can barely see them, even when they are right in front of your nose. Yet if they can bear one's weight and there are plenty of them, they form a "route," a step-by-step set of moves, providing a vertical path all the way to the summit.

Along most routes, there is typically one maneuver far more difficult than all the others. Unusual obstacles make it the toughest spot on the climb. It doesn't matter how far you've come or how easy the climb has been, when you get to this one point, you have three choices:

1. You can back down. Put your gear back in the car and head for the familiar comforts of home.

2. You can stay there for a while, hanging on as long as you can, until you are fairly certain you can make it.

3. Or you can just go for it. Take a calculated risk. Push ahead and make the move, finishing the course to the top.

It's called the "crux move, " and it can challenge your mind as much as it does your strength. Often the risk is unprecedented.

Crux moves are scary and uncomfortable. They can be stressful too. To make matters worse, people are often watching. If you choose to make the move and fall, you face certain embarrassment for and most likely serious injury.

As you face the crux move, all sorts of questions begin zinging through your head. *Do I have what it takes? Is there something there that I will be able to get a hold of? Will the rock hold? What am I doing here?!*

❦   ❦   ❦

Up to this point, this book has been a relatively easy climb. You may have stretched your paradigm a bit as we've investigated bios, *zoe*, mental maps, and behavior. But none of this has been too demanding and none of it has required a difficult, stretching move. So far so good, but now we've come to a critical section on our route.

*. . . your authorities are those things that actually direct your life.*

There are a number of reasons you may be reading this book. Are you looking for a novel approach to the gospel? More information? Your own healing? A deeper relationship with God? My hope is that you will find here the route toward true freedom, abundant joy, and deep rest for which we all seek. But before we can continue much further, there is a difficult move that must be made.

This chapter is the "crux move" of the book. And just like a climber out on the face of a rock, you will be faced with three choices at the end of this chapter:

1. Put the book down and go back to old, familiar, but dissatisfying comforts.

2. Hang here for a while, honestly considering the options before you.

3. Or you can make a committing move of faith and go for it!

For those who are ready to press on, we've arrived at the one obstacle that makes many people turn back. But hang on, you won't be sorry. Though the maneuver may not be comfortable, I guarantee if you are willing to take the risk, our destination, which is beyond anything we could hope for, dream or imagine, will open before us.

## Authority

"Authority." Most of us are repulsed at the word. We think of crabby teachers in elementary school, world leaders who've abused their authority, and clergymen who've smeared it. Bumper stickers remind us to "Question Authority." Teens test it. At work or at play, authority is usually something we try to avoid. But stay with me just for another moment while we take a closer look.

Rather than asking *who* is your authority, let's first ask, "What is an authority?" The bottom line is this: an authority is anything that directs your will. Since your will is what you use to make decisions and choose actions every day, your authorities are those things that actually direct your life.

Think about this. Most of us regard an authority as a person (such as a world leader, a policeman, the manager at our workplace, or our dad) who is trying to get us to do one thing or stop doing another, and we usually feel like they are forcing us against our desire. In contrast, I'm not just talking about people who have the power to control some of your actions, but rather the real bosses — *the real authorities in our lives—the beliefs that dictate our thoughts and decisions.*

These authorities exist for each of us and are constantly at work in our lives. Unlike the heavy hand of a tyrant, we usually aren't even aware of their subtle power over our attitudes and decisions. Most of the time our lives appear to be run by default. It seems like we just do things and just think things. But it's not that way at all. Behind every thought and action, an authority is at work.

Few people will argue the fact that they have authorities. Still most can't readily identify them. In chapter three we talked about the different sources of input that have influenced our "mental grids" and have shaped our view of the world and life in general. These influences include: family, friends, culture, religion, experiences, circumstances, and education. They not only shape our view of the world, but also can become authorities, depending on how much persuasion they have in our lives.

## External Authorities

External authorities are those people and things that we allow to mold our beliefs from the outside in. Their influence is always present, like background music playing quietly in our brain, affecting specific choices we make every day whether for good or bad. Such was the case for me the other day.

Over the past several months of work on this book, I've found it almost impossible to write at the office so I made the decision to write in other locations where there wouldn't be so many distractions. This plan was working pretty well until one of my friends said, somewhat in jest, "Hey, Bill, I haven't been able to get a hold of you at the office lately. It must be nice to show up whenever you want!"

> "They are a dreaded and feared people because their authority originates from within themselves."
> —Habakkuk 1:7

You might guess what a comment like this did to my "performer" flesh and my belief system that insists I must never appear irresponsible. I knew my buddy's comment wasn't a big deal to him, yet I was bothered that he was making an undeniable statement about my perceived productivity. His words began to gnaw at me.

*I've never been unreliable, and quite frankly, I'm not going to appear to be now!* I reckoned. Without conscious effort my friend's comment started to take root and soon my choices started centering on how I was being perceived while the book was in progress. I felt I had to explain everything I did and where I went during counseling center hours. My belief system allowed one comment to become a new authority.

A multitude of external authorities just like the voice of my friend infiltrate our minds over the years. Some we recognize and choose to ignore. We turn away many blatantly harmful messages, but in the process of life, our *external* authorities influence and shape the development of our *internal* authorities. Internal authorities influence our own process of reasoning and our emotions.

## Internal Authorities

In general, it's safe to conclude that our feelings and our reasoning have become our internal authority in almost all situations. "If it feels good, do it!" we say, or we just do what seems right to do at the time. The question is not whether or not you are sitting in the driver's seat of the control of your life. The question is this: Which authorities are you renouncing and which ones have gained your allegiance? What do you rely on as your primary and final authority when it comes time to make decisions?

*"There is a way which seems right to a man, but its end is the way of death."*

*—Proverbs 14:12*

In the overwhelming trend toward individualism especially here in America, the phrase "master your own fate" has almost become a mantra. In many decisions of life, one's emotions and reason (shaped and molded by the world) have become the final authority. This is nothing new. In fact, in the ancient time period of 600 B.C., God spoke through a prophet named Habakkuk who described a group of people called the Chaldeans. This is what he said, "They are a dreaded and feared people because *their authority originates from within themselves*" (Habakkuk 1:7, italics mine).

Dreaded? Feared? This might sound a bit extreme at first, but remember our mental maps? Our vision is skewed and our grids are incomplete and badly distorted. That means that our reason and emotions are leading us astray. How far do you want to travel with someone following his or her own self-centered compass? Do you anticipate he or she will have your best interests in mind? What keeps a person from corruption if their authority originates from within themselves?

"One day we will all find out that being respectful and sincere does not give us license to be wrong," says Ravi Zacharias. "Truth demands investigation and commitment. Our conclusions must be in keeping with truth that can be tested. To be handcuffed by a lie is the worst of all imprisonments."[2] When we move away from God's authority, we move away from God. Any path venturing away from love, truth, and life leads us toward lies, death, and separation from our Creator. In the words of wisdom written by King Solomon, "There is a way which seems right to a man, but its end is the way of death" (Proverbs 14:12).

When we can begin to correctly answer the questions, "Why do I do what I do?" and "Why do I believe what I believe?" we will begin to understand who or what our true authorities are. We tend to just keep doing what we've always done while listening to the authorities we are most familiar with. But are they right? Is your way working? Are you fully satisfied?

In Ezekiel, God speaks through a prophet to His people so that He might expose a faulty authority system. God said, "Yet you say, 'The way of the Lord is not right'.... Is it not your ways that are not right?" (Ezekiel 18:25). A person makes decisions based on authorities he or she believes are trustworthy. But, when that authority is anything less than perfect, wrong choices will soon follow.

*The "crux move" you face now is deciding whether you will accept God's Word, the Bible, as the primary and final authority for guiding your life, or whether you will continue to rely on your own feelings and intellect.*

Jan David Hettingta in his book, *Follow Me*, says:

> The ultimate issue in the universe is leadership. Who you follow and what directs your life, is the single most important thing about you. Tell me who your leader is and I can immediately tell a great deal about you ... even if your leader is yourself.[3]

Because God is all-knowing, all-seeing, good and sovereign, He is the only trustworthy and reliable authority. "Blessed be the name of God forever and ever, for *He alone* has all wisdom and all power ... He gives wise men their wisdom, and scholars their intelligence. He reveals profound mysteries beyond man's understanding. He knows all hidden things . . ." (Daniel 2:20-22, *Living Bible*). The "crux move" you face now is deciding whether you will accept God's Word, the Bible, as the primary and final authority for guiding your life, or whether you will continue to rely on your own feelings and intellect.

## Why the Bible?

Have you ever considered the amazing concept of a mailing address? I have. When cruising along the Interstate in South Dakota, such mind-boggling topics often come to mind. Humor me for a minute. There are nearly seven billion people on this planet, yet with only five little bits of information on a postcard, you can send a message to any one of those seven billion people. How? By the process of elimination—the five-part address removes any other possible option. If you write U.S.A. on the card, it eliminates all other countries. If you write South Dakota, you eliminate all other forty-nine states. The city, street name, and house number do the same thing. Finally, the name singles out the exact recipient of the postcard.

Our mail system works because each bit of information disqualifies all other seven billion incorrect alternatives. The Bible does exactly this: it eliminates all of the wrong possibilities in order to get us to the right Person.

*The Bible is critical to us because it is the only exact source through which we can find, identify, and get to know the true Jesus.*

You may say you choose to seek life in God, through Christ, but many of today's cults say they are doing the same thing. How do you know you've got the right one? The problem is that "many false prophets will arise, and will mislead many" (Matthew 24:11). Jesus is more than just a name. He is a real person. And if you have the wrong address, the right name will not bring you to the correct person. Jesus said Himself that on a certain day in the future, "Many will say to Me on that day, 'Lord, Lord, did we not prophesy in Your name, and in Your

name cast out demons, and in Your name perform many miracles?'"
But His answer will be, "I never knew you; Depart from Me ..."
(Matthew 7:22-23).

Do you know Jesus, Son of God, or are you merely familiar with
a name esteemed as a wise prophet or teacher by many religions
and faiths? Is He a symbol of your salvation; would you recognize
Him? How will you be sure it is Jesus and not a
false prophet? Follow His address!

An invisible God of cosmic proportions has made
His address known and invited us to know Him. How
can this be? How profound it is to think that God, the
Creator of the entire universe, has an eternal plan
with us in mind. When considering the awesomeness
of His purpose, C. S. Lewis wrote, "The whole thing
narrows and narrows, until at last it comes down to
one little point . . ."[4] God's plan narrowed down to
a point so tiny it was unseen within the body of a
young, virgin Jewish girl at the very point an ovum
was impregnated by the Holy Spirit.

*. . . "sufficiency of Scripture" defines the inherent quality of Scripture in guaranteeing and providing, in Christ, all that humanity will ever need for life and godliness. . .*

How do we find the house of this incarnate
God? In the jots and tittles written upon the pages of Scripture.
Only at this address will we find Christ the Messiah. Eliminating all
other options, Jesus said, "I am the way, and the truth, and the life;
no one comes to the Father, but through Me" (John 14:6). The Bible
is critical to us because it is the only exact source through which we
can find, identify, and get to know the true Jesus. "The Word became
flesh, and dwelt among us ..." (John 1:14).

"The Written Word is an extension of the Living Word, and as
such, takes on the same character as the One Who spoke it," states
Jim Craddock in his book, *Be Transformed*. "Consequently, the Bible
is sufficient to address every human problem and need, because
Christ is sufficient."[5]

## Sufficiency of Scripture

The term "sufficiency of Scripture" defines the inherent

quality of Scripture in guaranteeing and providing, in Christ, all that humanity will ever need for life and godliness (2 Peter 1:3). Whenever the truths of Scripture are applied to one's life, a transformation takes place as real as if we'd heard the voice of the Master speak or felt His hands touching our face.

The Bible makes radical claims about what it can do in our search for *zoe* life as it applies to every aspect of our being: body, soul, and spirit. For example, Psalm 19 says that God's laws can "restore the soul ... make the simple wise ... enlighten the eyes ... and warn the servant. . . ." I am especially fascinated with the claims made in 2 Timothy 3:16: "All Scripture is inspired by God and profitable for teaching [knowing what is right], for reproof [knowing what is wrong], for correction [knowing how to get it right], for training in righteousness [knowing how to keep it right]."

God has lavishly provided in Scripture for our every need for any given circumstance, and delights to do so! Were you weary this morning? His Word revives. Do you need understanding with your child? His Word gives wisdom. Is your heart grieved over the loss of your job? His Word comforts.

### Inspiration of Scripture

*... the Bible is absolutely reliable and relevant in every moment and situation of life.*

What do you expect as you open your Bible? Do you anticipate finding upon its pages truth as fresh and alive now as when it was whispered into the minds of its writers? They made claims such as, "For the word of God is living and active ... able to judge the thoughts and intentions of the heart" (Hebrews 4:12).

"We should approach our Bible with the idea that it is not only a book which was once spoken," said A. W. Tozer, "but a book which is now speaking ... God's speaking is in the continuous present." We must not only look to Scripture for wisdom from time to time but rather come to the pages of God's Word daily to encounter Him, to be renewed by His Spirit, and so we may be reminded of Whose we are. Reading the Bible isn't just an exercise of devotion to God; it brings us to the very heart of God!

When we talk about the inspiration of Scripture, we mean that it is literally the out-breathing of God. His words are made alive to our spirit in the same way that God breathed His breath into the nostrils of Adam. Just as Jesus, the "Word became flesh" (John 1:14), stepped into a room of terrified disciples and breathed on them saying, "Peace . . ." (John 20:19), so the Holy Spirit (*pnuema*, the same word associated with breathing) blows His life into our moments of confusion, fear, or uncertainty.

## Authority of Scripture

God's authority is man's final and supreme authority in all things that pertain "to life and godliness, through the true knowledge of Him" (2 Peter 1:3) as expressed in and through His Word. Whether or not we acknowledge it in our lifestyle, the Bible is absolutely reliable and relevant in every moment and situation of life.

This reliability is also reflected in volumes of research and mounds of archeological evidence that show the Bible is historically sound, has been transmitted accurately throughout the ages, and has been translated truthfully into our modern age.

This may be an area where we must become aware of old grids that block our view of God. "There's a sticky suspicion lurking in the back of our minds—something deep within us that is stubbornly reluctant to lower the final defenses and trust God completely," says Jan David Hettingta.[6]

If you struggle against the thought of God's Word being the last word, consider this: Our authority begins and ends with the Author of perfect love. So to be ruled by His Word is to be subjected to none other than the purest form of love. "To trust Him is to understand that total immersion into what He is doing with our life is the best thing that could ever happen to us."[7]

## The Crux Move

"You may as well quit reading and hearing the Word of God,

and give in to the devil, if you do not desire to live according to it."[8]

— Martin Luther

I am claiming that Jesus Christ must be the primary authority in the decisions you make in your life. Regardless of what feels right or what others have led you to believe, I'm telling you that the Bible is the only trustworthy description of Him. And if you commit to this, you will be changed both inside and out. The Bible is the guide that points us to the One who is our Life. "You belong to the power which you choose to obey," instructs J.B. Phillips.[9] Which power will it be?

In your quest for Life, are you willing to use the Bible as your primary and final authority? Whether or not we've read and memorized Scripture since the day we first learned to read, the step to be taken here is not a trivial one. We each must be able to ask ourselves, *"Is it possible the Word of God is not my authority in certain decisions of my life?"* An honest assessment may require a revolutionary change and entirely new focus in some areas of your life. Are you willing to reexamine your standards, belief systems, and feelings? Are you ready to allow major changes in how you deal with yourself, others, and your church?

*. . . know Him, live with Him, invite Him to replace both external and internal authorities.*

"He who has found his life shall lose it, and he who has lost his life for My sake shall find it" (Matthew 10:39).

You say you believe the Bible, but what does your behavior say?

Please know when I speak of the "crux move" I'm not merely referring to the exercise of "reading the Bible." Jesus said it Himself, "You search the Scriptures, because you think that in them you have eternal life; and it is these that bear witness of Me; and you are unwilling to come to Me, that you may have life" (John 5:39-40).

I once counseled a woman who had a rigid regimen of Scripture reading. The problem was she became so focused on keeping the requirements of her discipline that she missed Jesus. Because she felt compelled to read one Proverb every day, one Psalm every day, one Old Testament chapter every day, and one New Testament chapter every day, she couldn't afford the time to pause and meditate on what God was saying specifically to her in any one verse along the way. In order to listen and absorb His truth for us each day, we must somehow get past the drill, past the print on the page, and just *be* with Him.

Jesus didn't go to the synagogue because He was a holy figure with a reputation to keep. He hungered and thirsted for righteousness. The Messiah meditated daily, waiting and listening carefully for His Father's voice to infiltrate His spirit so that He could remain fully dependent on God's will and walk in it. Likewise, our study of the Bible isn't just an exercise of devotion to God. It is our source of life. Our modern culture offers little in the way of encouraging us to model Jesus as He lingered with God in His Word so we might hear Him speak. Richard Foster in *Celebration of Discipline* reminds us:

"The discipline of meditation was certainly familiar to the writers of Scripture. The Bible uses two different Hebrew words to convey the idea of meditation. These words have various meanings: listening to God's word, reflecting on God's works, rehearsing, and more. In each case there is stress upon changed behavior as a result of our encounter with the living God. 'I think of Thee upon my bed, and meditate on Thee in the watches of the night' (Psalm 63:6). The Psalms sing of the meditations of the people of God upon His promises. "My eyes are awake before the watches of the night, that I may meditate upon Thy promise" (Psalm 119:148). [10]

God spoke to the psalmist not because he had special abilities but because he was willing to listen. Meditation is not an exercise belonging to spiritual gurus. One of our fathers of the faith, Deitrich Bonhoeffer, wrote ". . . just as you do not analyze the words of someone you love, but accept them as they are said to you, accept the Word of Scripture and ponder it in your heart, as Mary did.

That is all. That is meditation."[11]

Come expectant and open to God's truth and wait for Him to speak. Toss away your goals and ask what He has for you today. Perhaps one word, one verse, is more than enough for your day. Build a monument and remain with Him there. Know Him, live with Him, invite Him to replace both external and internal authorities.

St. Ambrose said, "As in paradise, God walks in the Holy Scriptures seeking man."[12]

The question now is this: "Will you be found?

*Tempted and lured to act independent of His Father, Jesus relinquished His fleshly desires and chose to rely on the Word of God no matter how He felt.*

◊ ◊ ◊

It was a battle for truth, a battle for belief, and therefore, a battle over personal authority.

"Then Jesus was led up by the Spirit into the wilderness to be tempted by the devil. And after He had fasted forty days and forty nights, He then became hungry. And the tempter came and said to Him, 'If You are the Son of God, command that these stones become bread.' But He answered and said, 'It is written, "Man shall not live on bread alone, but on every word that proceeds out of the mouth of God."' Then the devil took Him into the holy city; and he had Him stand on the pinnacle of the temple, and said to Him, 'If You are the Son of God throw Yourself down; for it is written, "He will give His angels charge concerning you"; and "on their hands they will bear You up, lest you strike Your foot against a stone."' Jesus said to him, "On the other hand, it is written, 'You shall not put the Lord your God to the test.'" Again, the devil took Him to a very high mountain, and showed Him all the kingdoms of the world, and their glory; and he said to Him, "All these things will I give You, if You fall down and worship me." Then Jesus said to him, "Begone, Satan! For it is written, 'You shall worship the Lord your God, and serve Him only.'" Then the devil left Him; and behold, angels came and began to minister to Him" (Matthew 4:1-11).

In a calculated, well-crafted attempt to regain control of the earthly throne of God in Christ, Satan places before Jesus three classic temptations. "Make these stones become bread," he taunts. *Physical pleasure awaits you and you will hunger no more.*

"Throw Yourself down," he challenges. *Words are cheap; prove you are the Son of God and do something spectacular.*

And finally, "All these things I will give You," he begs. *Anything and everything I have, I will give you. Have it all, use it all, keep it all.* Tempted and lured to act independent of His Father, Jesus relinquished His fleshly desires and chose to rely on the Word of God no matter how He felt.

Three times Satan approaches Jesus. And what strategy does Jesus use in his defense? On what grounds does He respond to these attacks? "For it is written …", He responded. He chose Scripture as His ultimate authority. Each and every time, Jesus uses Scripture to combat the temptations Satan hurls at Him.

When offered the opportunity to avoid pain and find life, Jesus evaluated each bargain not on the basis of what felt right or even what might have seemed reasonable. With all physical strength gone, He was able to reject each temptation only while relying on the words of His Father found in Scripture. If Jesus, who was conceived and formed complete with God's spirit within, clung for His life to the authority of God's Word, how foolish is it to anticipate that we can win the battle for our soul with our own tainted authorities?

## In Summary

As I come to the close of this one brief chapter, I wish I could have embarked on describing the eternal wonders revealed to us through God's Word! But I have not. Rather this chapter is simply a practical challenge for you to grab hold of the truth—to set your trust on a foothold toward the life God promised you. It's time to fully engage! "True life," said Pascal, "can be found neither in ourselves nor in external things, but in God and in ourselves as united to Him."[13] The journey is going to be strenuous but beyond all description.

Here it is … the Crux Move.

# Reflection ∿

The crux move of your life is here. Carefully consider your three options:

1. I'm going to back off this climb and continue to use my feelings and my reasoning to guide my life.

2. I'm going to hang here for a while and think this over. This is a significant decision that I'm not ready to make yet.

3. I choose God and His Word as my ultimate authority. From this day forth, I pledge to be His disciple—His follower, and refuse to put anyone or anything else above Him, My Sovereign Lord. When I fail, I commit to being honest about it and making every effort to run back to my gracious heavenly Father. And remember, there is grace at His throne!

You might consider writing this commitment out, signing it and keeping it in a significant place. You may want to purchase a piece of jewelry or something that will symbolize and serve to remind you Who your authority is.

• Can you think of an example when someone said that God was their authority but their behavior indicated otherwise?

• Now do the same with yourself and some of the decisions you are making for your own life.

• Lastly, if you're brave enough, ask a close friend if they see anything in your life that might indicate that God is not your true authority.

# God's Desire ∿

"But know this first of all, that no prophecy of Scripture is a matter of one's own interpretation, for no prophecy was ever made by an act of human will, but men moved by the Holy Spirit spoke from God."
—2 Peter 1:20-21

"I am the Lord, and there is no other; besides Me there is no God."
—Isaiah 45:5

"For in Him (Jesus) all the fullness of Deity dwells in bodily form, and in Him you have been made complete, and He is the head over all rule and authority."
—Colossians 2:9-10

## *Your Response* ⌇

*Father help me to come to see and understand that to be ruled by Your Word is to be subjected to nothing less than the purest form of Love. Please remind me of the danger of walking under any other authority, even when the authority is myself (my intellect or my emotions), independent of You.*

# 7

# Bringing Law to Light

"Men never do evil so completely and cheerfully
as when they do it from religious conviction."
— Pascal[1]

hat are the chances that yours, like most families, has not just one but several Bibles in your home—beautiful, leather-bound with gold embossed edges, perhaps a study Bible or one with a special devotional guide for women, teens, or fathers. If you are like many Christians, you carry yours to and from church and know a few select verses that you memorized in Sunday School or at camp, but recently your daily reading has suffered because it has been pushed aside by more urgent demands on your time.

Did you know "the Bible is the most bought yet least understood book"? In his collection of fascinating facts about the Bible, Jerry MacGregor says, "Nine out of ten Americans own a Bible, but fewer than half ever read it."[2] The majority of the world truly appreciates the wisdom and message written in Scripture. Its poetic and ancient verses are commonly found in our music, public prayers, and literature. Still, I'd venture to say, few make the commitment to grab hold and heave themselves over the ledge, thus making Scripture their foremost authority. Why?

The Bible brings us great comfort in times of fear and tragedy. Many of us feel especially sentimental about passages such as the 23rd Psalm displayed on plaques like the one above grandma's kitchen sink, or the Lord's Prayer because it was sung at dad's funeral. But deep down, we tend to believe we can be freer, more in control of our destiny by relying on other modern sources and our own internal authorities.

For many people the Bible seems like the ocean — deep and broad, mysterious and somehow threatening. Its words often seem distant and disconnected from our current surroundings. We want to enjoy it without really getting caught in its waves. We shy away from its laws and seemingly harsh standards of piety that we don't understand.

Have you ever committed yourself to a purchase or a project only to find out later there were specific conditions that had to be met as part of the deal? Feeling high, you signed up for an interest-free credit card, only to discover in the small print that if the balance isn't paid off within ninety days you'll be charged twenty-eight percent interest on the entire amount owed. Or how about the time you applied for that seven-to-ten hour-per-week job, only to find that the position required no fewer than thirty hours of intense work? Coming from a chapter on authority, rules seem inevitable. We figure that where there's authority, there must be laws, and that means a set of rigid guidelines. After all, we've got plenty of testimony from Christians exhausted from trying not to sin. How can we be sure we're not trading the bondage of one authority for another?

*How can we be sure we're not trading the bondage of one authority for another?*

Remember Sue and her biker husband, Jim? Sue's traditional Christian concept of victorious living was to avoid vulgar actions and do "right" ones. Believing she was truly set free, Sue diligently studied God's Word, learning all the things she felt she must stop as well as the things she must start. She believed wholeheartedly that the Bible was her ultimate authority. Focusing on all the rules of the Christian life, she refused to share life with her husband as she once did. Instead she looked to her pastor for his guidance. She felt secure being told where she could go and where she could not. She became convinced that if she could only do the right things, she'd grow spiritually and enjoy an abundant Christian life.

Instead her choices made her husband grow continually more sullen and angry, which Susan took to be religious persecution from a non-believer. She wanted to keep a sweet spirit, but soon bitterness began to take over, spreading like a cancer. Bound to do what she thought ought to be done, she mistook her standards as "the Christian life."[3]

*Bound to do what she thought ought to be done, she mistook her standards as "the Christian life."*

Susan thought she was living by the standards set by the Bible, but she often felt like giving up. Christians are often confused by the commands set forth by God. What are we who live in the 21st Century to do with the laws that permeate Scripture? We could claim the Bible to be our authority, and upon opening the book of Deuteronomy get stuck. Is the Old Testament with all its unfamiliar statutes meant to be our authority? Are they simply an ancient record of Israel's history? These are necessary questions but more importantly, I believe we must ask, *What does our perception of the law tell us about God's character and what does He desire or demand of us now?*

❁   ❁   ❁

In my basement there is a full-sized popcorn popper just like the ones in theaters, a comfy couch, and life-sized posters of famous old movie stars.

There's nothing I like better than a good movie with scenes that powerfully illustrate a significant truth, a moment that reflects the deep realities of life, or something that just makes me laugh. Besides, it's fun to stretch out on the couch snuggled up with my wife or sit next to my boys, and escape the reality of life this side of the silver screen.

Two Hollywood characters get the honor of adorning my basement wall: Clint Eastwood and "The Duke," John Wayne. In my opinion, some of the greatest movies ever produced were old black-and-white westerns starring my heroes of decades past—you know, dirt flying, guns blazing, and bad guys frying!

In the classic western, everyone knows the plot will soon take a significant turn when "The Law" ambles through the saloon doors, donned with a shiny badge and two long-barreled pistols. No matter how bad things look, everything will soon be okay. Sometimes it might take a while and may include a scuffle or two, but after some sort of showdown between good and evil, we know the law will prevail; freedom and peace will be restored. The law isn't necessarily friendly, in fact, often it seems merciless and maybe even abusive to those who resist its standards—still we know its purpose—to bring justice and protection.

Is the law good? Is it bad? How should we respond to it? Do we fight it? Deny it? Cooperate with it? Throughout history, Orthodox Jews are known for meticulously keeping "the law." With undying devotion, they love the Torah and many have even given their lives for it. *But what are we to do with it? How can we rest after discovering all the demands of God?*

The Law demands our attention today because through it God gives us clear directives that will ultimately allow us to know Him more fully. Without delving too deeply into a subject almost as old as humanity itself, this chapter and the one following provide missing links to knowing why we are disillusioned and short-changed on victory in our lives. God's truths regarding the law are fascinating and contemporary; in fact, they were written with you and me in mind!

## What is "The Law"?

In taking a good look at biblical law and what it means for us, we must first recognize the inherent limitations of literary translation. Much of our confusion results from the English language having only one word, "law," to cover the many unique and differing shades of meaning provided in Scripture, spanning from God's general precepts to personal standards. Of the many Greek renditions for the word, "law," I will focus on only two here: the written law (nomas) and unwritten law (ethos).

Since the time the Law first came into existence on Mt. Sinai (when God gave Moses the Ten Commandments), its scope has expanded and now generally emerges out of three sources: 1) all the laws of the Old Testament as well as the commands of the New Testament; 2) the rules of our society and religion; and 3) our self-imposed standards of performance.

OLD TESTAMENT LAW AND NEW TESTAMENT COMMANDS

*(nomas)*

The earliest references to the Old Testament are known as "the law of Moses," "the law of the Lord," or simply "Moses." Additional writings were considered the work of prophets so the common term became "Moses and the Prophets," or something similar. By New Testament times, "Scripture" or "the Scriptures" became the common term used. The simplest generic term for the collection was "writings," often coupled with "sacred" or "holy."[4]

While the Ten Commandments are the most familiar of all the laws given in the Old Testament (Exodus 20), they were just the beginning of a comprehensive set of rules still to come. These Old Testament laws established the standard for what was required to be "okay" with a holy God. In fact, the Law, known as the Torah or the Laws of Moses, was much more than a law or set of rules. It encompassed Israel's history and her identity.[5] It was not to be perceived as harsh restrictions, but rather a standard of living that reflected the nature of God's character being uniquely different from that of the rest of His Creation.

If Israel would keep the Torah, then she would be kept safe and prosper.[6] Like an old Chinese sage giving wisdom to a young apprentice, so the Law was meant to be a creed for instruction and direction. Similarly, God guided His children, Israel, patiently leading them with His testimonies, His teachings, commandments, and judgments. When I refer to the written law (nomas), the reference is to God's primary instruction to His people as recorded in the canon of Scripture.

The Levitical priests in the Old Testament were called "those who handle the law" (Jeremiah 2:8). Their role was to teach precepts of the Law and to follow its regulations (Deuteronomy 17:11; 33:10). Sadly they became arrogant and forgot God (Isaiah 57:11), whose wisdom they were to teach. Over time they became more and more corrupt using the Law to enhance their own power and wealth (Zephaniah 3:3-4). The Old Testament tells the story of how God was filled with sorrow and sent His prophets to call His beloved Israel back into safety with true obedience to His standards (2 Kings 17:13).

Some generations responded to God's call, but down through the course of history, God's people, like angry teenagers, rebelled against His standards and eventually came to misunderstand the Law, seeing it as something which was imposed for its own sake rather than what their Creator intended the Law to be. In other words, "the means became the end." Separating themselves from the intimate relationship God so desired, His people made the Law only a cold, hard set of standards.

*By the time Jesus was born, the Law. . . had become a heavy, external set of rules under which people had become imprisoned.*

By the time Jesus was born, the Law, instead of being understood as a guideline based in love, had become a heavy, external set of rules (Acts 15:10) under which people had become imprisoned.

Following Christ's death and resurrection, the failure of His people to understand the perfect law of liberty (James 1:25) perpetuated the practice of severe legalism taught by the Judaizers in the First Century. Since all written Scripture is wise instruction from the Master Teacher to His children, the commandments of the New Testament are included as well. In the New Testament, Paul, too, found himself wrestling with issues of living under the Law and he took great care to define its true purpose for all people (both Jews and Gentiles) in Romans, chapters 1-8 and Galatians, chapters 1-3.[7]

## Purpose of the Law (Nomas)

The same Law (nomas) recorded thousands of years ago through which God gave His people guidance, still has a very important purpose for us today. We are not to disregard any Scripture. Being pure and perfect, God's Word reveals His love, defines His nature, and establishes His standards of holiness. The Law (Scripture) serves to protect mankind, to reveal sin, and finally, leaves no doubt that we are sinful and in need of reconciliation.

### GOD'S LAWS DEFINE HIS NATURE AND STANDARD OF HOLINESS

The pure and perfect nature of the written Law (nomas) reflects God's nature. God's statutes reveal that He is not only loving but also holy, absolutely fair, and just. "The law of the LORD is perfect, restoring the soul. . . the commandment of the LORD is pure, enlightening the eyes" (Psalm 19:7-8). Says Steve McVey in his book *Grace Walk*, "The law is a codified expression of God's righteousness, an external picture of God's eternal purity."[8]

God is the standard of holiness by which all else is measured. As a picture of God, the Law demonstrates to mankind pure holiness, perfect righteousness, and relentless love. An atomic clock in Fort Collins, Colorado, gives a great illustration of this. The clock provides the most accurate standard of time down to milliseconds, displaying the perfect time to which all other clocks must align if they are to reflect the true time. This is what the Law of God does as it reveals God as the absolute standard of holiness.

## GOD'S LAWS ARE TO PROTECT MANKIND

*Nomas* in its broadest sense is given to protect mankind from the dangers in life. No longer equipped with God's Spirit as their guide after the Fall, mankind was left vulnerable to the schemes of Satan. God knew man and woman would search for *zoe* life without His internal counsel. Therefore, He provided them with an external set of guidelines to shield them until the time would be fulfilled for the Messiah to come. Only then would we be given the internal instruction of the Holy Spirit to keep us safe from harm.

When we as loving parents told our son, Jess, "Don't go down on the pond, it's not safe because the ice is not strong enough," We were not telling him he's not a trustworthy or good son, but rather the rule was to protect him from dangers he couldn't see or understand. Likewise, God wants us to keep His commandments for our own good, so that we can live a long and prosperous life (Deuteronomy 6:2).

## GOD'S LAWS REVEAL WHAT SIN IS

"Sin" is a word loaded with heavy connotations and perverse images. Originally, however, the definition of the word "sin" stemmed from an old archery term that means "missing the mark." If you took your bow and arrows down to the range and you shot an arrow that landed anywhere except in the bull's eye, it would be considered a "sin." So it is with our lives. The Law defines the bull's eye. If we don't hit the mark dead center, it is sin, plain and simple. Perfection has not been met.

Without the law a person has no gauge for right and wrong. This principle is inseparably linked to God's laws. Says the apostle Paul, ". . . I would not have come to know sin except through the Law; for I would not have known about coveting if the Law had not said, 'You shall not covet'" (Romans 7:7).

## GOD'S LAWS DECLARES US SINFUL

Without the Law there would be no way to recognize our need for salvation or forgiveness. This need becomes clear only after the

Law reveals how we have fallen pitifully short of the standards of the infinitely holy God. It leaves no room for question or argument that we are desperately in need of a Savior. Even for those of us who already have the Spirit of God living within, the written law (nomas) continues to expose sin, revealing it to us when we go astray.

*The Law cannot make us right, but it is a good indicator showing when we do wrong.*

The Law cannot make us right, but it is a good indicator showing when we do wrong. Like an x-ray machine, God's standards of holiness reveal our inner illnesses. Obviously an x-ray machine is not designed to cure us of disease. In the same way, the Law was never designed to cure sin. The Law *reveals* sin, but living by it cannot heal us from sin. ". . . by the works of the Law no flesh will be justified in His sight; for through the Law comes the knowledge of sin" (Romans 3:20).

GOD'S LAW IS A GUIDE

How can we tell if something is wrong even when others say it is right? God's precepts have been given to help restrain and lead – to show when we are out of bounds. The Bible defines certain actions that clearly defy His Word, letting us know we're not walking according to the Spirit. Isaiah 30:21 says, "And your ears will hear a word behind you, 'This is the way, walk in it,' whenever you turn to the right or to the left." God's Law provides a path for us to walk, like a street with two curbs letting us know when we are in or out of bounds.

We must admit, then, just as Paul did in Romans, the Law is very good and it does an excellent job of demonstrating God's holiness, defining sin, exposing sin, and providing guidance for those not walking in the Spirit. Is the Law good? Yes. Purposeful? Absolutely. But how can you and I live under the Law? Just when we think we might be doing enough, we discover that it demands unconditional perfection. Attempting to keep God's standard of holiness on our own will destroy us.

Did you know that when we feel frustrated, discouraged, exhausted, and ready to throw up our hands in surrender, we are exactly where we're supposed to be? The purpose of the Law has been fulfilled. In contrast to God's profound beauty and perfection, our very best efforts can't even get the arrow near the target! We realize how terribly short we fall. We are small and helpless. In no way can we make ourselves righteous enough to find our way back to God.

In Psalm 51:1-4a, we see David's exasperation and desperate cry for God's deliverance. "Be gracious to me, O God, according to Thy lovingkindness; according to the greatness of Thy compassion blot out my transgressions. Wash me thoroughly from my iniquity, and cleanse me from my sin. For I know my transgressions, and my sin is ever before me. Against Thee, Thee only, I have sinned." The king pleads with the Lord to purify him (v. 7), wash him (v. 7), blot out his iniquities (v. 9), and to create in him a clean heart (v. 10).

*Attempting to keep God's standard of holiness on our own will destroy us.*

## GOD'S LAW LEADS US TO CHRIST

The Law is not intended to leave us at a point of desperation about our sin. God gave us the Law for one last magnificent purpose: to lead us to our Redeemer. Our loving Father longs to be reunited with us so we will find the Law leading us to Christ, our redeemer and hope, the One who beckons to us who are weary and heavy-laden so He can give us rest (Matthew 11:28) from the burdens of trying to keep standards of holiness.

In the days of ancient Greece when systems of education were first being made available to the masses, men were hired to escort the children from home to school and back. These "tutors" also helped students rehearse their lessons along the way, thus providing our concept of a modern day tutor. However, unlike our private aides who are usually friendly and encouraging to students struggling with certain topics, the first-century tutor was a paid servant of the government. Because his main function was to lead the student to the teacher, he often carried a whip and used whatever force he found necessary.

Paul knew the people in Galatia were familiar with this arrangement so while writing to them he used the metaphor of "tutor" to explain the role of the Law. "But before faith came, we were kept in custody under the law, being shut up to the faith which was later to be revealed. Therefore the Law has become our tutor to lead us to Christ, that we may be justified by faith. But now that faith has come, we are no longer under a tutor" (Galatians 3:23-25).

*But now that faith has come, we are no longer under a tutor."*

The apostle Paul made clear that our focus is not to be on the guide, but on Jesus, our great Teacher Who waits for us until we come to Him, that we might find forgiveness and acceptance. The Law's job is to guide us (even by force, when necessary) to see the futility of living in our own ignorance and weakness and to see our need for a Savior. It tutors us, leading us to Christ so we can learn to walk with Him in faith.

The tutor has been dismissed. Now that faith has come, we are no longer under its supervision. Paul writes to the Romans, "For Christ is the *end of the law* for righteousness to everyone who believes" (Romans 10:4, emphasis mine). The word "end" in this verse means goal, or completion, but not extinction. Jesus perfectly accomplished, or fulfilled, the requirements of the Law. Man no longer comes to God through the Law because Christ has finished it.

Perhaps you wholeheartedly embrace the fact that Jesus came to set you free from the "old" Law but you are still frustrated by not being able to live up to the standards set by Him. You may wonder, *the tutor has been dismissed, but what if I still struggle with living up to the standards of the Teacher? How can I ever please Him?* It's true; Christ's teachings are even more demanding than the Law!

Jesus said justice not only requires "an eye for an eye" (Matthew 5:38), but also your whole life! Luke records these words of Jesus, "But I say to you who hear, love your enemies, do good to those who hate you ... pray for those who mistreat you. ... And whoever takes away your coat, do not withhold your shirt from him either"

(Luke 6:27-29). "Not returning evil for evil, or insult for insult, but giving a blessing instead ..." (1 Peter 3:9). This really does seem impossible for most of us, doesn't it? What did Jesus mean?

The Pharisees believed they must observe thousands of petty rules and regulations, but nothing could have been further from the kingdom of God founded on love. By raising the bar to even higher standards than the Pharisees had ever achieved, Jesus left no shadow of doubt that to live up to the holy perfection of God was *humanly impossible*. He said that to keep the Law one must be perfect even as our Father in heaven is perfect (Matthew 5:48). Jesus left no room for doubt that humanity is in a desperate state of helplessness and frustration. Jesus gave unreachable demands so that we would recognize our need for an entirely different way to live—a whole new way of life.

The misuse of authority by the Pharisees and their false teaching not only kept them arrogant, but also they became dangerous. Jesus' law exposed the Pharisees' inadequacies. He accused the false teachers of laying heavy burdens on men and women without lifting a finger to help (Luke 11:46). In addition to God's law, they loaded down the common people with hundreds of rules and regulations – heavy laws of human traditions in the name of God. When the people failed, they felt guilty and spiritually defective. Times haven't changed much.

I'm going to make a bold statement here. I believe the majority of stress and heaviness we Christians feel today is not primarily a result of life's difficult circumstances, but rather the consequence of weight placed on our shoulders by someone other than God. We are in desperate need of a whole new way to live. Why have we come to accept the idea that struggling to live under such a paralyzing weight of standards and regulations is the life Jesus would have us live in order to attain spiritual growth?

*I believe the majority of stress and heaviness we Christians feel today is not primarily a result of life's difficult circumstances, but rather the consequence of weight placed on our shoulders by someone other than God.*

## Living Under the Law

"Now we know that whatever the Law says, it speaks to those who are under the Law, that every mouth may be closed, and all the world may become accountable to God" (Romans 3:19, emphasis mine).

What comes to mind when you think of a guide? One can be led by the gentle prompting of a shepherd. In some cases guidance comes by force, such as driving cattle with a prod or a whip. A bit and bridle in the mouth of a horse acts as a guide, as does a yoke over the shoulders of oxen. Unlike the words of a gentle leader, a yoke typically conjures up the image of a heavy, wooden beam over the shoulders used to steer two animals in the same direction, or to balance a heavy burden. The symbol of a yoke is often coupled with life under the Law.

THE YOKE OF THE LAW

In his book, *Healing Spiritual Abuse*, Ken Blue gives a clear picture of the oppression brought to the people of Jesus' time by the weight of the Law:

> The Pharisees spent many of their waking hours memorizing and discussing God's law and the thousands of man-made refinements surrounding it. They referred to this discipline as "coming under the yoke of the law." Those who mastered this yoke had occasion to boast, but for the common person, who had neither the time nor the means for such mastery, the yoke became an oppressive burden.[8]

No one in the New Testament was more committed to studying the Scriptures than the Pharisees. These religious leaders thoroughly knew the content of their Old Testament because they poured over it daily and could quote long passages from memory. But Jesus said, "You search the Scriptures, because you think that in them you have eternal life; and it is these that bear witness of Me; and you are unwilling to come to Me, *that you may have life*" (John 5:39-40, emphasis mine).

The Pharisees' approach to the Bible was just a more extreme approach than that taken by many of us. Christians are focusing on doing all the right things, but are missing the life of Christ in what they do, because their perspective is based on law. Just as the Pharisees missed Jesus and therefore life, we must wonder if even with our best intentions we, too, have been denied or are denying *zoe* life to those around us.

The traditions of the church have been handed down in much the same manner as the traditions of the Pharisees. God's written law was intended to guide, or tutor, all people ultimately to the Master Teacher, and was then dismissed through our faith in Him. Coming under the yoke of the law, however, means taking on "any standard or tradition *a person believes he or she must meet* to be okay with God, others, or him or herself." From this point forward our discussion centers on living under the law. It is here that we introduce the unwritten law, *ethos.*

**The Law**
FIG. 2

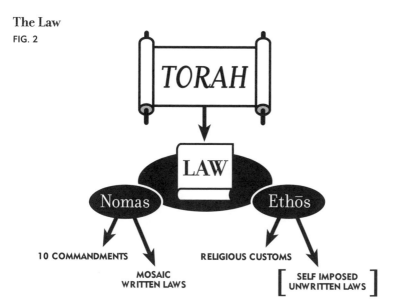

## Rules of Religion and Society (Ethos)

When Paul addresses the role of the law in Romans and Galatians, he not only addresses the written Law (*nomas*), but also the law as it applies to any unwritten standard, or ethos. This being the root from which our word "ethics" is derived, we can see how it has come to play an integral role in religion, society, and self-standards. Who determines what is moral, honorable, virtuous, decent, and proper?

RELIGION

You can see how ethos makes its way into religion. Laws of religion are intended to hedge us in and distinguish between those who belong and those who don't. While a few of these creeds can be found clearly stated in Scripture or in church codes of conduct, most are arbitrary standards describing how one must dress, act, speak, and behave, typically being heavily influenced by the cultural standards of the area. These rules include a vast array of expectations about how one should pray, vote, serve, dance (or not), drink, eat, spend time on Sunday, spend money, educate children, and worship. The laws of one's doctrine may even give the particulars about how to spend "quiet time" with God each day. These expectations become "law" when we feel we must live up to them in order to feel adequate or acceptable to our communities, our church, other Christians, ourselves, and maybe even God (Isaiah 29:13-14; Mark 7:6-13).

SOCIETY

Written or unwritten, *ethos* laws are ones with which our society defines acceptable and unacceptable conduct. Unlike the Old Testament law which was carefully written down, most of the laws of our modern society are a bit fuzzy, and are usually defined by values or virtues such as "honesty," "integrity," and "charity." Some are also written such as the federal, state, and local laws that tell us what we can and can't do. Societal laws tell us what it means to be a good neighbor and how to be a productive member of our community.

The laws of society certainly have a purpose to fulfill. A city or nation with neither the "laws of the land" nor the Spirit of

God would be filled with total chaos. We have seen it displayed
in pockets around the globe – riots in Los Angeles, genocide in
Uganda, or junior high band rooms when the instructor turns her
back.

## Self-imposed Standards of Performance (*Ethos*)

As if the standards of religion and society are not enough,
we also develop our own set of personal "laws." These personal
standards for performance might include a 3.5
grade point average, a certain level of athletic
performance, or financial status. They are *Though unique*
different for everyone and can vary widely such *to each individual,*
as maintaining a good physique, home schooling, *the personal stan-*
housekeeping, or spending money carefully. *dards or demands*
Remember, we are now discussing ethos, the *we create are just*
law as set forth in traditions and standards a person
believes he or she must meet in order to be acceptable *as real and carry*
to God, others, or oneself. Though unique to each *the same heavy*
individual, the personal standards or demands we *consequences of*
create are just as real and carry the same heavy *any law derived*
consequences of any law derived from Scriptures, *from Scriptures,*
society, or religion. They become most obvious when *society, or religion.*
we "blow it" and cannot do or be what we feel we
must in order to be acceptable.

Without consciously being aware of it, my *ethos* drove my
Christian life just as strongly as it did my athletic goals. I simply
traded my performance as the Iron Man for memorizing more than
three thousand Scripture verses. My law weighed heavy.

Why do we often feel trapped in behaviors or roles we don't
necessarily want? Our *ethos* is learned from the day we are born,
and our belief systems demand that we live up to these laws in
order to be accepted. Below you will find the process by which we
come under the yoke of our own personal law (*ethos*).

## Self-imposed Standards

(Derived from Jim Craddock, SCOPE Ministries)

1. I discover that I am accepted—not on the basis of who I am as a person—but on what I do.

2. Since I am not accepted as a person, I adopt artificial standards to guarantee acceptance and approval. These standards become part of my lifestyle.

3. Block-by-block, layer-by-layer, mental fortresses (sometimes called strongholds, citadels, or belief systems) are built up in my mind. Soon they produce their own thought patterns, coloring what I see, hear, sense, and feel.

4. The lies that I believe about myself produce a poor self-image, which, in turn, affects my behavior.

5. This inaccurate perception of self reinforces the need for artificial standards to gain the acceptance, approval, and recognition that does not come unconditionally.

6. Every standard that I accept as truth becomes my authority. My life is governed by these standards.

7. A conflict emerges within me between my desire for unconditional acceptance and the demands of my standards.

8. The standards that I accept affect all my relationships, forcing me to try to become the person I think you want me to be. I cannot be myself and, consequently become a phony.

9. The fear of rejection and disapproval is so strong that it continually reinforces these standards.

10. The system of rewards and punishment that most parents, schools, and places of employment follow tend to reinforce these standards.

When we speak about being under the confines of the law, this undoubtedly includes the standards of "performance-based acceptance" that we place on others and ourselves. Perhaps the most devious and subtle form of "law," these standards can crush the heart and feel like a ten-ton yoke on the shoulders. The words of 2 Corinthians 3:12-18 have become very real to me, and the presence of *nomas* and *ethos* in my life have become clear to me also as "the veil" has gradually been lifted from my eyes. In years past, it became fairly easy to recognize the harsh legalism of first-century Judaizers, the piety set forth by Church of England, and the traditions of Catholicism in my childhood. But more recently and more painfully, I've come to see clear examples of unwritten standards expected by my current church and our counseling ministry. Then one night as I was teaching on this topic at a conference, God began showing me how these expectations have appallingly permeated my own home.

Whether played out in different denominations or our own parenting, we have all come under the yoke of the law. I've yet to find a person in all my years of counseling who is not living under some dictates of man-made standards. We've learned our survival strategies well. And for this reason Paul specifically warns us not to be conformed or squeezed into the world's mold by believing we can be something apart from God based on our own performance (Romans 12:2).

## Take My Yoke

Why isn't your life abundant and free? Have you or someone you love placed you under certain requirements in order to gain acceptance or approval? Jesus says, "Come to Me, all who are weary and heavyladen, and I will give you rest. Take My yoke upon you, and learn from Me, for I am gentle and humble in heart; and you shall find rest for your souls. *For My yoke is easy, and my load is light*" (Matthew 11:28-30, emphasis mine).

When Jesus speaks of his yoke in this passage, He is referring to "a new law," His law. In other words, Jesus says that standard you have been carrying is much too heavy for you to bear. Can you hear the tenderness in His voice? He kneels beside us when we are beaten down and asks if we want to trade. When Jesus says, "Come to Me," He is inviting us to an intimate relationship with Him. Overcome with compassion, Jesus is personally asking you, "Take My law of love upon you and know Me. Learn of My gentle acceptance and My rest."

Says Ken Blue to those who need to be freed from the prison of performance:

> "Though we fail, Christ never fails. As our Savior He meets every standard on God's test of perfection and He credits our account. We don't know how to worship perfectly, but He does. We don't know how to pray perfectly, but He does. We don't know how to trust and obey perfectly, but He does. We don't know how to love perfectly, but He is love."[10]

## In Summary

When I find myself weary and under a burdensome situation, when I'm being drained and on the verge of burnout, I know I've been shouldering the wrong yoke. Principles only demand more and more from me. I've found that Law doesn't require a relationship, but Christ, on the other hand, looks me in the eye and asks if I might come to know Him, to learn from Him, and to find rest. God is not interested in guiding us with a whip or a prod, or steering us with a bit and bridle; He wants to walk with us.

God's sacred Law is perfect, defining His nature and standard of holiness. Not only was His Law set forth to protect mankind, but also it ultimately allows us to know Him more fully. We recognize our desperate need for His redemption from our sin, and His Law leads us like a tutor to Jesus in whom the Law was perfectly fulfilled. One command fulfills all other commandments —"Love."

Is your Christian life weary and burdensome? God's answer is not a longer quiet time, a firmer commitment, attending one more conference, or another trip to the altar. God's solution for spiritual tiredness is rest—rest in the loving acceptance of Jesus and His perfect load-carrying work for you. "Come to Me."

## Reflection ⌇

Are you still trying to be "good enough" to be acceptable to God? Completing the following sentences will help you see areas in you life where you are "living under the law."

God would love and accept me more if . . .
I would be a better Christian if . . .
I would love and accept myself more if . . .

After reading this chapter, what are some laws that you recognize in your own life?

## God's Desire ⌇

"Therefore, my brethren, you also were made to die to the law through the body of Christ, that you might be joined to another, to Him who was raised from the dead, that we might bear fruit for God."
—Romans 7:4

"It was for freedom that Christ set us free; therefore keep standing firm and do not be subject again to a yoke of slavery."
—Galatians 5:1

## Your Response ⌇

*Father, teach me the way to live in freedom—not freedom to live in whatever manner I choose, but freedom to live in the new way of the Spirit—not under law but in grace.*

# ❧ 8 ❧

# Escaping the
# Stained Glass Prison

"For Christ is the end of the law
for righteousness to everyone who believes."
—Romans 10:4

I travel and speak to many groups of people, including pastors and godly leaders from different states and countries. As I stand before these respected men and women of prayer and faith, I hold a glass cup out in front of me. I then ask my audience to pray and believe that the cup will not fall to the floor when I let go of it. Do you know, in all my years of teaching and all the hundreds of men and women I've asked to do this, not a single person has ever kept the cup from falling to the floor. Why? The earth was created with the physical law of gravity.

Just as surely as this physical law guarantees a cup will fall and smash on the floor, spiritual laws regarding living under the Law abound as well. God says that if you choose to live by the Law, you will fall under its dictates and be subject to the consequences of life lived under the Law.

I like this illustration because I've always been interested in the laws of science and religion. In my childhood, there were moments when these two laws seemed to come together in a way that was magical, even electrifying. Some of these moments took place on Sunday mornings, at about 10:25 A.M., when I was fulfilling my duties as an altar boy during communion.

*God says that if you choose to live by the Law, you will fall under its dictates and be subject to the consequences of life lived under the Law.*

It all started with the scientific law that says when plastic (such as that found on the soles of an altar boy's shoes), is rubbed against wool (such as that found at the altar of a church sanctuary), little electrons are rubbed off the carpet and stored in the body of the altar boy. The more friction he creates with each rub of his shoe on the carpet, the more electricity his body stores. It is also a simple law of science that this static electricity can be rapidly discharged through a metal object (such as a communion plate) into the body of another human being—such as another kid.

One particularly glorious morning, as the congregation lined up three by three for communion, my job was to hold a metal plate under the priest's hand as he served the communion wafer to the next potential "victim," (I mean recipient). And God be praised, in my line was my buddy, Neal Danielson.

Neal tried to avoid my gaze at first. He knew this game all too well. Though no scientist, he was an altar boy himself, and he occasionally utilized the same laws of science to singe the peach fuzz from my cheek. When our eyes met, he knew it was payback time. Rub, rub, rub.

He fidgeted nervously back and forth as the line shortened. Was there an alternative? Switch lines perhaps? He looked to the front of the left line, but there was my brother, Joe. Rub, rub, rub. He looked right, but there was my next-door neighbor, Tom. Rub, rub, rub. He looked back at me helplessly. We all had the same devious smile on our cherub faces.

He was stuck with nowhere to go. At that moment he was securely held under both the laws of science and the laws of religion. As the organ played on, excitement grew between the electrons. Neal's turn at the altar had come. Solemnly he knelt at my feet like a criminal before an executioner.

The priest offered Neal the round wafer and he dutifully tilted his head back ever so slightly, leaving his mouth open to the priest and leaving a clear shot of his Adam's apple open to me. As the priest brought the bread to Neal's lips, I brought the plate closer to his neck. Closer, closer, until that beautiful instant when the laws of science, the laws of religion, and the laws of retribution all meshed together in one wondrous, yea even shocking, way.

Simultaneously, when all of the excess electrons decided they were close enough to make the jump, there was a brief flash of light and ZAP! If my memory serves me right, the light bulbs above the altar flicked instantaneously, the priest's heart skipped a beat, and for scientific reasons I do not fully understand, the gray hair on the heads of the old ladies in the front row stood momentarily on end, rousing them from their slumber. Then all was quiet. Neal began breathing again and looked up with a calm, religious smile—but wild, fiery eyes. Next week, his mind raced, *I'll be the altar boy and the laws of science and religion will again manifest themselves.*

The laws of science guarantee a cup will fall and hit the floor and that excess electrons will arc from a metal plate to skin. In the same way, living under the law, whether written (*nomas*) or unwritten (*ethos*), can bring only a destructive sense of responsibility. Attempting to accomplish good things for God may sound admirable, but it can actually produce long lasting and damaging consequences.

The apostle Paul realized that no one could ever fulfill such demands completely. In Romans 5:6-10, he describes mankind prior to receiving Christ as "helpless," "ungodly," "sinners," and "enemies." Sin (anything less than perfect holiness) renders us totally incapable of pleasing God through our own efforts.

The coming of Christ ended everything Paul had been taught

about the Law's role in making him right with God. To the Galatians he wrote, "the whole Law" is fulfilled in the one commandment of love, "You shall love your neighbor as yourself" (Galatians 5:14). On the other hand, to consider living under any other obligation meant living a cursed life. Any voice (external or internal) which demands that we do more and try harder to merit divine or human acceptance results in what Paul refers to as "the curse of the law."

## The Curse of the Law

"All who rely on observing the law are under a curse."
– Galatians 3:10

Curses are the consequences that come with trying to keep the law. Curses may sound a bit mystical to our modern ears but the results of living under the law are very similar to being under a spell. Because the law demands perfection, there is no way to do it halfway. My friend, if you choose anything other than the Law of Love by believing there are rules that you must keep in order to be okay with God, others, or yourself, there are a number of curses under which you *will* be chained.

"...Cursed is everyone who does not abide by *all* things written in the book of the Law, to perform them." (Galatians 3:10; Deuteronomy 27:26, emphasis mine)

## CURSE #1: Perfection

If you are trying to keep the law in order to pass God's class, you need to know right up front that God doesn't grade on the curve. There's not a single "C" or "B+" in His book. It's "pass" or "fail," and nothing in between.[1] Second, you need to know that in order to earn an "A," you must score perfectly one hundred percent of the time.

And if that isn't intense enough, Jesus requires a *higher* standard than the laws presented in the Old Testament. Number seven of the Ten Commandments says, "You shall not commit adultery" (Exodus 20:14), but Jesus said, "... every one who looks on a woman to lust for her has committed adultery with her already in his heart" (Matthew 5:28). Jesus raises the bar of the Law to include not only one's actions but also one's *thoughts*! And again, the standard of purity is one hundred percent.

The laws of society, religion, and self aren't perfectly holy and just as God's laws are. The people of society and religion can cut you some slack if they want to because they aren't holy and just like God. However, there is no guarantee that they will, unless you live up to all of their ideals all of the time.

That was part of my trap in baseball. Not only did I have to be good, I had to be the best. I needed to hit the *most* home runs. I needed to have the most runs batted in and the highest batting averages. I could not fail, lest I fall short of the law of society and the personal requirements of performance I had created for myself.

*If you are "under the law" in these situations, be prepared to become fearful and a phony as you try to be what everyone else says you should be.*

In 1978, my home run and hitting statistics dropped slightly. I was second best in the Minor League AA and I was *devastated*. I couldn't believe how affected I was by this until I learned that "whoever keeps the whole law and yet stumbles in one point, he has become guilty of all" (James 2:10).

The standards of society and religion waver on almost every "law" (abortion, taxes, marriage, and divorce—all differ from state to state or church to church). Even the laws of society regarding one's appearance change constantly. What is sexy or macho today is bound to be dorky tomorrow. If you are "under the law" in these situations, be prepared to become fearful and a phony as you try to be what everyone else says you should be.

It's a tough way to live, but if you are living under the law, you might as well get used to it, particularly when you are trying to make yourself right before God. Even if you do it all right ninety-nine percent of the time, with one mental slip you might as well have committed all sins—you've missed the bull's eye. Regardless of whether it is God's law, the law of others, or your own laws, if you believe you need to keep these standards in order to be okay, perfection is the only way to be sure.

## CURSE #2: Distraction and Bondage

My altar boy experience was a fun example of how seriously distracted we can become from the beauty of God's truth in practices such as communion. If we are living under the law, it is impossible to walk with God by faith because we are focusing on rules and not on Him. "...we were kept *in custody* under the law, being *shut up* to the faith which was later to be revealed" (Galatians 3:23, emphasis mine). *In custody* and *shut up* sound an awful lot like jail, and it is. Trying to make ourselves "okay" with God through the law will not only distract us from experiencing *zoe* Life, it will imprison our soul. The consequences of distraction and bondage are serious when it comes to our relationship with God.

*Trying to make ourselves "okay" with God through the law will not only distract us from experiencing zoe life, it will imprison our soul.*

Personal standards distract us and keep us bound from living the life of freedom Christ intended as well. Take for instance when a young lady (we'll call her Amanda) goes bowling with some friends. She steps forward to take her position and with her team and spectators watching, tries to concentrate on her next roll. But she can't focus on the pins at the end of the alley or the position of her ball for the only thing on her mind is, "Does my butt look too big in these pants?" Self-conscious and miserable, the game is no longer fun for her. She throws a gutter ball and sits down as quickly as she can, bound by her personal laws of appearance.

Like Amanda, many of us live bound under the laws of society and self. A dad might be physically present at his son's soccer game but be so mentally distracted by issues back at the office that he misses his son's first goal. Other people are tied up by their personal laws such as, "I can't rest or have any guests until my house is clean and orderly," or "I can't play until all the work is done." The only problem, of course, is that the work will never be done.

### CURSE #3: Destructive Sense of Responsibility

After adding the curse of perfection to the other curses of distraction and bondage, the law begins to feel very heavy, doesn't it? Now heap on the fact that you are fully responsible for keeping this law totally on your own. If we are so bold to state, "God, I can earn your love and acceptance," we must do so out of our own strength. If I'm in love with God and I'm trying to impress Him with my behavior, it doesn't help for someone else to step in and take my place. I'm alone with this destructive sense of responsibility. I have to do it myself even though I am trying to do something I was never created to do.

With any *ethos* or personal standard, it is our responsibility alone to keep it. Can we earn the Diety's favor or make Him love us just a little more? To this Paul exclaims, "Are you so foolish? Having begun by the Spirit, are you now being perfected by [your own] flesh?" (Galatians 3:3). Rather than focusing entirely on Jesus, living "under the Law" leads us into three deceptive lies: I can keep the Law, I *must* keep the Law, and I am *responsible* to keep the Law.

### CURSE #4: Aroused Sinful Flesh

It gets worse. When we live under Law and try to use it to gain righteousness, we are actually giving power to the very things we are trying to flee. Did you know the law actually arouses and stirs up the very things we wish would fade away, making it impossible to do what is right? The Bible says, "For while we were in the flesh, the sinful passions, which were aroused by the Law, were at work in the members of our body to bear fruit for death" (Romans 7:5, emphasis mine).

Now consider this. I don't want you to sin. In fact, I'm insisting that you don't. Do NOT sin. I will help ensure that you don't by telling you exactly *what* you shouldn't do. Don't even *think* about it. (Remember Proverbs 23:7 says, "For as he thinks within himself, so he is.") So, right now, I specifically do not want you to think of a swear word that begins with the letters, "sh".

How did you do? It didn't work so well, did it? Why not? I specifically told you what not to do, and you found it impossible to obey. What is going on here? Before I told you not to think of the "sh" word, it hadn't entered your mind!

You just experienced how the law arouses sinful flesh. How many of us can tell of diets that made us obsess over the food in the pantry, or attempts to stop an addiction that made us drive headlong into its clutches?

Why is that? There are two reasons—first, in order for sin to move in your life, it needs a *vehicle*, and that vehicle is your body (Romans 6:12-13). Second, sin needs fuel to propel your body into unrighteous actions and thoughts. Did you know the Bible says that the fuel your body needs is the law itself?! "The sting of death is sin, and *the power of sin is the law*" (1 Corinthians 15:56, emphasis mine). Since we can't get rid of our body, the only other way we can cut out this "arousal of our flesh" is to get rid of legalism in our life.

*It is critical to understand that trying to live by the law is impossible because the law gives power to the very things that make us unrighteous.* The law stirs up sinful flesh, making it impossible to do what is right. And the harder we try, the worse it gets. It's one thing to try to not think about the "sh" word, but what about lust, jealousy, or pornography? If we tell people to "just say no!" to these things, *will we not arouse the very sin we are trying to prevent?*

*It is critical to understand that trying to live by the law is impossible because the law gives power to the very things that make us unrighteous.*

"...the sinful passions, which were aroused by the Law, were at work in the members of our body to bear fruit for death. ...for I would not have known about coveting if the Law had not said, "You shall not covet." But sin, taking opportunity through the commandment, produced in me coveting of every kind; for apart from the Law sin is dead" (Romans 7:5, 7-8).

## Curse #5: The Trap of Self-Righteousness

Maybe you've convinced yourself up to this point that you really have been making the grade. You've had to dismiss minor "shortcomings" or slight "mess-ups," but those are just little things, right? When it comes to the important things, you've done what you've needed to do. Your family is in good shape, and your friends and neighbors hold you in high esteem.

Even though you might never verbally admit this, it's quite obvious when you compare yourself to others that, indeed, you are doing better than most. You're doing what it takes, you've gone the extra mile, avoided the pitfalls, and have set yourself apart from others who share neither your commitment nor your sacrifice. Your beliefs, theology, and actions have put you in position to compare yourself to others.

Congratulations! You are now part of an elite group of Christian "performers". In your own mind, you have met the challenges put forth by the laws of God, society, religion, and self. Through your efforts and abstinences you now feel worthy in God's presence and can project your standards of performance upon others. You want to feel pretty good about that, but understand this—Jesus showed more anger toward people like you than He did anyone else (see Matthew 12: 34; 15:12-14; 23:13-19, 33). Personally, I fall for this often. When I am succeeding at living under the law, self-righteousness invades my heart like a poison.

"I do not nullify the grace of God; for if righteousness comes through the Law, then Christ died needlessly" (Galatians 2:21). These are sobering words. The Law was never intended to justify us or make us acceptable. If any of us choose to live under the Law of God, the laws of society and religion, or the laws created by ourselves, we must know they come hand-in-hand with the curses described above.

❂ ❂ ❂

It should be clear by now that living under the law is not where you want to be. The curses are devastating, the demands overwhelming, and failure is certain. What can you do? Imagine yourself for a moment in a movie much like the westerns I love. In this scene there are three main characters: you, God, and the Law. The scene fades in where an encounter of epic proportions is about to take place.

◊  ◊  ◊

Tumbleweeds blow through a dusty, vacant town. The worried eyes of a few residents peer through dirty windows of shanties lining the street. Two figures stand alone in the empty street. One is you. The other is the Law. Sometimes very vocal, sometimes in silent disapproval, for as long as you can remember, the Law has been your constant companion. It is legally binding—you were born into it and have lived with it in a world that fuels it. With the Law you have been "sealed for life, till death do you part." The Law begins dragging you with an unmerciful grip down the middle of the rutted street.

The air is thick with danger. Your throat is constricted and dry, making it impossible to swallow. Searching for a trace of compassion, you are met only with accusation from your silent, disapproving companion—and rightfully so. Though you've tried to live up to perfection, you've messed up—again and again. Always in small ways, sometimes in big ways—and the Law reminds you of every fault.

The Law isn't wrong. In fact, it's right. Unmercifully right and right all the time, revealing your weaknesses, pointing out your failures, constantly reminding you that you fall pitifully short of all that is required by God.

The Law isn't mean, just unbending. It's not evil, just heartless. You've tried everything in your strength to please, but this spouse's standards can never be met. You've tried harder and harder, to find only that still more is demanded.

Stopping now in the town square, you stand alone with the Law—exasperated, exhausted, and near despair. You have looked to the Law for direction and protection, stability and security. Instead you have found only criticism, higher standards, and the constant, irrefutable charge that you never have been and never will be good enough.

"You are a failure, you know," the Law reminds you, again.

The tears welling up in your eyes are met with a cool stare. "I just wanted to be loved," you whisper.

"Sorry, just doing my job," comes the reply, as the grip on your wrist tightens again. Can anyone rescue you from this bondage?

At high noon the pounding of hoofs can be heard in the distance. Squinting into the blazing sunlight, you see someone approaching on the horizon. It is God Himself, coming in the form of a man, galloping into town on a blazing white stallion... and He is riding right toward you! Could it be? Could deliverance be near?

As the stallion nears, the Law stands unflinching, unmoved, unintimidated. He has every right to your life. You were born in sin and have lived always under the Law. According to the Law of this land, you are rightfully, legally bound to the Law.

Your desperate eyes meet those of your Creator. What does He see?

The warmth of His gaze draws you in and for a blissful moment you realize He sees not only your sins, but He actually sees YOU, all your hopes, dreams, and fears. "I knit you together delicately, each thread of personality tenderly woven," His heart speaks to yours. "I created you for splendor and unity with me. You are My bride, but betrothed to another. Your beautiful heart formed by My own hands, now so stained and discarded belongs with Me!"

He knows you as you've never been known before. All you know is that this is who your heart thirsts for.

Looking toward the heavens, Jesus pauses. Unhurried, He dismounts and walks toward you. The town's people dive for cover as He slowly approaches. Your heart beats faster.

The moment of deliverance from the Law has come! Jesus pulls you to His chest, but the Law's grip remains firm and unrelenting. There is a brief shuffle of feet and the undeniable sound of a gun being unholstered, its hammer being pulled back. The sound of a shot rings out and a severing pain rips through your heart. Filled with shock, your mind screams, "This can't be! I'm, I'm bleeding!"

Looking up, you then find to your horror that He too is falling to the ground, bleeding from the hands, feet, and side. Having taken the same bullet that will end your life, your Savior holds you firmly, and with eyes filled with pain and peace, He looks deep into your eyes.

"It is finished," Jesus says, His breath and yours fading. As your heart beats slower and slower and finally beats its last, the Law's grip on you loosens and your arm falls to the ground, lifeless and free. Jesus breathes His last as well, the smoking gun still in His hand.

Another tumbleweed rolls by. All is quiet except for the rustle of the wind. The scene fades.

This is not quite what you were expecting, is it? If you are like me, you anticipated your hero would kill the Law. But, my friend, that could never be. That was never part of the script. Jesus said, "Do not think that I came to abolish the Law or the Prophets; I did not come to abolish, but to fulfill" (Matthew 5:17).

The western movie scene might be a bit dramatic, but the analogy of us being married to the Law certainly is not. In fact, in Romans chapter seven, Paul uses marriage as an illustration of our bondage to the law, signifying that the relationship can be broken only by death. "Or do you not know, brethren. . . *that the law has jurisdiction over a person as long as he lives?* For the married woman is bound by law to her husband while he is living; but if her husband dies, she is released from the law concerning the husband" (Romans 7:1-2, emphasis mine).

*Only through death can our bondage to the Law be broken.* There is nothing to warrant the death of something holy and right, and we've already seen that the Law is perfect, so the only option left was our death. At the deepest core of our being, our sinful, God-forsaken spirit has once and for all been crucified with Him. Paul explained, "For through the Law I died to the Law... I have been crucified with Christ; and it is no longer I who live ..." (Galatians 2:19-20).

If this story leaves you feeling baffled or uneasy, open the Bible to Romans seven and read again. *It is imperative that each of us grasps the truths written here.* Be encouraged, you will soon find this is not the end of the story, but rather just the beginning! The next scene opens with resurrection to new life.

With the death of our old spirit, our binding marriage to the Law has ended and an entirely new era in our lives begins—one in which we've been made completely new in Christ. A future filled with hope awaits us. Not only are we free from sin's consequence of eternal separation from God—we are free now from the tyranny of rules and regulations. Together crucified—together, we are raised with Jesus Himself.

*A future filled with hope awaits us.*

"But now we have been released from the Law, having died to that by which we were bound, so that we serve in newness of the Spirit and not in oldness of the letter" (Romans 7:6.)

"You also were made to die to the Law... that you might be joined to another, to Him who was raised from the dead, that we might bear fruit for God" (Romans 7:4).

We are free, free from the Law. We are now a new creation designed by God to be containers for the very life of Christ—with Him living His life through ours, with His Spirit guiding and empowering our spirit. The commands of Scripture can now fulfill their God-designed purposes, but we are no longer bound to them as requirements that we must meet in order to be acceptable to God. Through our spiritual death and rebirth, Christ has made us alive with Him, bound to Him, unified with Him, and empowered to walk by faith, in the Spirit, fulfilling the purposes that He has prepared for us.

Christ came to fulfill the Law. He forgave us all our sins,

"having canceled out the certificate of debt [the written code against us and which was hostile to us] *and He has taken it out of the way, having nailed it to the cross . . . Therefore let no one act as your judge . . .* " (Colossians 2:14,16, emphasis mine).

Making reference to prison, Paul anticipates his readers will be familiar with the practices of legal punishment of the day. In Biblical times, if one was convicted of a crime, he was kept in a cell and a list of offenses with the penalty incurred was kept on record. When the prisoner had served the time required for a certain offense, that "debt" was then crossed off the record. This continued until the entire debt had been paid. When the certificate of debt was nailed to the door, he was "forgiven the debt" and free to leave.

Our debt was paid by Christ. Jesus canceled your debt, taking it away and nailing it to the cross. When He died, He paid the price, once and for all, for your sin and your failure. When you died, the legal bond you had to the Law was broken. No one can rightly judge or condemn you any longer!

From the day of your death and rebirth , your life never needs to be the same. The movie ends and your life begins with you resurrected, contemplating the future with Him alone as your companion and guide. As the sun dips toward the horizon, you are free to leave your dismal life of living up to standards and traditions in that dusty little town of legalism. If you so choose, you can be free from the Law and the curses of the Law, free to ride into the sunset, together with Him in His love.

## Reflection ～

• According to Colossians 2:20-23, living by standards and laws "appears" to be beneficial, but actually has *"no value."* In your opinion, how does the law appear to be beneficial?

• What are the standards you use to judge the acceptability of others? Hint: What are your pet peeves? What behaviors make you disgusted or disappointed in others?

• What criticisms from others especially hurt or anger you? What personal standards are revealed by your reactions?

## God's Desire ～

"I didn't want some petty, inferior brand of righteousness that comes from keeping a list of rules when I could get the robust kind that comes from trusting Christ—*God's* righteousness."
—Philippians 3:9 *The Message*

"If you have died with Christ to the elementary principles of the world, why, as if you were living in the world, do you submit yourself to decrees, such as, "Do not handle, do not taste, do not touch!" (which all refer to things destined to perish with the using)—in accordance with the commandments and teachings of men? These are matters which have, to be sure, the appearance of wisdom in self-made religion and self-abasement and severe treatment of the body, but are of no value against fleshly indulgence."
—Colossians 2:20-23

## Your Response ～

*Father, open my heart to understand and receive Your perfect love for me. Help me to see that Your love for me never changes because it is not based on my performance. May I begin to understand that living under standards only brings bondage, the very bondage for which You died to set me free.*

# ❀ 9 ❀

# Me, Myself, & I Am

"Men go abroad to wonder at the height of mountains,
at the huge waves of the sea, at the long courses of the rivers,
at the vast compass of the ocean, at the circular motions of the
stars; and they pass by themselves without wondering."
—Saint Augustine

For me, an automobile is one necessary form of earthly evil, which, like root canals, must be endured in order for us to function in society. To me, even the word "automobile" seems a farce. As far as my vehicles go, there doesn't seem much about them that makes them "automatically mobile." My cars are more often automatically immobile.

Just get me there and back in one piece on time. Beyond that, I don't want to know anything else about my car. When it breaks down, which is only when I'm in a hurry, I hope that somebody within the radius of a screwdriver and a wrench will know how my car is put together and how to get it back on the road.

I admire and depend on people who know what my car is made of, especially when it breaks down. In fact, I've developed a lasting relationship with my mechanic. We depend on each other in special ways – namely, Ray keeps my car on the road, and I pay for his kids' college education.

As I write out the checks, he teaches me a little about the car I drive and the part that has most recently called it quits. Over the years I've learned that the workings of a vehicle can be dissected into three systems: the drivetrain, the fuel system, and the electrical system. I've also learned that when one of these systems comes apart, it costs about a semester's worth of tuition at an Ivy League school to get things rolling again.

Now I'm certainly no mechanic, but I am a counselor and people are a lot like cars in some ways. For example, when our life is broken down, it's very important that we have a clear understanding of the "systems" we are made of so that we can repair the parts of our life that are broken.

The same goes for a life that is sputtering at an important intersection or not operating to its full potential. This particular person might be able to get by for a while, but unless someone with an understanding of the human design comes along to help make necessary adjustments and modifications, he or she might never experience life as God intended.

The Bible clearly states that humans, like cars, are made up of different systems. The book of 1 Thessalonians ends with the prayer that "your spirit and soul and body be preserved complete . . . " (1 Thessalonians 5:23). Several other passages also allude to the distinct components that make us who we are. For example, the greatest commandment, given in Deuteronomy 6:5 and quoted in Matthew 22:36-38, says that we are to love God with all our "heart," "soul," "might," and "mind."

Now back to the car analogy for a minute. I've known mechanics who hang around the garage arguing about which system is what or how many individual systems there are in a car. Take for instance the electronic fuel injection. Is it part of the electrical system or part of the fuel system? From what I understand, it's debatable. Regardless of the position one may take, a good mechanic who uses the right tools and the appropriate manual will be able to fix it.

Likewise, there are theologians who argue about which components of humanity belong to which system. For example, some would insist that humans have only two basic components: material and immaterial. Others suggest that man has three distinct parts. It isn't essential that you agree on all points with the model of humanity presented in this chapter. In fact, we've found that anyone using God's Word and a few tools to properly interpret it, can go to work on life's most difficult issues and respond to them from a godly perspective.

The point is that the Bible says we are made up of different components and that distinctions should be made between them. Hebrews 4:12 says that, "For the word of God is living and active and sharper than any two-edged sword, and piercing as far as the division of soul and spirit, of both joints and marrow, and able to judge the thoughts and intentions of the heart."* The word "division" here comes from the Greek root merizo that means "to divide, to differentiate between." The Bible does exactly that. It makes distinctions between the different systems that make us complete as humans.

*Like a healthy body that is strong and vibrant, functioning to its fullest potential, so too our entire being, when working together in unison, begins to fulfill God's vision for us—to be fully alive.*

And that's the purpose of this chapter. I'm going to describe in practical detail three divisions that can be deciphered within our being: the body, the soul, and the spirit, and the specific roles of each. When these systems work

* A commonly asked question is: Where does the Bible's use of "heart" fit into this model? The word for heart typically used in Scripture means "the middle of something." It is typically used to interpret the totality of man's inner or immaterial nature. It is also a synonym for "mind." As such, the heart is the seat of the will. In Psalm 51:10, the psalmist cries, "Create in me a clean heart, O God ..." and in Psalm 119:2, "How blessed are those who ... seek Him with all their heart." One of the things the Lord promises us in the New Covenant is a new heart, "Moreover, I will give you a new heart and put a new spirit within you; and I will remove the heart of stone from your flesh and give you a heart of flesh." (Ezekiel 36:26)

together in unison as they were intended to do, abundant life is absolutely possible. God has fashioned a marvelous design for us, and if we have an accurate understanding of this design, we will be able to powerfully apply all the things we are learning about mind influences, life, and law. Like a healthy body that is strong and vibrant, functioning to its fullest potential, so too our entire being, when working together in unison, begins to fulfill God's vision for us—to be fully alive.

## The Design of Man[1]
FIG.3

## A Body to Relate to the World

"God made all the delicate, inner parts of my body, and knit them together in my mother's womb. Thank you for making

---

[1]Although we have been careful to be gender inclusive when possible, we find it less clumsy in places to use the term, mankind (or the design of man), throughout this chapter and following. Furthermore, we recognize the revelation of the Trinity is expressed through personal attributes including both masculine and feminine traits. Inasmuchas, we don't want to use any generality to make our Creator seem less personal so we choose to rely on the Biblical tradition of masculine pronouns for the great I AM.

me so wonderfully complex! It's amazing to think about. Your workmanship is marvelous. . ." —Psalm 139:13, *The Living Bible*

The body is truly remarkable in its intricate complexity. Once the union of a sperm and an egg begins the process that ultimately produces a human being, a plethora of unending miracles is silently orchestrated. Within the period of approximately nine months, an astounding world of cellular microbiology is delicately woven into what we know simply as *bios*, our physical life. "The mere existence of that [first] cell," writes Lewis Thomas, "should be one of the greatest astonishments of the earth."[2]

We are without a doubt, as the psalmist says, "...fearfully and wonderfully made" (Psalm 139:14). The same sovereign hand that orchestrates the rising of the sun, choreographs the microscopic interaction of each cell of the body. Tim Hansel describes it this way:

> "You and I produce about three billion red blood cells every day, about a million a minute ... We've got approximately sixty thousand miles of capillaries running through our bodies. In some places, the cells have to line up one by one in order to do what they are supposed to do. And this is all choreographed without the least bit of conscious thought on our part."[3]

Not only are the mechanics of the body itself beyond comprehension but when we consider the body's ability to absorb sensory input and interact with other people in our world, we can't help but marvel at its workmanship. As the sun crested the tops of the trees this morning, I looked out my window at the beautiful Black Hills and was amazed at God's matchless creation. I then turned to see my wife gazing out the window as well. My wonder was instantly transferred to her as the morning light danced in the specks of brightness in her eyes. I cannot look into the windows to my wife's soul, a profound work of intricate detail fashioned by the Master Himself, without awe for her Creator. I am fascinated with the knowledge that the human eye can see an estimated eight million different colors with an estimated two million signals hitting our nervous system every second.[4]

How can we not marvel at the meticulous care God took in providing this dynamic, living organism through which we can relate to our physical environment and enjoy it immensely?!

Tragically, some dismiss the intricacies of the human body for fear that we might become overly fond of it. Centuries of old Puritan and Victorian practices (as the agnostics that Paul addressed in Colossians) have stained the intention of our Creator, marking the body as the enemy of the spiritual life. But no such thing is true. Our body was elaborately fashioned by God, created as the dwelling place where our spirit and soul are to reside with Him.

*Our body was elaborately fashioned by God, created as the dwelling place where our spirit and soul are to reside with Him.*

Contrary to common religious traditions, we are not to deny or despise the body. While speaking to husbands and wives, Paul matter-of-factly states, "no one ever hated his own flesh, but nourishes *and cherishes it*" (Ephesians 5:29, emphasis mine). It must have brought God deep sadness to cover the beauty of Adam and Eve's bodies with animal skins after they sinned. Just as certain, God's disappointment is perpetuated by our daily despise and neglect for our bodies, or our obsession with how they look. Overworking them, denying them necessary exercise and nutrition, burdening them with debilitating stress—His glory is dimmed when we loathe or ignore the magnificence of the human body.

We are to enjoy and appreciate our ability to touch, taste, feel, and hear, while being wise stewards of our physique. Yet, the simple fact that our bodies are the most visible part of our being does not mean they are to demand more attention than the soul and spirit.

Certainly, the core essence of who we are is not found in our bodies. But the body is vitally important as the vehicle of expression through which we, together with God, display our inner self. It conveys and reveals what is going on inside, and is the only tool we have to relate to our environment and serve those around us, so take care of it! Keep it tuned up and filled with gas so it can be ready and willing to respond to God's Spirit at any given time.

## A Soul to Relate to Others

Whereas the body allows us to relate to our surroundings and our world, our soul gives us the ability to connect with ourselves, others, and God in deep and meaningful ways. Andrew Murray once said ". . . the soul is the meeting place, the point of union between body and spirit.... Standing thus midway between two worlds, belonging to both, the soul has the power of determining itself: of choosing or refusing."[5]

"The soul stands between the 'spirit' with its openness to the spiritual world, and the 'body' open to the physical world ... having the power of choice as to which shall control the entire man,"[6] said Jessie Penn-Lewis. As such, the power of choice and the seat of our personality reside in the soul. In the soul we find three major components of decision making which guide our every step in the quest for Life. Those three components of the soul are the mind, the will, and the emotions.

The "mind" is a fantastic component where tremendous amounts of information are processed, evaluated, and stored away in our *belief systems*. This also seems to be the doorway from the soul to the spirit, through which God's Spirit can speak, lead, and comfort.

The "emotions," on the other hand, can only react to input they get from the world and the body. Emotions don't have any intellect of their own and can only respond to our mind and body. As such, they can tell us a lot about what we perceive is happening in our quest for *zoe* Life.

Finally, we have the "will." The will is the great control and command center of the soul, and is therefore the "boss of the body." The will makes the decisions, and the will gives the orders.

The activity of the soul must be carefully considered because it is the center of our choosing. The soul also embraces one's personality and character, enabling each individual to have meaningful

135

relationships with others. But that's not all it does. Just as the body is the vehicle of the soul, so the soul is the vehicle of the spirit.

### A Spirit to Relate to God

Simply and profoundly, our spirits were designed to house the Spirit of God. While our bodies relate to our world and our souls relate to ourselves and to others, our spirits were specifically fashioned to relate to God. This is the place where the supernatural intertwining of His Spirit and our being can take place.

*While our bodies relate to our world and our souls relate to ourselves and to others, our spirits were specif-ically fashioned to relate to God.*

But God's Spirit does not come into our spirit automatically or as part of our natural birth. Jesus made it very clear that we are *not* spiritually connected or alive to God by nature or birth. "That which is born of the flesh is flesh; and that which is born of the Spirit is spirit" (John 3:6). After Christ ascended to the right hand of the Father, He sent His Spirit to unite with believers in Christ and to dwell within them. Acts 2 describes this incredible change in the course of human history when God, for the first time, took up residence not only *with* human beings, but also *in* human beings. Today, when our soul responds to His call to have a relationship with Him, only then does His Spirit come into our life.

Therefore, we must understand God in order to truly understand humanity. Our spirit, living in unity with God's Spirit, is where the core of our identity is found. *This* is the part of our being that is created in God's image. Unlike the animals that have a body, a soul, and an instinct to guide them, we are inbuilt with the capacity and privilege to reflect the glory and image of God while being guided by His Spirit through our spirit.

The practical reality of this relationship is unfathomable. "At the heart of the Christian story lays the promise of direct correspondence with the unseen, a link so profound as to be likened to a new birth, and the key to life beyond organic death," said Philip Yancey.7 There is no way to measure the depth of its implications from our limited human perspective, but we are fashioned to know its truth.

When God imparted spiritual life to Adam, the life He gave was His own. His Holy Spirit inhabited man's human spirit – giving *zoe* Life to man's spirit. God and man had a pure relationship, together in the same temple. Perfect intimacy is what God intended to be "normal." God designed the human spirit as a vessel in which man and God should live together united.

But this perfect, ideal condition was not to last. When Adam and Eve turned their backs on God's original design, they began a legacy of corruption, destruction, and death that has been passed down for generations through our bodies, our souls, and our spirits. This inheritance of death has left us with a multitude of problems we all wish we could fix.

*When God imparted spiritual life to Adam, the life He gave was His own.*

## Determining What Needs to Be Fixed

Most often, I find that people know they need help but aren't sure where to get it. Where do we turn when our car isn't firing on all cylinders? Trying to live "our own way" will guarantee a long and jerky ride.

"This is as good as it gets!" we're assured. Society slaps us on the back and says that we're perfectly normal. "Keep on going—you're actually doing better than most!" But deep in our hearts we know we are here for a greater purpose—we know that the emptiness and confusion we face are not what we were created for. In quiet, honest moments, we know that repairs and renewal are deeply needed. But where do we start? Knowing which component of our being needs to be fixed in order to address a certain problem is the key.

Consider the sex addict. Very often he will question his salvation. "How can I be a Christian and do *this*?" He thinks something is wrong with his spirit, but most often, the battle for lust is won or lost in the mind, which is in the soul. Consider the young executive, who may be dealing with mental fatigue and overwhelming feelings of failure. He may think he is having an emotional breakdown in his soul, but maybe he just needs a good rest for his brain and his body. And it wouldn't hurt to have someone remind him that true *zoe* comes through a relationship with God in his spirit, and not through his job.

Consider yourself. You too may be broken in an area you've tried to change for many years. You've prayed, wept, and denied it, yet it still hangs on your back like a dead man (Romans 7:24). But if you've been trying to fix the wrong system, you are going to continue being frustrated, hopeless, and angry. You can try and try, but if you're focusing the "fix" on something that's not broken, while another problem goes unchecked, your troubles will remain.

Being careful not to oversimplify, we must keep in mind how fantastically complex we are as human beings. Please know that many people need repair in more than one area, and often problems in one area directly affect others. Some biological problems such as stress-related illness are closely linked to decisions made by the soul. Those poor decisions of the soul could be the direct result of someone desperately trying to find *zoe*, an issue of the spirit.

It's not always cut-and-dried simple, but differentiating between body, soul, and spirit is enormously helpful in understanding and dealing with the human condition.

*Each individual's spirit is dead to the ways of God until it is reborn to commune with Him.*

## WHEN THE SPIRIT IS DEAD

Our core spiritual problem was inherited from our ancestors, Adam and Eve, and has a profound effect on all other areas of our being. Each individual's spirit is dead to the ways of God until it is reborn to commune with Him. When I say dead, I don't mean *partially* dead. I don't even mean *mostly* dead. I mean *dead* dead. In 1 Corinthians 2:14, the Bible says that man without the Spirit cannot comprehend the Spirit of God. Ephesians 2:1 and 2:5 tell us that we are "dead in trespasses and sin," "dead in our transgressions."

In this crucial area, many people make the error of trying

to fix a spiritual problem with soul solutions. The "self-help" movement, the "New Age" movement, transcendental meditation are all attempts to fill a spiritual void by enhancing the awareness and experiences of the soul. Through religion many of us have been taught that if we live a moral life or remain true to our "faith," a relationship with God comes automatically. But this is not so. Even though we might *feel* or *think* we have a relationship with God, *zoe Life does not originate in the soul.* Neither is it a product of our intellect, emotions, or a choice to do right.

*... even in the midst of an otherwise busy and fulfilled physical and soulful existence, we may become aware that an entire dimension of life is missing.*

*A dynamic, intimate relationship with God begins in the spirit.* Only when our spirits are alive and quickened by the fullness of God's Spirit can we express our worship and have communion with the Creator. John 4:24 states, "God is spirit, and those who worship Him must worship in *spirit* and truth" (emphasis mine).

That's why Jesus was so emphatic that we must be "born again." Consider His words carefully,

"Truly, truly, I say to you, unless one is born of water and the Spirit, he cannot enter into the kingdom of God. That which is born of the flesh is flesh, and that which is born of the Spirit is spirit. Do not marvel that I say to you, 'You must be born again'" (John 3:5-7).

In quiet moments, during a crisis, or even in the midst of an otherwise busy and fulfilled physical and soulful existence, we may become aware that an entire dimension of life is missing. This realization can come as a moment of enlightenment, but most often it is a disturbing experience. Echoes of thought and desire can haunt the soul, finding nowhere to rest. Perhaps you've had such an experience. Your life might include an abundance of material goods for the body. On the soul level, your life might display happy emotions and a disciplined will that makes good and moral decisions. Your existence may even be filled with deep philosophical and religious insights of the mind—yet your spirit, the core of your entire being, is dark, empty, and dead.

Please, please, stop for a moment and consider all of this. You may need to quit reading for a while, close this book, and get very honest with yourself and with God. If you've never responded to His invitation to come into your life and make you a new creature, I want to invite you to seriously consider doing so. Right here, right now, you can call on His name, thank Him for His forgiveness, and ask Him to make your spirit new, pure, and filled with his presence.

"For whoever will call upon the name of the LORD will be saved."
—Romans 10:13

"Behold, I stand at the door and knock; if anyone hears My voice and opens the door, I will come into him, and will dine with him, and he with Me."
—Revelation 3:20

◊ ◊ ◊

I'm trusting that you really did take some time to consider all that was said above. There is no possible way that I could overemphasize the central importance of accepting Christ's offer to come into our spirit and make us alive with Him.

Here is something else to consider—once God's transformation of our spirit has taken place, it cannot be made any more "alive." God didn't make our spirit *partially* alive or even *mostly* alive. It's *alive* alive. Our spirit cannot get any holier or more righteous—it simply cannot be improved upon. Ephesians 4:24 clearly states that we are to "put on the new self, which in the likeness of God has been created in righteousness and holiness of the truth." That is simply incredible! God has regenerated our spirit. In its *present* state of union with Him, it is pure and magnificent. Think about it. Could a perfect and holy God reside in anything less?

## WHEN THE BODY IS BROKEN

Every day we encounter physiological breakdown, whether in our own bodies or those we love and care for. Due to living in a world plagued by the results of sin and abuse, we suffer from many bodily ailments. Not only did the Fall of man bring disease into the world, generations marred by sin and selfish endeavor leave a legacy of environmental toxins, high stress, danger, and poor nutrition.

As a result of being born into such a world, my body breaks down and suffers affliction. Even with as much care as I've taken in remaining healthy and fit, I still get colds, I suffer from muscle pain, and I see my doctor monthly to check for recurring skin cancer. When you are dealing with a physical problem or ailment, seek a physical solution. Eat well, rest enough, and go to your doctor when needed. Exercise that body to keep it working as well as possible.

At the same time, never diminish God's willingness or ability to heal us physically. One of God's names in the Old Testament is *"Jehovah Rapha"*, the "Great Healer" of the human body. Not only does He have the power to regenerate and redeem our spirits, but also our bodies. The book of James addresses medicinal issues I find so fascinating and of such importance that I hope to devote an entire book to the topic of Biblical healing in the future.

The tension between faith and physique is complex to say the least. Often the issues are gray, and we must extend grace to others and ourselves. But know that applying physical solutions to bodily problems is not a compromise of spiritual convictions. When you are trying to figure out what to fix, biological needs (such as high blood sugar, chemical imbalances, or fatigue) should always be ruled out before embarking on a complicated spiritual or emotional diagnosis.

There was a time not long ago when several theological questions tangled around my mind. It got to the point that I couldn't make sense of spiritual truth. Feeling confused and defeated, I set an appointment to seek wisdom from two godly men whom I have come to love and admire greatly: Jim Craddock and George Sanchez. While trying to explain my quandary, I thought perhaps I needed deliverance from demonic oppression, or at least a better grasp of Biblical truth to set me free.

During our meeting in Albuquerque, New Mexico, Jim and George listened patiently and carefully. After I had blurted out all my disjointed questions, they both offered the same quiet response. "Bill, you're extremely tired and your body needs rest. Get away to a quiet place and sleep soundly. Then take a day or two away from everything including the telephone, teaching, counseling, and your family. Then call us again."

I did as they advised and sure enough, with needed rest I was refreshed. My confusion cleared and my troubled thoughts dissipated. Only a couple of my questions remained, and I could then talk through them with these wise friends. What had appeared to be a serious spiritual issue was instead physical fatigue—a bodily breakdown.

WHEN THE SOUL IS OUT OF SYNC

Issues of the soul bring people to my office most often. The majority of the personal struggles we face are either directly or indirectly related to our souls. Remember that the soul is the bridge between the spirit and the body. Comprised of the mind, the emotions, and the will, the soul handles an intricate network of thoughts, feelings, and decisions. When these components are out of sync with the spirit and each other, problems are inevitable.*

Let's face it. The soul of humanity is in bad shape. We've grown up allowing our emotions and intellect to make decisions about our direction in life when only the Spirit and Scripture can truly define us and bring fulfillment. Even after receiving Christ, we tend to ignore the leading of the Spirit and may not be at all sure of how to apply Biblical truth to our daily lives. Instead, we keep using strategies from a world filled with lies, hoping that God will offer His help when we get ourselves really stuck.

---

* The biological dimension of emotion is often baffling and incredibly complicated However, due to the specific approach we take in this book, we will not address this issue in its entirety.

We must acknowledge the subtle danger presented by shopping malls, movies, magazines, and escapist literature, all of which are designed to help people retreat from the harsh pressure of daily living and feel intense emotions in ideal, larger-than-life fantasies. Don't get me wrong, I love few things better than a well-made movie that grabs all my senses and takes me to another place for a couple of hours. The break from focusing on human tragedy is a pleasant respite for me, and the heightened sense of ecstasy is a thrill. The media, however, is best to be enjoyed in small doses and must never take the place of the Holy Spirit and the timeless truths of God's Word.

> *We will never realize our full potential as the visible and audible image of God until we relinquish "our way" and tune into seeking zoe — "God's way."*

We can easily become so accustomed to how our emotions respond to the screen and the mall that they become the anticipated norm for home. I guarantee disappointment and bitterness will soon take over when real life doesn't measure up, even in small degrees. We are doomed to a life of discontent until we learn to listen daily with our spirits to Him who is the Giver of all we desire and truly need. Do you believe that? We will never realize our full potential as the visible and audible image of God until we relinquish "our way" and tune into seeking *zoe* — "God's way."

## Seeking Life Our Own Way

We have been conditioned to determine truth by how we feel, basing our decision-making process on emotions. "How can this be wrong when it feels so right?" we ask ourselves. We naturally allow our feelings to convince our mind that *what we feel is right*. Our will, in turn, commands to the body to act on these things that *feel* right. "If it feels good, do it!" Right? Wrong.

Let's say a fellow wakes up one morning after a hectic month of sick kids, financial stress, visiting in-laws, and a broken water line that just destroyed the new carpet. As he rolls over he's troubled by the notion that he doesn't feel anything toward his wife. She isn't very appealing this morning, she's crabby, and he just wants out of the house. It doesn't take long for his mind to say, *This marriage has been going down the tubes for a while now. I'm not sure I'm in love with her.* This thought, initiated by his *emotions*, bumps up against his *will*, and his *body* begins to carry out the commands of his mind. He storms off in his truck. As he pulls up to his office, he is greeted by a pretty secretary who gives him coffee just the way he likes it, focuses her attention on all his needs throughout the day, and lets it be known that she happens to be available for a drink after work.

His body begins naturally responding to what his soul is telling it. He stands taller and goes out of his way for her. His body tingles because she not only looks fantastic, but also smells delicious. His mind is bombarded with thoughts fueled by aroused emotions. *I've never felt more alive and at peace than I do when I'm with her,* he thinks. *She cares about me and she accepts me. I think she is actually my soul mate, the one God intended for me to have all along.*

> We've been convinced that what we feel is real, and these feelings are often reinforced by the lies that constantly bombard us from the world.

His body begins responding to these messages and soon his behavior reveals his new belief: He is in love with his secretary. Obviously, his spirit has been hushed and his actions are giving a visible, audible image of living life independent from God. When we do what feels right, without first conferring with the Holy Spirit and the Bible, our emotions act as our compass and we begin to be controlled by "the desire of flesh" (Galatians 5:16).

Why do Christians have about the same rate of relational brokenness, anxiety, and financial failure as nonbelievers? Our choices are piloted by a compass set on feelings rather than on God's truth, and we try to navigate by an old map heavily influenced by external input such as daily conversation, books, media, and old habits. We've been convinced that what we feel is real, and these feelings are often reinforced by the lies that constantly bombard us from the world. Our bodies then serve as the vehicle to carry out the desires of the flesh. No wonder we get in so many messes!

## Seeking Life Man's Way

1. External influences and/or my emotions and/or mind tell me that what I feel or think is "truth."
2. My emotions conclude this must be true because of what I feel.
3. My emotions and mind command my will to make choices consistent with what I feel or think.
4. My body carries out the commands of the soul.
5. My actions give a visible and audible image to the world of a person acting naturally, apart from God, according to what seems right based on feeling and intellect.

Since birth, our identity and purpose have been defined by our beliefs, traditions, and powerful influences from the world rather than by our Creator. But to be truly "whole" we must rediscover and learn to live through His Spirit — our source of *zoe* Life.

## Seeking Life God's Way

The implications of the transformation of our spirit, and the practical implications of God's Spirit now being in communion with ours, is nothing short of fantastic. You were created to be in relationship with God. This is what He intended for all of humanity. He yearns for His people to know Him through His Word and through His presence each moment of the day, while communicating through His Spirit to ours.

This is how it works:

• God's Spirit communicates wisdom and guidance through our spirit.
  • Romans 8:16; 1 Corinthians 2:12
• Man's spirit instructs his mind, advising it of the guidance of Christ.
  • Proverbs 20:27
  • John 14:26
  • I Corinthians 2:16

• The mind evaluates this spiritual communication through its chosen authority, the Word of God, in order to verify its origin.

    • Acts 17:11

• Recognizing the Truth, the will submits to the guidance of Christ, regardless of feelings or how things look.

    • 2 Corinthians 5:7

    • Galatians 2:20

• The body obeys the will.

    • John 14:15

    • 1 John 5:3

    • Colossians 1:29

• Finally, the actions give a visible and audible image of God to the world.

    • Genesis 1:26-27

    • 2 Corinthians 3:2-3, 18

The Bible calls this "walking by the Spirit" (Galatians 5:16). It starts in that amazing connection our spirit has with God. The Holy Spirit actually communicates through our spirit, and the thought is passed on to our mind. Our minds then evaluate whether the thought is true by checking to see if it lines up with God's character and His Word. When we verify that the thought is consistent with God's Word, our will can then submit to truth, whether or not our emotion is in line with it, and our body carries out the command of the will.

To know, think, and choose right in fullness of life and inexpressible joy—this is God's ultimate plan for you! Your soul, the meeting place between body and spirit—choosing the wisdom of the Spirit rather than fleshly knowledge and desire, walking in ongoing relationship with God, remaining open to the things of the Spirit, and verifying them by God's Word. Then your soul can be set free from the death grip of sinful strongholds, addictions, and desires of the body. Then you can begin to choose what that will lead to genuine *zoe* Life for you and those around you.

◊ ◊ ◊

My wife likes to dance. I'm good at hitting a ball with a stick. I like to be in control and dancing for me is not a controlled event. Even when I try practicing at home, I feel like I'm having a seizure. I'm sure I look even worse. I'm guessing I resemble a worm dying on the sidewalk after a rainstorm.

I also don't like being embarrassed, and a worm trying to wiggle his way around a dance floor blushes plenty. But my wife likes to dance, and I love my wife, so sometimes a man's got to do what a man's got to do, no matter how loudly his testosterone objects.

One afternoon, God's Spirit prompted my spirit to take Nancy dancing. In fact, I'm sure that it must have been God. I don't get these thoughts on my own, particularly when it's a beautiful day for a motorcycle ride or there is a great new movie at the cheap theater. Why else would a rational man think such a thing?

The thought coincided with what I understand the Bible to say about putting my wife's needs above my own and loving her as Jesus loves us. So my mind reluctantly accepted this dancing idea as a good thing.

But now a debate begins between my emotions, which are under the control of my darkest fears, and my lips, which are under the control of my will:

"Nancy?" my lips say.

*"Don't do it, you'll regret it!"* my emotions warn.

"I was wondering," my lips say.

*"You can't do this! Save our reputation!"* my emotions cry out.

"Would you like to go d-d-d-d. . ."

*"Get out while you can!"* scream my emotions. "Ask her to go out d-driving or to d-a mall shopping. Anything except. . . ."

"D-d-dancing?"

There, I said it. But that's not the end of it. After Nancy regains consciousness, we get our coats and head out the door, and my emotions rebel even more. But my will proves stronger and I find I can even open her car door, turn the ignition, and drive downtown. So far, so good.

My mind, being the intellectual center of my soul, chooses a place with lots of people to hide among so hopefully no one will recognize me. But isn't it amazing how you can pick the busiest dance floor in town and the minute you step foot on it, one woman decides it's time to go to the bathroom (which means that all the women decide it's time to go to the bathroom), and you're left there alone with your wife, surrounded by a bunch of guys with nothing to do but wait for their dates—and watch you d-d-dance?

Yes, that was some evening. Though I'm not sure that my actions gave "a visible and audible image of God to the world," I am sure people there still remember the night they called 911, thinking the new guy out on the dance floor was having some sort of an attack. My wife, however, remembered the night for what it was, cherishing my effort, and receiving it as an expression of my love. I will remember it as one of the nights when God's Spirit spoke to mine, and one of the evenings where my will proved stronger than my emotions.

## In Summary

The model of seeking Life through the Spirit (rather than according to what feels natural), heavily impacts our celebrations, our grief, our work ethic, and our dearest relationships. Knowing what needs to be fixed is the key to becoming fully healthy and alive again.

Unlike cars, "we are not machines that can be repaired through a series of steps—we are relational beings who are transformed by the mystery of relationship."[8]

If we have accepted Christ's offer to come into our life, God's Spirit has entirely transformed our spirit and by faith we can trust God in His goodness to be fully restored. Only then do we become whole, complete, and adequate. As Peter wrote, "His divine power has granted to us everything pertaining to life and godliness, through the true knowledge of Him who called us by His own glory and excellence" (2 Peter 1:3). Herein lays the key to abundant and victorious living! By fully grasping this truth, we realize that, "every person who begins his [or her] Christian life, begins it with everything he [or she] will ever receive."[9] When we finally understand the implications of this, the rest of the story comes into view.

## *Reflection* 〜

How would you define the body, the soul and the spirit? How would you describe the function of each?

Review the section, "When the Spirit is Dead." It is essential that you know whether your spirit is dead or alive to God. I John 5:11-12 says, "And the witness is this, that God has give us eternal life, and this life is in His Son. He who has the Son has the life; he who does not have the Son of God does not have the life."

What is something that you know you should do but don't "feel" like doing (for example, showing love to someone you don't like or praising your spouse when you "feel" they are not doing enough). Realize that you can operate contrary to your emotions and in truth by activating your will. If necessary, enlist the help of another in activating your will in your particular instance .

## *God's Desire* 〜

"Now may the God of peace Himself sanctify you entirely; and may your spirit and soul and body be preserved complete, without blame at the coming of our Lord Jesus Christ."
—I Thessalonians 5:23

"Do you not know that you are a temple of God, and that the Spirit of God dwells in you?"
—1 Corinthians 3:16

"Moreover, I will give you a new heart and put a new spirit within you; and I will remove the heart of stone from your flesh and give you a heart of flesh. And I will put My Spirit within you and cause you to walk in My statutes, and you will be careful to observe My ordinances."
—Ezekiel 36:26-27

## *Your Response* ⟿

*Father, thank you for giving me a brand new spirit. Help me to grasp the awesome gift of a spirit that is completely righteous and holy and to realize that there is nothing I can do that can cause it to be any more righteous or any less righteous.*

*If you are not convinced that you have received this new spirit by responding to Christ's offer of this gift, we invite you to pray the following:*

*Father, I recognize that because of sin, I am born separated from You and unable to bring myself out of this state on my own. Thank You for taking my sins upon Yourself on the cross and paying the penalty for them that was due me. I accept Your offer to be my Savior and the Lord of my life. Thank You that by receiving You I am given a new spirit and that You take up residence there forever.*

# ❧ 10 ❧

# New Creation

"Therefore, if any man is in Christ, he is a new creature;
the old things passed away; behold, new things have come."
—2 Corinthians 5:17

T he law can be especially brutal to those who don't look or
act "right" in the eyes of society. In biblical times, lepers
were required to cry out "unclean!" and people with a past
reputation, or those crippled and impoverished, were separated
from others by the strict social systems of their day. Unfortunately,
times haven't changed much for the unfit and unlovely.

We too live in a world that demands certain standards of beauty
and success in order to flourish or even survive. How are we to live
under these current conditions without falling prey to the curses
of the law? You may be thinking, *I know Jesus came and paid a high
price to set us free, but riding off with Him into the sunset seems only a
storybook fantasy. I'm still here!*

We can't deny the world's impact as it molds and defines us by our gender, race, and financial status. We want to become all that we can be and we want our kids to achieve well beyond us. Our sense of worth seems destined to be defined by external standards of success. But we know if we are to live free from the expectations and demands of others and ourselves, our meaning and purpose must originate elsewhere. Have you ever asked yourself: What am I worth?

## Outside/Inside

*Have you ever asked yourself: What am I worth?*

Everything created by God is intrinsically valuable. Whether the CEO of a mega-international corporation or a drunk in the town park, our fundamental design as human beings project our Creator's likeness. In fact, our very existence is an expression of worship to Him because we are "fearfully and wonderfully made" (Psalm 139:14). Unarguably, our potential has been marred by generations of sin, but we are never left to doubt that human life is sacred because it bears the *imago dei*, the image of God.

We are all made in our Creator's image, but likewise, in all of us, our true image is distorted. We are born into sin and because of this birth defect, we are, at best, misshapen images of God. Regardless of the value assigned by others according to our external image, God's reflection has been broken and fragmented by sin.

FROM THE OUTSIDE

Since the dawn of humanity, individual worth has been defined by bloodlines, caste systems, and education – in other words, from the outside in. Living in South Dakota, I am often asked to counsel Native Americans whose displaced and broken history as a people carries pain and discouragement into all walks of life. What retribution is sufficient for a people stripped of their culture, disbanded after great slaughters, and exiled to waste lands? In addition to the promise of eternal life, what hope do I have to offer to these tribes of people – or any other broken human being for that matter? What does the gospel, the hope for abundant life, mean for them?

The good news, friend, is that not only are we offered a fresh start in Christ, but also we are given a brand new identity!

## A CHANGE IN COVENANTS MEANS A NEW IDENTITY

Every term of the law has been satisfied by Christ and through His death. Through His sacrifice on the Cross, we have entered into a New Covenant which is an entirely different arrangement for relating to God. The death of our old self released us from the punishment and dictates of the law. Our spiritual birth joined us to Christ, making us righteous and releasing us from the demands of the law. But our spiritual rebirth does something even more profound.

"For this reason Christ is the mediator of a new covenant, that those who are called may receive the provided eternal inheritance—now that He has died as a ransom to set them free from the sins committed under the first covenant. In the case of a will, it is necessary to prove the death of the one who made it, because a will is in force only when somebody has died; it never takes effect while the one who made it is living" (Hebrews 9:15-17 NIV).

Spiritually, at the innermost core of our identity, we've been grafted into the family line of Abraham, Isaac, and Jacob – God's chosen ones! Do you know what this means for you? Under the New Covenant we are given a new inheritance. We now belong to the house of Judah. Have you ever seriously considered your place within your spiritual clan? Old Testament stories don't just provide answers for Bible Trivia games and flannel graph characters; when you've been grafted into this spiritual clan the promises made to Abraham, Isaac, and Jacob *are now your promises*. When God blesses the house of Israel, He blesses your house! No longer does your family name, your career path, or your appearance define your true worth.

*No longer does your family name, your career path, or your appearance define your true worth.*

I think many Christians perceive their identity in Christ somewhat like being in the witness protection program instead of being reborn and entirely new. In the movie *My Blue Heaven*, Steve Martin plays the role of an ex-con who must testify against a crime boss. To ensure his safety, he is moved to a new city with a new "history." As the movie progresses viewers watch as the plot reveals a man who may have been given a new name and identification yet is still the same person on the inside. Does this sound like you?

In the late '70s I would have confidently told you that my self-worth was totally found in Christ. Still, my image of success was being defined by my role on a professional ball team. I was young and fit and even in demand for the occasional interview. When people asked for my autograph, I can't deny the fact that my view of myself definitely improved.

Shortly after my shoulder injury, however, everything drastically changed on the outside. My baseball career was history and I was working at a local convenience store. Whereas fans could once recognize me from the stands with my team jersey's lucky number 11, I was now wearing a little red smock! Needless to say, I wasn't getting many requests for my autograph at my new job. Instead, I had ill-tempered motorists demanding that I pour them fountain drinks. My new four dollars an hour wage afforded a little house where we had a great view of the outside – through cracks in the walls. In a few short weeks, I lost thirty pounds and the physique I had worked so hard to build atrophied and disappeared.

Yes, I was frustrated. Of course, I was stressed when the bills came due, and I agonized through some dark moments. But through it all I was reassured by a quiet voice inside that God was about to show me who I truly was, apart from my performance on the ball field. In the darkness, bound by my own definitions of personal value, I cried out to God because I knew something within me needed to awaken.

FROM THE INSIDE

I knew the Life of God had already been implanted within my spirit. *Zoe*, the fullness of Life, God Himself, was within me. I just had to allow it to seep into the folds of my understanding so I could accept who I was and grow into my new identity. So often we accept Christ as our personal Savior, but fail to recognize the radical and total transformation that He has brought about in our spirit. "The work of Christ," says A.W. Tozer, "sweeps away both one's good and evil and turns him [or her] into *another person* . . . transformation *as deep as the roots of human life*. If it does not go that deep, it does not go deep enough"[1] (emphasis mine).

## Birth/Being

Not only are we inherently valuable as created beings in the image of God, God *recreates* us as beings that are born of noble worth when the Holy Spirit enters our life. We are now valuable because of who we are: God's dwelling place—His children. We are born into God's family, therefore taking on the holiness and righteousness of Christ. It is by rebirth, not performance, that our worth is determined and our identity settled.

*It is by rebirth, not performance, that our worth is determined and our identity settled.*

Imagine with me, proud parents looking at their newborn child. As they witness this miracle of life they pray together that one day their baby will grow up to be a human. That's ridiculous, isn't it? We know that a baby is as much a human as someone who is twenty, thirty, or eighty years old. The baby may not be able to do adult things, but with growth and training he or she will.

Preston Gillham explains how this illustration relates to our spiritual birth.

"Babies are not human because they act like humans;" Gillham states. "They are human because they are conceived and born human. In the same vein, your performance does not determine your true identity, but your birth does."[2]

Let's consider once more the biker couple. After meeting with Susan to reexamine her grids and belief systems, she came to know who she was as a new creation in Christ. She no longer needed to force her standards and rules on her husband because she began to realize her true value and worth didn't come from him or his actions and appearance.

At the time of their first meeting, I don't remember having a proven therapeutic strategy in asking Jim to enjoy a motorcycle ride rather than being interrogated about his less-than-holy behavior. I do remember experiencing a bit of sheer terror in the presence of a couple that was toxic with anger and frustration. At the prompting of the Holy Spirit, I had excused Jim while encouraging his wife to reconsider why she was so miserable. Little did I know that by doing this, I connected with Jim and he felt welcome to return when he was ready.

*"The Christian who believes he's a "sinner saved by grace" denies that his identity was changed through identification with the crucified and resurrected body of Christ . . .*

Several months later Jim came back to see me. Well, actually he found me first. Some buddies of mine and I had been taking lessons to be certified in scuba diving, and afterward we'd stopped by a lounge with a big screen TV. While we were catching up on the game, Jim sat unnoticed over in corner having a beer. After a while he shuffled over, towering above me, and growled, "Do you remember me?"

My friends were a little jumpy, wondering what I'd gotten myself into. Jim looked even rougher than he had our first meeting. After we became reacquainted the biker asked me if we could meet at the lounge the next evening. He seemed much more comfortable in this setting so I agreed.

The next night I would discover how Jim was not only astonished by the fact that his wife had quit nagging him, but also that her life had changed dramatically since our counseling sessions. He saw genuine contentment and joy, and it didn't take long to realize she now had something that he didn't. Jim thought he had been happy, but life wasn't all that he had made it out to be. Now he was being swayed toward Christ by the behavior of his wife, without a word being spoken on her part. (See 1 Peter 3:1.)

After meeting a couple of times, he too accepted Christ. As he grew in his understanding of the reality of becoming a new creation,

Jim's old, wild life passed away. Don't be mistaken; Jim didn't give up the open road. He still loves riding his Harley with the wind in his face. He wears heavy boots and leather chaps over blue jeans, and his hair is still pulled back in a long braid down his back. Some scars from bar fights will remain on his flesh forever, and the tattoos will permanently tell of his past, but he's an entirely different man now. Though some habits linger, his entire countenance has changed. What once defined Jim are now only outer garments, patterns, and shadows of the past. In 2 Corinthians, chapter five we're told that from now on we are to "recognize no man according to the flesh" (v. 16). In his spirit Jim is as innocent and clean as a baby.

Our spiritual identity defines us rather than our flesh. Jim's scars and tattoos no more determine his worth than my DNA, economic status, or education. His value and identity is not predetermined by his ancestors' bloodline, or even his past performance. Now, as a child of God, he deserves acceptance, love, and respect only because of what Christ has done for him.

You've heard it said, "I'm just a sinner saved by grace." Whether it's meant to communicate one's humility or is used as an excuse for not living "up to par," Preston Gillham says it simply does not line up with who Jesus says we are.

"The Christian who believes he's a "sinner saved by grace" denies that his identity was changed through identification with the crucified and resurrected body of Christ . . . Understanding your true spiritual identity is crucial to abundant living. Believe you're a sinner saved by grace, and you'll act like it; believe you're a purified saint who sins at times, but hates it, and you'll be highly motivated to act like a saint. You can no more be a sinner saved by grace than you can be a married single person. When you came to Christ, you were crucified as a sinner (Galatians 2:20) and then reborn with a new identity, a saint. Birth, not performance, determines identity."[3]

*Birth, not performance, determines identity."*

"If anyone is in Christ, he is a new creature; the old things passed away; behold, new things have come" (2 Corinthians 5:17). Did you know the word "creature" in this verse comes from the root word "create" which means to make something qualitatively new, something that has never existed before?

When God creates, He performs like no other artist to follow in His footsteps. In Genesis we learn that God spoke, setting in motion fresh mountain streams coursing through snow capped mountains, from whose peaks the Master Himself could view oceans, valleys, and skyscapes, all created from . . . nothing. That's right, the Creator of all creation fashions and sculpts out of nothing.

Set your imagination free because only then can you begin to grasp this most revealing truth about the supreme power of God. The same word "create," used in describing the genesis of our spectacular world, is the word chosen to explain the miracle of our new birth. We too were made a new creation out of nothing! During the radical transformation of our spirit, God didn't simply tweeze out some good stuff to begin sculpting our new life before throwing away the old scraps. No, God said He fashioned something fantastic and eternal out of nothing. Ephesians 2:10 says that, "We are His workmanship, created in Christ Jesus for good works, which God prepared beforehand, that we should walk in them." He started over; recreating, transforming, exchanging His life for ours, so we might be of exquisite worth.

*The same word "create," used in describing the genesis of our spectacular world, is the word chosen to explain the miracle of our new birth.*

## A Radical Transformation

Are you living undercover? Or have you allowed the truth of this spiritual birth to take hold and transform your life? If so, your days, your relationships, and your outlook on life should be markedly different. Three vitally important things happened when the Spirit of God took over your spirit:

1.   Your old spirit is done away with. You died. (Romans 6:3)

2. You are given a new spirit. (Romans 6:4)
   "Therefore if any man is in Christ, he is a new creature; the
   old things passed away; behold, new things have come. Now
   all these things are from God . . ." (2 Corinthians 5:17-18).
3. God's Spirit comes to reside in your new spirit.
   God spoke through the prophet Ezekiel foretelling, "I will
   give you a new heart and put a new spirit within you. . .
   I will put My Spirit within you and cause you to walk in My
   statutes. . . " (Ezekiel 36:26-27).

Jesus, before He was crucified on the cross, told His
disciples of this coming *infusion* of God's Spirit with theirs
saying, "the Spirit of truth. . . you know Him because He abides
*with* you, and will be *in* you" (John 14:17, emphasis mine).

Though these words are fairly simple and may sound familiar,
the implications are incalculable. Could this really be true? God
Himself, living in us, relating to us, and relating through us to the
world? The following verses certainly claim it to be so:

"However, you are not in the flesh but in the Spirit, if indeed
the Spirit of God dwells in you. But if anyone does not have the Spirit
of Christ, he does not belong to Him" (Romans 8:9).

"And because you are sons, God has sent forth the Spirit of His
Son into our hearts" (Galatians 4:6).

The possibility of Christ's Spirit being our very center is an
incredible truth to grasp, but Scripture says that it is a reality.
Regardless of what shape the world's mold has squeezed us into
(by what we do, what we have, what we look like), God has given
us our true identity. He knew we would need to be reminded again
and again of our new life in Him; therefore, we Believers are called
saints approximately fifty times in the New Testament. The name
"saint" literally means "holy one" and identifies us as "one set apart
from the world to God."

Whether we immediately *feel* like it or not, our will can choose
to accept our new likeness. Remember, we must act according to
the truth, regardless of how awkward it may feel. "Hypocrisy" is not

acting different than we feel. "Hypocricy" emerges when we don't act according to the truth. "Considering what God says about you, is it possible that you are a hypocrite?" challenges Preston Gillham. "God says we are saints; that we are righteous, holy, and forgiven. That doesn't mean we're perfect but it does mean we're new."⁴ Being a saint does not describe what we do, but rather who we are born to be.

When we were "born again," God did not tell us to shape up and become valuable. No! He created a new man that was already of infinite value. Though we live temporarily in the same body the old man used to occupy, the person living here now is brand new. At the deepest level of our beings, we've been changed even though there are times we don't act like it (an issue we will deal with in chapters to come).

Romans chapter six emphatically states, "Do you not know that all of us who have been baptized into Christ Jesus have been baptized into His death? Therefore we have been buried with Him through baptism into death, in order that as Christ was raised from the dead through the glory of the Father, so we too might walk in newness of life" (v. 3-4). To be baptized, *baptizo*, literally means "to place into," "to change the identity of something or someone."⁵ It is a term used for placing a piece of fabric in a vat of dye. It's not like dipping a person into a pool of water and then bringing him or her out and watching droplets of water evaporate, leaving the person a dry version of what once was soaked. Being baptized into Christ is like immersing a fabric in dye. The dye penetrates into the very fiber of the dye, and the cloth and the dye are inseparably united. When the piece of fabric comes out of the vat, it comes out wrapped in the dye; covered in the dye, it looks the same as the dye. Once baptized with Him, we can never be separated. What happened to Jesus physically in His death, burial, and resurrection literally happened to us spiritually.

*Once baptized with Him, we can never be separated. What happened to Jesus physically in His death, burial, and resurrection literally happened to us spiritually.*

In his book, *A Gentle Thunder*, Max Lucado tells of a young family's visit to Disney World. The story goes something like this: On this particular spring day, the inside of Cinderella's castle was packed with wide-eyed children and their parents. Suddenly all the little tourists rushed to one side. Had the castle been a boat, says Lucado, it would have tipped over with the momentum. Cinderella had entered.

Cinderella, perfectly typecast by a gorgeous young girl, had arrived. Beyond the sea of children stood the princess with each blonde hair tucked neatly into place. With flawless skin and a beaming smile she soon stood waist-deep in kids, each reaching out to touch and be touched.

The other side of the castle was now vacant except for two young boys. The one's age was hard to determine because his body was so terribly disfigured. Dwarfed in height, his deformed face could hardly be seen as he stood, watching quietly and wistfully, holding the hand of his older brother.

He surely wanted to be with the other children, longing to be unnoticed in the middle of the kids reaching for Cinderella, calling her name. But instead of uninhibited childhood ecstasy, the contorted face held eyes clouded and withdrawn from resignation and fear. The high cost of rejection and the possibility of being taunted or mocked locked his little feet in place.

Just then Cinderella noticed the boy and began making her way over to him. By inching through the crowd of children, she finally broke free. Walking quickly across the floor, she knelt down at eye level with the stunned boy and placed a kiss on his cheek.

"Rather than a costumed princess of Disney," explains Lucado, "we've been approached by the Prince of Peace." In both cases a gift was given. In both cases a gesture of love beyond words was made. In spite of our hesitation and fear of rejection, Jesus comes to us, breaking past all the barriers between us, and crouches down to our level.

As touching as the gesture of tenderness shown by a young girl dressed like Cinderella was, it hardly compares to the gift extended to us by Christ Jesus. Jesus did so much more than exhibit kindness to those of us who are unsightly or rejected by society. The costumed princess gave only a kiss and when she stood to leave, her beauty went with her. The boy was still deformed.

Unlike Cinderella, Jesus takes on our disfigurement, leaving us with His beauty. "For God took the sinless Christ and poured into him our sins. Then, in exchange, he poured God's goodness into us!" (2 Corinthians 5:21, The Living Bible).

Charles Trumbull expresses this work of Jesus perfectly in his book *Victory in Christ*, when he says:

> I had always known that Christ was my Savior; but I had looked upon Him as an external Savior, one who did a saving work for me from outside, as it were; one who was ready to come close alongside and stay by me, helping me in all that I needed, giving me power and strength and salvation. But now I know something better than that. At last I realized that Jesus Christ is actually and literally within me; and even more than that: that He has constituted Himself in my very life, taking me into union with Himself—my body, mind, and spirit—while I still have my own identity and free will and full moral responsibility.[7]

While building a case for Christianity, the great theologian and Cambridge professor, C. S. Lewis, also knew from personal experience the depths of this life-giving transformation described by Trumbull. Following his own wrestling match with understanding *zoe* life, Lewis writes in *Mere Christianity*:

> *Bios* has, to be sure, a certain shadowy or symbolic resemblance to *zoe*, but only the sort of resemblance there is between a photo and a place, or a statue and a man. A man who changed from having *bios* to having *zoe* would have gone through as big a change as a statue which changed from being a carved stone to being a real man.[8]

Let the Spirit of God invade your heart anew with the radical truth of His exchanged life. Breathe deep the breath of God and be transformed from the inside out. Have you been immobilized by your past? Act like a statue no more. We are born again into a new spiritual clan—recreated, revolutionized, and baptized in His likeness.

## In Summary

There are two ways to keep a man from breaking the law. You can either put him in prison, or give him a new heart. God chose the second option, offering us a brand new heart, purified and inhabited by His Spirit. Until Christ came, the law kept men in custody. But God chose to set us free saying, "I will cleanse you from all your filthiness. . . I will give you a new heart and put a new spirit within you. . . I will put My Spirit within you and cause you to walk in My statutes. . . " (Ezekiel 36:25-27).

*There are two ways to keep a man from breaking the law. You can either put him in prison, or give him a new heart.*

What are you worth?

"You are a chosen race, a royal priesthood, a holy nation, a people for God's own possession, that you may proclaim the excellencies of Him who has called you out of darkness into His marvelous light; for you once were not a people, but now you are the people of God" (1 Peter 2:9-10a).

# Reflection ⌇

Have you ever considered your lineage as being determined by your spiritual birth rather than by your physical birth?

Let's begin to take a look at this new creation—the new you! From the list below, choose some "lies" you believe. Begin to renew them by reading, writing, and meditating on the appropriate scripture and "What is True About Me."

| What I Feel or Think About Myself | Scripture | What Is True About Me |
|---|---|---|
| I am unworthy/ unacceptable. | Romans 15:7; Psalms 139 | I am acceptable/worthy. |
| I am alone. | Hebrews 13:5b; Romans 8:38-39 | I am never alone. |
| I feel like a failure/ inadequate. | 2 Corinthians 3:5-6; Philippians 4:13 | I am adequate. |
| I have no confidence. | Proverbs 3:26; Hebrews 10:19 | I am confident in God. |
| I'm confused/fear I'm going crazy. | 1 Corinthians 2:16; 2 Timothy 1:7 | I have the mind of Christ. |
| I don't have enough. | Philippians 4:19 | Christ supplies all I need. |
| I am a fearful, anxious person. | Psalm 34:4; 1 Peter 5:7; 2 Timothy 1:7 | I am free from fear. |
| I am defeated. | Romans 8:37; 2 Corinthians 2:14; 1 John 5:4 | I am victorious. |
| I am in bondage. | Psalm 32:7; 2 Corinthians 3:17; John 8:36 | I am free in Christ. |

| I am unloved. | John 15:9; Romans 8:38-39 | I am very loved. |
|---|---|---|
| I am unwanted and don't belong. | Romans 8:16-17; Galatians 4:5; Ephesians 1:5 | I am God's chosen child. |
| I have no strength. | Acts 1:8, Ephesians 1:19; Ephesians 3:16 | I have the Spirit's power. |
| I can't reach God. | Ephesians 2:6; 1 Peter 2:5, 9 | I have direct access to God. |
| Nothing will ever change. | 2 Corinthians 5:17; Ephesians 4:22-24 | God gave me new life. |

## God's Desire ～

"Therefore from now on we recognize no man according to the flesh; even though we have known Christ according to the flesh, yet now we know Him thus no longer. Therefore if any man is in Christ, he is a new creature; the old things passed away; behold, new things have come."
—2 Corinthians 5:16-17

"What marvelous love the Father has extended to us! Just look at it—we're called children of God! That's who we really are!"
—1 John 3:1a

## Your Response ～

*Father, please show me what steps of faith and action You want me to take in order to begin experiencing my new identity. Help me to recognize when I'm living out of my old identity rather than as the new creation you've made me!*

# ❦ 11 ❦

# One Nature Under God

"Do you believe in ghosts? I'm not speaking here of the Holy
Ghost. Daily I listen to Christians who still seem to be taking
a beating by a phantom. They call it the 'old man.'"[1]
—Charles Trumbull

I don't know if you can relate, but in spite of all I've known
about God's love, there have been times in my life when the
casual expression of godly confidence I've worn has hidden
my feelings of being a giant loser. I know in my spirit who I am, and
though everything in me wants to do right, I still fail. And when I do,
I certainly don't feel like a saint!

I know I've not been alone in this. I've met with many a friend
and client who struggle too and have basically said, "Bill, if you
really knew me, you wouldn't be encouraging me to be free. I think
I need a little bit of law. I can't be trusted!"

❦　　❦　　❦

In the late 1980s, a dark shadow spread over public Christianity, marring an image that many had worked diligently to protect and to present in a polished, clean light. It was a sobering season for Believers, a time when it was tempting to scrape the fish decal off the back of our cars.

The integrity of Evangelical Christianity seemed to go up in smoke when the five o'clock news broadcasts aired shameful stories of a couple of flamboyant, prime-time preachers working overtime with their secretaries, and laying hands on prostitutes for purposes other than healing and deliverance. Extravagant luxuries were revealed, all bought at the expense of trusting supporters. Rolls Royces and gold plated bathroom faucets merely added fuel to the fire.

After the media's feeding frenzy began to die down, even sadder stories seemed to ignite in small towns and churches where cases of infidelity among Christian leaders began to surface. These men and women weren't money-grabbing televangelists; they were some of the most respected leaders of churches and ministry organizations throughout the world! It seemed as though every other week or so, a high-profile Christian was falling. In the smoldering trail of caring relationships gone amuck lay destroyed marriages, broken families, and disgraced ministries.

I was embarrassed, and I was also afraid. If these "saints," many of whom I personally admired and respected for their spiritual strength and passion for God, were waking up in the wrong bed, where did that leave me?

This newfound insecurity of mine grew close to paranoia. I was nearly immobilized by this secret fear of potential sin. You see, I love people; they are my life. My heart breaks with their pain and I'm swept up in their glory. I adore children, I admire men . . . and the mysterious beauty of women awes me. Soon I was easily convinced that this passion for people and the uncertainty of sin was a lethal combination. I came to believe that when I least expected it, some primal instinct could take over and shove me into the bed of a sensuous woman, whether I consciously wanted to be there or not. I'd break out in a cold sweat as I imagined headlines splashed across the pages of religious periodicals, *Bill Ewing: Another Saint Fallen From Grace.* The really crazy part of this story is that I was gripped by fear without even having a woman in mind! Just the possibility of uncontrolled desire taking over me was enough to haunt me.

> *Because of the new spirit God put in me, the core of who I am truly desires what He wants!*

During this period of time (several weeks) when terrifying scenarios stormed through my head, I was also teaching classes regularly at the counseling center about the Believers' new identity in Christ and how we are designed with the righteousness and holiness of God. I would teach during the day and wrestle my fears at night until one day the truth dawned on me. I was going about this "affair scare" all wrong, and my fears were grossly misplaced.

I finally came to accept that indeed, I'm as capable as the next person to get caught in the snares of an affair, perhaps even more so because of my deep love for people. But then I realized, that as a Christian, a sexual temptation can't just leap on me and drag me down into destruction, nor can any sin for that matter. Because of the new spirit God put in me, the core of who I am truly desires what He wants!

The essence of my redeemed nature longs to do right because it is literally baptized into Christ. It can never be separated from him. Just as you would find "apple-ness" inside an apple tree, at my core you will find Jesus. I'm not saying I'll never sin. You and I will most definitely be tempted and there will be times we give in, but not without having made conscious choices all along the way. And when we do, the sin will be contrary to the true "us!"

We must not confuse our new nature with the old, dead one. Saint Augustine described our state of being *before* Adam fell, as *posse pecarre*, i.e., "able to sin," meaning that Adam created with a free will had not yet sinned, but he was "capable of sinning." However, *after* Adam fell, according to Augustine, he became *non posse noa peccare*, or "not able <u>not</u> to sin."[2] This means that in and of himself, Adam was unable to break free of sinning. In other words, sinning was in accordance with his very nature after the Fall. As a result of Adam's choice, we too are all born with this same fallen nature (Romans 5). It was this sin nature that made up the core of the "old man" *before it was crucified and we were made alive with Christ.*

My old nature's lusts and passions often ran unchecked with little desire to resist temptation. The media and my peers could easily persuade my old nature that I had no power over what felt good. Selfish ambition often ruled, even if serving my needs came at the expense of someone else. Therefore, I can't tell you how relieved I was to discover that my old nature is dead and gone! I had no reason to fear or be haunted by it any longer. No evil thing could bubble up within me and overtake my will. My enemy was the fear itself, not my phantom old man.

All along I had been trying to re-crucify my old nature. Somewhere in my Christian upbringing I had learned that we have a dual nature, an old and new—that there's a "bad dog" hiding inside of me waiting to take out my "good dog." But as I searched God's Word, I couldn't find this concept anywhere in the Bible. What Scripture *does say* is that my old nature was crucified. It died!! Scripture also says there will be a continual struggle with my flesh (see chapter 14), but not with my core spiritual nature. I am alive; I am one with the Spirit of Christ Jesus. My true nature is to live out my life as He designed it, at His lead.

The battle isn't between a bad nature and a good nature. I was fighting a battle that didn't exist. In fact, my wayward thinking was only making it worse. Living under the law of not sinning allows temptation to consume our thoughts and can actually drive us into the very sin we are trying to avoid! (see Chapter 8) When we really understand who we are, we can walk away from this lonesome, needless fight that so many men

> *When we really understand who we are, we can walk away from this lonesome, needless fight that so many men and women battle, and rest in who God has fashioned us to be.*

and women battle, and rest in who God has fashioned us to be.

For the Christian, engaging in sin comes as the result of a deliberate, poor, conscious choice, or a series of wrong choices. In order to sin, we must *choose* to act contrary to who we are. That's why sin makes us feel so miserable. The Holy Spirit doesn't just wag a finger or tug gently at our heart when we deliberately sin; His Spirit united with ours is repulsed. Our insides constrict with godly sorrow.

"For if we have become united with Him in the likeness of His death, certainly we shall be also in the likeness of His resurrection, knowing this, that our old self was crucified with Him, that our body of sin might be done away with, *that we should no longer be slaves to sin; for he who has died is freed from sin*" (Romans 6:5-7, emphasis mine).

In response to this scripture, D. Martyn Lloyd-Jones says:

"This is, to me, one of the most comforting and assuring and glorious aspects of our faith. We are never called to crucify our old man. Why? Because it has already happened—the old man was crucified with Christ on the cross. Nowhere does the scripture call upon you to crucify your old man; nowhere does the scripture tell you to get rid of your old man for the obvious reason that it has already gone. Not to realize this is to allow the devil to fool you and to delude you. . . . He [the old man] is non-existent; he is no longer there. If you are a Christian, the man that you were in Adam has gone out of existence; he has no reality at all; you are in Christ."[3]

Fundamentalist and Evangelical Christians are most widely known for their personal claim to be "born again," but have you ever sat and seriously pondered your need for rebirth? Why must we be born again? And if we are, what exactly does that mean?

To "reckon" ourselves dead is to accept what God says, "Now if we have died with Christ, we believe that we shall also live with Him" (Romans 6:8). Christ did not come into the old heart to try to make some improvements, but to make an end of the old heart by a complete removal, by death. He then replaced it by implanting within us a new heart that would *want* to walk with Him (Ezekiel 36:26, 27).

To be "born again" means to be "complete, made whole" in our original design. Time after time in Scripture, we see Jesus encounter people with the anticipation and expectation that they were no longer the same. They would go on to live a victorious life after knowing Him. In fact, we find a definite finality in His words. He didn't suggest they join a support group and start working through their issues, He said, "Your sins have been forgiven your faith has saved you; go in peace" (Luke 7:48, 50). "Go your way. From now on sin no more" (John 8:11). How could He have such expectations? He was absolutely certain of the power He had in each of his followers.

## How Then Shall We Live?

I don't know if I've ever actually seen one, and maybe you can verify whether or not this is true, but I've heard of documentaries or movies based on the story of a child lost out in the wilderness who is the only survivor of a plane crash on a remote island or in the mountainous jungle of a far away place. At any rate, rather than being eaten by wild predators, the little human is adopted and raised by a pack of wolves.

You know how the story goes. When the young boy is eventually found years later, he is crawling around on all fours, sleeping in the den, growling at intruders, and howling at the moon. He has a grimy face, matted hair and, to keep the story rated PG, Wolf Boy has somehow acquired a leather loin-cloth from who-knows-where.

What would you do if you were on the expedition team and found a little wolf-child? How would you begin the process of "humanizing" him? Wouldn't it be foolish if you set your efforts on cutting off his tail, trimming off his ears, and filing down his fangs? Why would this be ridiculous and useless? Because he doesn't have them! He is already human, and only needs to see who he really is. When he understands and truly believes he is human, human behavior *will* follow.

It is equally foolish, ridiculous, and useless for the Christian to try to kill the "old spiritual nature" *because Christians don't have one.* Like I said, we will battle with our flesh, but we don't have to change a thing to be spiritually pure or perfect because we already are. When we begin to understand this and truly believe it, our behavior and choices will follow, naturally, because that's who we are!

So, let's say you discover the young boy and though you are there to rescue him, you know that without being forced, he will be drawn to you because you reflect who he was created to be. All you do is set up camp and allow him to watch and then come to you when he feels safe.

*Only when we approach Christ to watch Him, model Him, and let Him live out zoe through us, do we begin to discover and become who we are.*

I imagine that at first he is gripped in fear, but as he watches the expedition team, he discovers he has hands that grasp like yours, and soon he finds he can stand upright and ever so slowly he begins to recognize his true nature. The aroma of your food makes his mouth water and when he hears the voice of humans, something stirs deep inside him. He begins to understand, *"This* is who I am".

Similar to the little Wolf Boy, we've learned survival skills without knowing the full potential of who we've been created to be. We continue to settle for *bios* life without ever awakening to the true possibility of *zoe* life. Only when we approach Christ to watch Him, model Him, and let Him live out *zoe* through us, do we begin to discover and become who we are.

Our past actions and strategies of the "wild" once helped us survive, but are no longer needed and have since been forgiven. Old behavior is no longer consistent with who we now know ourselves to be. Sinning becomes as incompatible with our new nature as acting like a wolf would be to our true human identity. Most assuredly, we will fall short of being all we are created to be, but we do not need to fear condemnation (Romans 8:1). Rather, like the young boy, we're free to explore and discover all that we already are. We have one nature, and it is a good, pure, and perfect spirit that God has given us and then indwelt with His Holy Spirit.

If I know who I am, really believe it, and choose to act on it, then what I do is going to change. Furthermore, the motive for why I do what I do is going to change and my behavior will begin to live out my true personhood.

The wolf story makes for fun imagery, but is a bit far fetched. A seventy-nine- pound anorexic, on the other hand, believes she's fat even as she starves herself to death. This is a far more sad and realistic scenario. If prior to meeting her, I had only a description of her behavior (i.e., she continually diets, only drinks Diet Coke, won't wear a bathing suit in public), I'd believe she was heavy. But is she really? What is she ideally designed to be? Or what about the man who believes he's an uncontrollably angry person? By observing his behavior, one might conclude that explosive anger must be in his nature, but is that consistent with his new nature in Christ?

REFLECTIONS

The world offers us many types of mirrors . . . not only in unique styles and shapes, but in reflective quality too. Some mirrors, like those in department store dressing rooms, are more subtle than others and influence our self perception without us even realizing.

Imagine growing up in a room full of trick carnival mirrors. Without any other point of reference you would come to believe that you are squatty with a bulging head and short stumpy arms and legs. If this image was all you ever saw of yourself, you would come to believe this is you, right?

Now let's say, my office has a full-length mirror that accurately reflects a person's true image and to prove to you that you are actually quite stunning, I stand you in front of the real mirror. *"This* is who you really are," I tell you. What would your response be? Chances are, you would turn away in disbelief exclaiming, "That's not me!" I'm guessing there would be no *"Scripture tells us what we truly are. . ."* way I could convince you unless I could otherwise prove that my mirror revealed the truth. What if I took a measuring tape and held it up to your legs and then compared it to the measurement of your legs' image in the mirror, could you believe then?

We are often told the Bible gives us a beautiful picture of what we *should* be. "Nonsense!" exclaimed F.D. Maurice, "Scripture tells us *what we truly are*; it says, 'This is the form in which God created you, to which he has restored you; this is the work which the Eternal Son, the God of Truth and Love, is continually carrying on within you.'"[4]

*... we must keep the Word of God, our true authority, before us to remind us of who we are in Christ, lest we walk away and forget His face and ours.*

We encounter many mirrors in life reflecting wrong images that delude us—obscuring our identity. Since we will always perform out of the basis of who we believe we are, we must keep the Word of God, our true authority, before us to remind us of who we are in Christ, lest we walk away and forget His face and ours (James 1:24).

But I shouldn't just ignore my wrong behavior either. When my behavior is wrong, it's obvious that my thinking is wrong. I don't want to just do right; I want to think right. I must exchange the lie for the truth of God and worship the Creator who is blessed forever. "In humility receive the word implanted, which is able to save your souls" (James 1:21).

I *am* someone clean and new, even though I don't feel like it sometimes. No longer is my life an extension of what I think I know and what I perceive. It's no longer a reflection or a reaction to what's going on around me. Instead, in humility, I can fully embrace the Word implanted deep within, and I can choose to believe what God says about Himself and how that is reflected in me.

## Why Do I Still Sin?

A valid question at this point is: If my old self died, and the real me is made after the holiness and righteousness of God, then why do I still sin? The Bible offers four major reasons why people act in sin even after a new birth. First, our behavior is a display of what we believe to be true, whether it is or not. Second, Satan is a relentless deceiver. Third, we fail to recognize the power instilled in us to overcome temptation, and fourth, old habits die hard.

## 1. BELIEFS DETERMINE BEHAVIOR

We can try to "Christianize" ourselves and others, but if we don't know and don't believe who we really are, it's going to affect our whole approach to life. If we are acting out of a lie, our lives will continually be out of sync with our spiritual reality, leaving us in frustration and defeat. If we believe that we still have a corrupt, sinful nature ravaging our soul and overpowering our spirit, *this is how we will behave, even though it's not true.* If we believe that we are not pure, not like Jesus, *we will behave accordingly, no matter how hard we determine to do otherwise.*

If you *believe* you are wolf, you will act like one. If you believe you are a sinner, you will *act* like one. If you are to genuinely act as a child of God, it's critical that you know and believe what is genuinely true about you. If you don't, you may have wings but will never fly, you may be free yet never leave prison, and you may be victorious in the war with sin and still lose battle after battle.

## 2. SATAN IS A RELENTLESS DECEIVER

The second reason we sin must not be overlooked. One of Satan's primary tactics is a two-handed approach, one for sinners and one for saints. On the one hand, he tricks sinners into believing that they are actually pretty good people, while on the other, he deceives saints into believing they aren't saints after all. A good friend of mine, Bill Gillham, explains it something like this: "Satan is a liar, the father of lies, and his native language is lying" (see John 8:44). Three of the titles given to him as a liar are: tempter, deceiver, and accuser. (Matthew 4:3; 2 John 1:7; Revelation 12:10) Let's look at how this plays out in real life.

Satan is very familiar with our old ways. In the areas in which he knows we are vulnerable, he often presents an appetizing temptation tailored just for us. His next plot is to deceive us into being convinced that those tempting thoughts originated from within, that they are ours, and come from us naturally because we are greedy, gossipy, and lustful people. These temptations will sound as if they are coming from us because he uses words like "I, me, my, mine." His plan is to make us think that these are our own thoughts that originated from within. For example:

*"Why should I report that on my taxes, nobody would ever know if I didn't?"*

*"I can't stand the way she manipulates the boss. I'm going to tell Susie about this."*

*"She is so sexy. I wish my wife would say seductive things like she does! I'll just flirt with her a little."*

Did you know that "the father of lies" will use Scripture out of context to be even more convincing? He would love for you to think you are dark and untrustworthy at your core. Making you feel helpless, he may mix and match verses such as "The heart is deceitfully wicked. It cannot be trusted." As soon as Satan convinces us of our depravity, he attacks from his third title, "the accuser." He points a crooked finger, blaming us for being dirty, selfish losers. Once we have come this far we will either silently condemn ourselves or act out what we believe about ourselves, even when it is not at all true! Many Christians bring blame, guilt, shame, and condemnation upon themselves, believing they are a continual disappointment to God. Believing they acted ungratefully for all Christ did for them, they've fallen headfirst for Satan's snare.

## 3. FAILING TO RECOGNIZE OUR POWER

Another reason we Believers sin is that we either don't realize the power within us to do otherwise (see Romans 6), or we choose to make a willful decision to act out of our own strength and power, rather than relying on God to live through us. We were never designed to operate out of our own strength. When we attempt to do so, the results will always be inconsistent with our true identity and can often be disastrous.

## 4. OLD HABITS DIE HARD

Lastly, we have deeply ingrained habit patterns that take time to change. We easily fall into old grooves unless we begin to redirect and replace old behavior with decisions based on truth. Sometimes people know the truth, but they fall into automatic habits that must be broken. We will dedicate chapter 13, "Being Transformed," to this topic, and I think you will find this absolutely liberating.

◊  ◊  ◊

How, then do we defeat sin and overcome temptation? By trying harder to be something we wish we were? Absolutely not! We overcome evil by declaring what is already true about Christ and our new identity in Him. Throughout all of the New Testament we are shown our true reflection (see Romans 6:6; Ephesians 4:22-24; Colossians 3:9-10). "The greatest truth we can ever be told," says D. Martyn Lloyd-Jones, "is that our old self has gone ... the problem of [sin] becomes much easier once I realize that my old self has gone. My old self was an utter slave to sin. That self has gone; I have a new self, I am a new man."5 Will Christ, in you, act in a greedy manner? No! Will Jesus ever succumb to lust? No! Will He speak an unwholesome word about another person? No!

*We overcome evil by declaring what is already true about Christ and our new identity in Him.*

## Incredible Potential!

Not only do we no longer need to be preoccupied with sin, we can look to the future with great expectation. We are reborn to do what? Understanding our true identity found in "one nature under God" is absolutely essential to living in victory over the flesh and sin. But this is just the beginning. It gets even better. Understanding the incredible truths about who we are in Jesus sets us free and unleashes our *real* potential.

Lance Armstrong, arguably the greatest endurance athlete in the world and a survivor of the cancer that should have killed him, came back to be a multiple winner of the Tour de France, the mother of all bicycle races. Of course, he works hard, trains and rides with world-class teammates, and has fantastic equipment. But there is something different about Lance: his body can suck in and absorb oxygen at an exceptionally high rate. It's just the way God made him. Lance didn't do anything to get that special ability, but *he knows his potential and plans his life accordingly.* As a result he continually accomplishes what others claim is impossible.

Undoubtedly, there are dozens of couch potatoes who have the same capacity to use oxygen as Lance, but they either don't know it, or if they do, they disregard their God-given ability. They are missing the action. And how many Christians are out there warming pews for an hour on Sunday, and just getting by the rest of the week? What a waste!

Consider this seriously. Not only do we have a ready supply of oxygen, the life-giving force for *bios* life, we are made complete with *zoe*, the unlimited source of the essence of God Himself! Maybe you are just now discovering who you truly are and the real potential to be unleashed because of who you are in Christ.

Remember the words Jesus spoke to the woman at the well? He asked her for water for His body, but then He said, "If you knew the gift of God, and who it is who says to you 'Give me a drink,' you would have asked Him, and He would have given you living water" (John 4:10). He offered her *zoe* water, and He offers it to us today! Sure, we need water for our *bios*, but if we ask Him, He will show us the way into an incredible life, saturated with living *zoe*!

The truth is that we've yet to even scratch the surface of the implications of these truths. Because of who we are in Him, we can fly when we couldn't even crawl, sing when we couldn't talk, and perhaps most amazingly, dance without restraint in the presence of a God from whom we used to hide.

"Now to Him who is able to do exceeding abundantly beyond all we ask or think, according to the power that works within us, to Him be the glory in the church and in Christ Jesus to all generations forever and ever. Amen." (Ephesians 3:20).

## In Summary

The spiritual walk with God promises an exhilarating and unpredictable journey as His Spirit directs and teaches, making us into a unique and whole person—complete with our body, soul, and spirit functioning in harmony with Him, His Truth, and His creation. Spiritually, we are alive with Christ. Our old nature was put to death, and we've been raised with the newness of life. What is natural and normal for me now is to live in righteousness (those things I was designed to do).

I will experience the urge to howl at the moon from time to time for though my spirit is already new, my mind still needs more renewing to the truth of what happened in my spirit. But in the meantime I can rest. I can rest assured knowing the phantom old man is gone and that at the central core of my being, my spirit, I am exactly who I am supposed to be.

## Reflection ～～

Satan's definition of hypocrisy is "acting differently from how I *feel* about who I am." God's definition of hypocrisy is "acting differently from what is true about who I am."

How would believing your old man is dead and understanding your new identity make a difference in your relationships and the manner in which you deal with problems?

Choose an area you struggle in. What aspect of your new identity do you need to accept by faith and begin to live according to?

## God's Desire ～～

"What you're after is truth from the inside out."
—Psalms 51:6 *The Message*

"Knowing this, that our old self was crucified with Him, that our body of sin might be done away with, that we should no longer be slaves to sin; for he who has died is freed from sin"
—Romans 6:6-7.

## Your Response ～～

*Father, thank you for nailing my old man to the cross, freeing me from slavery to sin, and raising me a new creation in Christ. Holy Spirit, teach me to depend upon Your strength and power to live out the reality of who I am now, as a new creation.*

# ※ 13 ※

# The Forgiveness Factor
# Part 1

If possible, so far as it depends on you,
be at peace with all men.
Romans 12:18

Patricia is alone tonight, in a dim and quiet apartment. That's the way it's going to be every other weekend and alternating holidays for a very long time. She held it together during work today, but now, after dropping off the kids at her ex-husband's house, the world has seemed to collapse around her, pinning her down on her bed, even as it refuses to let her sleep.

As she stares at the ceiling, the events of the last year replay over and over in her mind. She longs to be free from them even as she desperately holds on to them. She should have seen it coming – the cool complacency that had descended on their marriage, his late nights at the office, his occasional out of town trips to see "old friends." Looking back, she can see that both of them were only pretending that the other didn't know. In time, of course, she had to face what everyone else in town already knew — Michael, her husband, was holding another woman in his arms and in his heart, and he would soon be leaving.

Since the explosive day when all was revealed, Patricia's life has been a blur of thoughts, emotions, lawyers, job-hunting, and apartment shopping. She has done her best to walk through it all with integrity. She has prayed. She has immersed herself in the Bible. She has known the comfort of friends. She has been faithfully going through the motions.

But Patricia can't remember a normal day. A day when she just talked about the new styles, when she felt normal around married couples, when she felt as though she was doing a half-decent job of mothering, when she wasn't stressed about paying the rent. She tries to block it all out, but her memories of the past and her concerns about the future are consumed by images from the present. Tonight, at this very moment, he has the kids, and tonight he is with her. Tonight they are a family ... and tonight, Patricia is alone — and the silence of the apartment is deafening.

Patricia feels as if her mind is being shredded cell by cell. She's been told that things would get better if she "gave it some time," if she "moved on," if she "put some distance between herself and the situation." But instead of healing, she knows she is only coping, and just barely coping at that.

Over several months, a heavy cloud of depression has descended on her soul. Some friends have recommended that she see a doctor and consider anti-depressants. One friend encouraged her to try therapy first, so after a referral from her pastor, Patricia made a counseling appointment with our counseling center for tomorrow morning ...

The world is not a happy place. Full of disappointment, hurt, and emptiness, life is a constant dance with pain. Relationships turn sour. Friends turn their backs. Family members wound us. Others unknowingly hurt us, leaving us with wounds that scar.

What are we to do when hurt comes our way? Equally important, what are we to do when *we* are the ones who have been the source of pain or disappointment in the heart of another? What are we to do with the weight of *our* guilt and the festering anger? We now know that we are new creatures, free from the constraints of legalism, but what are we to do when others cause us pain, and their actions imprison our hearts with anger?

In over twenty-five years of counseling, I can recall only a handful of clients that didn't have to deal with anger from the pain inflicted by another. Thankfully, God has not left us alone. Once we recognize anger and where it comes from, God has made a way to deal with it decisively.

## Goals vs. Desires

*Anger emerges anytime something we want to happen doesn't, or something we don't want to happen does.* Anger is fueled by the breaking of hopeful expectations, whether it's broken dreams or broken promises. We get angry when a "goal" is blocked or interfered with by someone or something. Whenever we can't get to something that we feel is essential to *Zoë* Life, we will get angry at the things or people that are standing in the way.

For example, you might *desire* your child or spouse act in a certain way. But remember, except for using handcuffs and straitjackets, you can't control them anymore than they can control you. A *desire* is something that you wish would happen, *but is ultimately out of your control.* A *goal*, on the other hand, is something that *you can* control. If you don't have all the resources to make something happen, it should be a *desire*, rather than a *goal*. Do you want a quick hint for radically reducing anger and stress in you life? Apply these two strategies:

1. *Pray for your desires.* God commands you to do this anyway (Matthew 6:9-13, John 16:24). You might desire that your children turn out to be honest, respectful, obedient teens, but that's not in your control, as any parent of a teen can tell you. Pray for them!

2. *Act on your goals.* In the case of parenting teens, don't try to change them. Instead, make it a goal to be a solid, gracious, guiding mom or dad, *regardless* of what they do. You can control what you do,

so act! Sure, you may have to ground them and provide firm barriers, but everyone will be a lot less angry (including you) if you are doing it out of a loving, serving heart — rather than out of anger because they aren't doing what you want — blocking your goal!

## The Many Faces of Anger

Much of the time, anger is displayed through "getting mad." But just as often, an angry person doesn't appear mad and may not even feel mad. Often anger is turned inward and a person feels hurt, offended, depressed, or withdrawn. When my wife Nancy and I used to get mad at each other, sometimes we vented our anger by giving each other "the silent treatment." We couldn't really yell at each other downtown or dump each other's clothes out on the street where the neighbors could see them. So we just clammed up and played it cool — *really* cool — like ice —and faced the other direction.

Although the ramifications of anger can be terrible, *anger itself is not our enemy.* Anger is not even a sin (Ephesians 4:26). When we recognize anger for what it is, it can be a powerful messenger, telling us when we have ungodly goals that are being blocked. As a messenger, anger tells us when it's time to change these goals into desires.

Anger can also arise as a *result* of sin. The wrong and evil actions of others often have a direct negative impact on us, causing anger to rise. In this common, recurring situation, anger is an indicator that someone needs to be forgiven for hurting us.

When anger is not dealt with as God designed, the angry person begins to descend into a dangerous, destructive pit that leads to relational, emotional, and even physical death.

## Anger's Progressive Destruction:

*In Cain's Life in Genesis 4*

* Hurt and Anger (Ephesians 4:26)  Genesis 4:3-5
* Bitterness (Hebrews 12:14-15)
* Resentment (James 3:14-16)  Genesis 4:9
* Vengeance (Proverbs 24:29)

- Hatred, strife (Galatians 5:13-20)
- Ungratefulness (Romans 1:20-21)
- Loss of Hope and Faith      Genesis 4:5-7,13-14
  Anger is reflected in
  Cain's facial expression.
- Depression      The fallen or downcast
  face expresses anger
  or depression.
- Death      Genesis 4:8&16
  (separated from God)

From the moment we experience broken expectations or blocked goals, anger begins to lead us, step by step, into this pit. Some say that "time will heal all things," but even after angry emotions diminish, they continue to simmer, waiting to erupt again. Adding distance from the hurtful event usually offers only a brief distraction from the anger, for we will always take our memories with us, no matter where we go. Sometimes we try to neutralize our anger by minimizing the true impact of the event. We say, *I guess it wasn't really that bad.* Or we justify the motives of the person who hurt us by thinking, *she wasn't herself at the time,* or *if only I had been different, he wouldn't have done this to me.*

Dealing with anger in these ways may cause you to forget about the initial hurt, but the underlying anger is still there. It has only gone below the surface and results in such maladies as withdrawal, sleeplessness, depression, anxiety, explosions of temper, etc. Then one tends to attempt to deal with these symptoms and wonders where they came from. The culprit is buried anger.

None of these strategies was ever intended to heal a hurtful wound or mend an angry heart. God designed one way and one way only to free our bodies and souls from the ravages of hurt and anger.

## Healing in Forgiveness

God is the Great Physician (Exodus 15:26). He embodies the true heart of a dedicated doctor. He is intimately acquainted with how we are made, for indeed, we are the work of His hands (Psalm 139). He is the Wonderful Counselor (Isaiah 9:6), knowing the intricate and integrated nature of our souls and our spirits. Like no one else, God is the One most qualified to prescribe a remedy for our pain and heal the destruction caused by our anger. As our Great Provider (Genesis 22:14), God not only offers His instruction, but also He has intervened and provided a strategic way out of the bondage of anger. It's called the way of *forgiveness;* it's the way that He Himself walked and it's the way that He now beckons us to follow.

Forgiveness is the divine transaction, paid in full by the blood of Jesus, which frees both the offender and the offended from the bondage of sin. The act of forgiveness follows in the footsteps of Christ to the very shadow of the Cross. Contrary to earthly wisdom and human conceptions of "fairness," true biblical forgiveness is built on the following principles:

*Forgiveness is the divine transaction, paid in full by the blood of Jesus, which frees both the offender and the offended from the bondage of sin.*

*First, forgiveness begins when you fully embrace the wrong that you have encountered.* When you've been hurt — either through a direct action or a broken expectation — the pain is real. Don't downplay that. Sin is personal. Recognize that you feel you have been personally wronged and identify the personal consequences that you experience as a result.

*Second, forgiveness is built on the understanding that all sin is ultimately against God, not us.* David recognized this fact when he repented of his sins of adultery and murder. He proclaimed, "Against *You, You alone,* have I sinned" (Psalm 51:3-4, NRSV). Whether we accept it or not, we are no longer our own (Romans 14:7-8). We belong to Him. He is the true owner of all that we are, and any attack against us is an attack against Him. When Paul was pursuing the destruction of Christians, Jesus knocked him from his donkey and cried out, "Saul, Saul, why are you persecuting *Me?*" (Acts 9:4). When others persecute you, they are persecuting Him, through you, as well.

As members of the church of God, we are members of *His* body (1 Corinthians 12:27). Each of us occupies a specific part in that body, but we are only a part of the whole; the "whole" is Jesus. An offense against one part is an offense against the entire body. If "Joe" gets stabbed in the back, the newspapers don't report, "A back was stabbed yesterday." They report, "Joe was stabbed in the back." Likewise, you might be an arm in the body of Christ, and when you get stabbed, the offense is *against Him* although it came *into the body* through you.

When someone sins against you, it's going to hurt. The sin is a blow by another, striking the part of Christ's body that happens to be you. Thus, we "share [in] the sufferings of Christ" (1 Peter 4:13).

This may seem odd, but it is a vital truth to grasp. When we understand that we are part of His body and that our life is truly His, we are able to bring the process of forgiveness all the way to the Cross — where forgiveness is completed. If we think the sin is ultimately against *us*, we will be left to deal with it in our own strength and wisdom — and we were never designed to do that. Forgiveness finds its origin at the Cross when we accept the fact that the sin was actually against *Christ* and dealt with by *Him*.

*Third, true forgiveness is empowered when we embrace the extent of God's forgiveness toward us.* Psalm 103:3-4 says that the Lord "pardons *all* your iniquities" and "redeems your life *from the pit....*" [Emphasis mine]. Paul further expresses God's forgiveness with these words:

> In Him we have redemption through His blood, the forgiveness of our trespasses, according to the riches of His grace, which He lavished on us (Ephesians 1:7-8).

> He made you alive together with Him, having forgiven us all our transgressions, having canceled out the certificate of debt consisting of decrees against us and which was hostile to us; and He has taken it out of the way, having nailed it to the cross (Colossians 2:13) [emphasis mine].

Note that these passages are in the past tense. God's forgiveness was perfectly paid for two thousand years ago. In order for us to authentically extend forgiveness to others, we must first realize that we have been forgiven. In Luke 7:47, Jesus goes so far as to say that those who feel they have been forgiven of little, love little; those who know that they have been forgiven of much, will forgive much. Understanding the incredible extent of God's forgiveness for *us* gives us a perspective from which we can extend forgiveness to *others*. We are just passing on something that we already have received from Him — we "forgive, just as the Lord forgave you" (Colossians 3:13). As a consequence of their sin, often those who have committed adultery and then repented lose everything: wife, children, finances, home ... but they gain a sense of grace, forgiveness, and humility that far surpasses those who haven't committed the same sin.

*Fourth, in order to be willing to forgive, we must first trust God with our feelings.* Forgiveness is an act of the will, not the emotions. It's a choice. If you follow your feelings, you'll never truly forgive, for your angry feelings will always get in the way. Your mind, not your emotions must lead the way. Satan and the world have caused us to get this backward. Most people don't forgive because they don't feel like it. If you trust God with those feelings, however, and choose to obey God's call to forgive, the peace will follow *after* you forgive.

*Fifth, forgiveness is something that God must do through us; it's not something we can do on our own (John 15:5).* Even if we understand *how* to forgive, we must realize that only He can *do* it. He alone was worthy to die as the perfect sacrifice for sin, and He alone is able to empower us to forgive others, having paid the price for their sin. As we choose to allow God to forgive through us, we actually get to participate in the power of God's love as it is extended through us and forgives those who have sinned against us.

## Reasons We Don't Forgive

The freedom and rest that wait on the other side of forgiveness can transform our lives, yet we all tend to hesitate to forgive — and often flat out refuse to do so. Here are some excuses we use to dodge God's command to forgive:

- The sin was too bad and hurt too much.

- We don't "feel like it."
- They aren't truly sorry.
- They may do it again.
- I don't like them.
- They haven't asked me to forgive them.
- They did it on purpose.
- I can't forget it.
- I'll have to be nice to them.
- I want to see them punished.

None of the above is a good enough reason not to forgive, and will only keep us in bondage. Forgiveness is a choice. If you ask God, He will give you both the desire and the power to forgive. If you choose not to forgive, however, some nasty consequences will be yours.

Consequences of Unforgiveness:

- A restriction of love, even to those who did not cause the pain. "I am not going to get hurt like that again."
- Stress and all its effects (a depleted immune system, ulcers, chronic degenerative diseases, premature aging, etc.)
- Inability to "get over it," resulting in bondage to the hurtful event or person.
- "Opportunity" is given to Satan (Ephesians 4:27).
- "Advantage" is given to Satan (2 Corinthians 2:11).
- Being handed over to "the tormenter" (Matthew 18:23-35).
- Depression (Genesis 4:6-7)
- A hindered relationship with God and others (Isaiah 59:2, Genesis 4:3-8 & 16).

This is not the way God has designed us to live, but that is where we naturally end up — unless we make the choice to forgive as God created us to forgive. Still, we aren't to forgive simply because it is highly beneficial for us to do so and very destructive to us if we do not. Our response of obedience to forgive is to reflect the moral nature of Christ Himself. Consider this quote from a Chinese pastor who was imprisoned in work camps for many years:

"You ask me, 'Is it right for someone to strike my cheek?' I answer, 'Of course not! But the question is do I only want to be right?' As Christians, our standard for living can never be 'right or wrong,' but the Cross. The principle of the Cross is our principle of conduct. Praise God that He makes the sun to shine on the evil and the good. With Him it is a question of His grace and not of right or wrong." — Watchman Nee, *Sit, Walk, Stand*

## Responding to God's Call

Forgiving by self-effort is impossible. Forgiveness was initiated by God, embodied in Christ's blood, and is empowered through the Holy Spirit. If you need to forgive, begin by asking God to work through you entirely, giving you the *willingness* and the *ability* to walk through the process.

## Steps to Forgiveness

1. Make a list of the specific hurts that were committed against you. List things they both did or didn't do that hurt you.

2. List all the ways this action has affected you. Your pain will help guide you to the consequences of the person's offense against you. For example, if someone steals your car, you might be mad that you have to walk to work. If your spouse has left you, you might be depressed because of how it has caused other couples to avoid you. The ramifications might be financial, social, mental, emotional, physical, or others.

3. Claim the truth that your life is Christ's and, as part of His body, you shared in His suffering. Thank God for His forgiveness *toward* you, and thank Him for forgiving the offender *through* you. Pass the sin on to the Cross, and since God has already paid the price for this offense, pass God's forgiveness on to the offender.

4. Release the responsibility for punishment to God. While you may still need to pursue recourse through church discipline, recognize that it is not your place to punish. Forgiveness doesn't necessarily mean you have to forget. If someone has sinned against you, you don't have to be foolish and set yourself up for further pain or abuse. It does mean, however, that in God's power, you free them from your condemnation and judgment, and choose to love them

... faults and all. "Vengeance is mine ..." says the Lord (Romans 12:19).

A prayer of forgiveness might sound something like this:
*Father of Forgiveness,*
*Oh, Lord, You are aware of the sins that have been committed and the effect they have had on me as Your Child. (Give Him the specifics.) I know that my life is Your life and all I am and all I do is through You. So, thank You for forgiving them through me. Thanks for paying the cost for their sin and mine when You died on the Cross, and when I was crucified with You. I trust in You to deal with them as You see fit. I choose not to do that in anyway on my own. Free me from my feelings of anger. Make me a blessing to those that have hurt me.*
*Your Forgiven Child.*

5. Destroy the lists. Destroying the list symbolizes that you are choosing no longer to carry the burden of their offense. You are letting it go and setting yourself free!

6. Give a blessing.

To sum up, let all be harmonious, sympathetic, brotherly, kindhearted, and humble in spirit; not returning evil for evil, or insult for insult, *but giving a blessing instead* (1 Peter 3:8-9) [emphasis mine].

An act of kindness toward someone who has done wrong seems to unleash the power of forgiveness and break the stronghold of emotion that Satan uses to control those who have been hurt. I've seen this time and again! When you respond to sin with obedient love, supernatural freedom is unleashed.

Proverbs 21:14 says, "A gift in secret subdues anger." We know it's not "fair." We know they don't "deserve it." But some sort of blessing given to the offender is great for *your* soul. You really have to experience this to understand it! But I'm telling you that giving some sort of "good" to those who have done you wrong is cleansing and liberating. It is so contrary to the way of the world and the flesh, but it will break any lingering attachment you have to anger and frustration and will be the final thing that sets you free from the sin that another has committed against you and Christ.

Before we continue, I want to encourage you to stop here. Let this soak in for a while. Pray for God's leading in what He now wants to do through you. Forgiving others is so vital to every aspect of our being – please don't just hear about it without pausing to let God unleash its' healing into your soul and body.

# The Forgiveness Factor
# Part 2

## The Hardest One to Forgive

O ver the last two decades, the counselors with whom I
have worked have become convinced of the importance of
forgiveness in the process of physical and mental healing.
Reconciliation with God is absolutely central to finding healing
and deliverance. Forgiveness also sets the stage for restoration in
earthly relationships. Time and time again, people are set free as
they begin to forgive. But many times, as a client walks through
the process, they get stuck. It seems that there is one person who is
harder than all others to release and forgive: *self*. How is it that you
can receive God's forgiveness, forgive others, and yet not be willing
to forgive *yourself*? There are several possible reasons:

- **You don't** *feel* **forgiven.** Guilt runs deep, and Satan loves
to stir it up. While we might feel forgiven for some sins, there

are others that we seem unable to let go of. Usually these are "biggies" in our mind. We feel we've gone too far to be forgiven and our feelings of guilt condemn us over and over until our minds believe that we really aren't forgiven at all. Be honest about those feelings. We know it's easier to forgive yourself for cheating on a spelling test than it is to believe you are forgiven for your abortion or your affair. Christ's sacrifice for those things is just as sufficient and God's forgiveness for those things is just as complete (Hebrews 10:14).

· **You hold yourself to** *higher standards* **than God does.** It's quite possible that even though you believe that God has forgiven you for certain sins, you won't forgive yourself for them. This reveals that your standards for acceptability are higher than God's. It reveals a vein of self-effort and a desire to be your own judge, or legalism — the very legalism that Christ died to free you from. Think about this logically: If a perfectly holy God now finds you completely acceptable because of Christ's sacrifice, who are you to demand more?

· **You think you need to** *punish* **yourself.** In essence it's thinking, "I must pay for my own sins. Christ didn't do the job well enough, so I need to punish myself before I can be forgiven."

## When You Don't Forgive Yourself

God has chosen to fully forgive you (that is a biblical fact), but you are the one who must choose to forgive yourself. If you choose not to, you will carry a burden of guilt that Christ has already carried to the Cross.

"Come to Me, all who are weary and heavy-laden, and I will give you rest. Take My yoke upon you, and learn from Me, for I am gentle and humble in heart; and you shall find rest for your souls. For My yoke is easy and My load is light" (Matthew 11:28-30).

Unless we forgive ourselves, we will always be prone to beating ourselves up emotionally, denying ourselves good things that God offers, and sometimes even hurting ourselves physically through eating disorders, overeating, self-mutilation, maybe even suicide.

"There is therefore now no condemnation for those who are in Christ Jesus. For the law of the Spirit of life in Christ Jesus has set you free from the law of sin and of death" (Romans 8:1-2).

## Feelings of Unworthiness

Satan rejoices when we feel like our sin has disqualified us from the Master's service and made us useless to His kingdom. God has always been in the business of using dented people for His glory. Numerous people in the Bible had to fall hard before they were willing to give up their self-effort and let God begin to live through them. Remember Peter's story? Peter denies Christ three times, still Christ gives him the assignment of "tending His sheep" (John 21:15-17). Paul recounts again and again his persecution of Christ by attacking Christians yet God uses him as few others to build His kingdom (Acts 26).

"For we are His workmanship, created in Christ Jesus for good works, which God prepared beforehand, that we would walk in them" (Ephesians 2:10).

If we don't forgive ourselves, we may begin trying even harder to make things right; thinking, If I just do such and such, I'll feel better about myself. Certainly, the earthly consequences of our sin might require quite a bit of effort to fix, if it can be fixed at all, but if we set out to make ourselves acceptable to God, we have missed the mark again and launch ourselves right back into self-effort – the very thing that got us in trouble in the first place.

"For the one who has entered His rest has himself also rested from his works, as God did from His. Let us therefore be diligent to enter that rest, lest anyone fall ..." (Hebrews 4:10-11).

If you are unwilling to forgive yourself, a tremendous amount of anger is turned inward, against yourself, causing significant mental and physical stress.

"When I kept silent about my sin, my body wasted away... My vitality was drained away as with the fever-heat of summer" (Psalm 32:3-4).

## Letting Go

God has done His part and our forgiveness is fully granted. But total reconciliation requires both parties to forgive. This is true in human-to-human relationships as well as our relationship with God. One person can forgive, but both parties must be willing to reconcile. God has forgiven you, but if you don't forgive yourself, you will hinder openness and intimacy in your relationship with Him. For reconciliation to be complete, you must be willing to let Him into those dark areas of your life so He can give you the desire and the power to forgive yourself too. If you have reached the point where you know that God is telling you that it's time to let go — that it's time to be free of the weight of your guilt and shame — talk to Him about it and consider praying something like this:

*My God and my Creator,*

*I have come to believe that You are a God of forgiveness. I believe Christ's sacrifice was sufficient and that I am forgiven for all the sin I have done and all the sin I will do in the future. I am so grateful for that sacrifice. Thank you for making me a forgiven person.*

*But Father, I've been unable and unwilling to forgive myself for ____ [List them for Him! All of them!] I now see that it is destructive and wrong to not forgive myself. I want to be free from the harm that this is bringing to me and those around me. I also see how this dishonors You and robs You of my praise and worship.*

*God, I can't forgive myself for these things on my own. Give me the faith, the desire, and the strength to forgive myself. I ask that You would do that now. By Your strength and an act of my will, I forgive myself and declare myself free from these sins because Christ has paid the penalty for them in full.*

*When my feelings try to drag me back into guilt and self-condemnation, quickly remind me of who I am as Your child. Continually remind me that I've been completely cleansed and forgiven of these things, no matter how I feel.*

*Lord, I praise You and I thank You for this new freedom; empower me to live as You desire.*

*Amen.*

Please don't continue reading this book until you have paused and let God minister to you in this area of forgiving yourself. Biblical principles are not about information; they are about *action* and *life-change*. A time of quiet and prayerful thought will reveal where you have refused to forgive yourself and where you are in bondage to past sins. Consider walking through the step-by-step process of forgiveness we covered in the last section ... only this time you will be extending the freedom of forgiveness to yourself!

## Seeking Forgiveness from Others

Once you realize that God forgives you, and after you extend that forgiveness to others and to yourself, you are ready to take one last (and often very difficult) step toward freedom and rest. When you have sinned against someone else, certain biblical principles must be followed to begin healing and reconciliation. Consider the words of Matthew 5:23-24:

> If therefore you are presenting your offering at the altar, and there remember that your brother has something against you, leave your offering there before the altar and go your way; first be reconciled to your brother ...

When you are in the wrong, and the other person knows it or has suffered in anyway from your actions, now is the time to ask for forgiveness. Now, not later! The pattern in Matthew suggests that even your normal routine of worship and service should be interrupted if you need to seek reconciliation.

These basic steps will help guide you — but more importantly, you will want to listen to the specific guidance of God as you approach the person you have hurt.

1. Clearly identify what you did and the impact it had on the other person.

2. Thank God for forgiving you (because ultimately, all sin is against Him).

3. Ask the person you sinned against to forgive you. Don't just say, "I'm sorry." Be specific and ask, *"Will you forgive me for ___?" "Will you forgive me?"* Or, *"I was wrong in what I did and am*

*truly sorry for offending you."* Do this without making excuses for your actions or words. Freedom always comes with a price. Forgiveness comes with humility and an awkwardness that the flesh would just as soon avoid. But I am telling you that it is worth it. When you pick up the telephone and say those words, healing from your actions takes place in your heart. If they forgive you, healing takes place in their heart as well.

4. If they don't forgive you, you are free, and the other person will have to carry the weight of your sin. If the person extends forgiveness, then both of you will experience freedom.

Asking for forgiveness does *not*, however, release you from earthly consequences of your actions. You may still face ramifications. One of those consequences may be living with a broken relationship. (There is no guarantee that the person you have hurt is going to forgive you.) The relational implications of your actions could be severing and severe. There may be legal, financial, and physical implications as well. But no matter what you've done or continue to do, it's never too late to do the right thing — and seeking forgiveness is the right thing.

Embracing the forgiveness of God, forgiving others, forgiving yourself, seeking forgiveness from those you have wronged — these are the privileges, the rights, and the responsibilities of those who walk in the shadow of the Cross. May we have the wisdom to daily allow the forgiveness of Christ to flow to us and through us.

❧ ❧ ❧

*Patricia's mind was swimming after her counseling appointments. There were so many new thoughts, so many verses from the Bible that had come alive. As she returned to her empty apartment, these new thoughts mixed with her thoughts and anger regarding her husband's affair, the divorce, the custody of her children; she was exhausted from the day, yet unable to sleep. Just before midnight, she got out of bed, sat at the kitchen table, and opened her Bible. As the clock ticked into the wee hours of the morn, she read, prayed, and cried, letting all her emotions from the past year spill out. On pages stained with tears, she made lists of the hurts of her husband, writing line after line of the pain, the pressure, and the ramifications that his unfaithfulness had brought upon her and their children.*

*She held the list close to her heart, and felt one more time the full weight of it. Then, with a thick, black, permanent marker she drew a bold cross over the words, giving each and every item to Christ. She thanked Him that He was taking the burden of each sin from her. When there were no more tears, she tore the list into pieces and threw it away. Back in the bedroom, she slept soundly for the first time in over a year.*

*The sun on her face woke her just before noon, but this was to be no day off. Deep inside, Patricia knew that there was still business to do. Back at the kitchen table, she prayed for God to search her heart and reveal her ways. As the Spirit and the Word shed light into her soul, the list of her own sins and shortcomings grew on the page. Some were minor. Some were major. Some revealed a controlling and critical spirit that overflowed into specific acts of anger and manipulation. Some revealed the life of sincere, but misguided self-effort to be like God, making herself responsible for things that only He should have controlled.*

*When He showed her nothing else, Patricia wrote the words of 1 John 1:9 over the list: "If we confess our sins, He is faithful and righteous to forgive us our sins and to cleanse us from all unrighteousness."*

*Then she tore up the list, disposed of the pieces, and prepared to make the most difficult telephone call of her life.*

*Against a flurry of mental, emotional, and undoubtedly spiritual opposition, Patricia took a deep breath, picked up the telephone, called her ex-husband, and asked him to just listen for a minute or two as she confessed her sins against him. Then, somehow, she uttered a heartfelt request: "Will you forgive me, Michael?"*

*Not normally a man to be at a loss for words, he stuttered through some sort of "sure, of course." (To this day, she's never been sure that he understood what she was asking or why, but as she hung up the telephone, a surge of tension was cut loose from her soul and her body.) Almost immediately, she began to feel with her emotions what her mind had been able to accept only by faith: receiving, extending, and requesting forgiveness sets you free.*

Still she knew there was one thing left to do. Later that afternoon she stopped at the stadium and bought a pair of tickets for her husband's favorite team. She put them in an envelope and sealed it with a sincere prayer that God would, in His own way, as He saw fit, bless each of them with the richest of His blessings. When she put the envelope in the mailbox and shut the door, she knew that something critical had been put to death. On the way back to her empty apartment, she began to smile, and then laugh, and then cry with a different kind of tears — tears of freedom, healing ... and rest.

## *Reflection* ~~

Forgiveness is something that must be applied in order to be understood, as it is absolutely contrary to the principles of the world and the desires of the flesh. Forgiveness requires a conscious decision on your part, enabled by the Holy Spirit within you. It's a process that you must personally go through with God.

As soon as possible (ideally right now) get alone with the Lord for an uninterrupted time of introspection. Meditate on the truths of Scripture that were presented in this chapter. Walk through the process of forgiveness in each of the critical areas:

1. Receiving the forgiveness of God for specific sins you have committed.
2. Forgiving others for the hurt they have caused you.
3. Forgiving yourself.
4. Asking for forgiveness from those you have hurt.

## *God's Desire* ~~

"And so, as those who have been chosen of God, holy and beloved, put on a heart of compassion, kindness, humility, gentleness and patience; bearing with one another, and forgiving each other, whoever has a complaint against anyone; just as the Lord forgave you, so also should you."
—Colossians 3:12-13)

"Therefore if any man is in Christ, he is a new creature; the old things passed away; behold, new things have come. Now all these things are from God, who reconciled us to Himself through Christ, and gave us the ministry of reconciliation, namely, that God was in Christ, reconciling the world to Himself, not counting their trespasses against them, and He has committed to us the word [ministry] of reconciliation."
—2 Corinthians 5:17-19

## Your Response ~~

*Father of Forgiveness,*

*Search my heart and show me Your ways. As my Redeemer, I praise You for forgiving me. Be now my courage, showing me specific areas where I have been hurt. Make me willing to be a channel of Your forgiving love to those who have harmed me. By Your power and the blood You shed for my sins, give me the obedience to walk through all the steps of forgiveness, that I might be healed and be freed from the wrongs that were done against me. Show me where I have yet to forgive myself, and make me willing to apply the biblical principles of reconciliation to myself as well as others. Father, where I have wronged others, give me the strength and courage to confess what I have done to them. Please give them a heart of forgiveness, that they might begin to heal from the hurt and harm I have caused them.*

*Amen.*

# ❊ 14 ❊

# *Grace Now!*

"Be strong in the grace that is in Christ Jesus."
—2 Timothy 2:1

Fnrom the windows of my mind I see a black man standing at the end of a lane. He stands precisely where his bare feet and providence have led him. From here the lane meets the open road stretching left and right, as far as the eye can see, reaching, straining toward both horizons.

The man stands perfectly still, naked except for thick calluses on his hands and a pair of ragged trousers. The southern sun beats down on the scars carved into the muscles of his back. Behind him manicured trees reach back, framing the white pillars of a plantation mansion—a mansion built and sustained by several decades of his backbreaking labor. But there will be none of that today. Today is a new day.

This day, bought with blood and tears and the lives of courageous ones, is his, all his. With the final stroke of quill upon paper, the page of his story was turned. Emancipation has been proclaimed. The slave, now at the crossroad, has been declared free. Free from the whip, free from the plow, free to a future open wide before him.

Yet now he stands still at the junction of the lane and road. "Right or left?" the road beckons . . . but he does not know the answer. Gone are the shackles; the whip lays still, its painful, familiar directives for the first time silenced. How will the answer come? "To the right or to the left?" He does not know, for he has never had to choose. The predictable days of bondage have left him without a notion. The crippling forces that dictated his every move remain on the plantation he's just left behind.

Here at the end of the lane it is so very quiet. "Right or left?" the road beckons.

◊   ◊   ◊

"And your ears will hear a word behind you, 'This is the way, walk in it,' whenever you turn to the right or to the left." —Isaiah 30:21

How are we to live? In freedom; Christ's freedom, so unpredictable, unimaginable, unconstrained, zoe can be compared only to the wind. We must awaken now to its power; for a whole new way of living awaits us. "Right or left?" I pray that you will discover love so far beyond your understanding, that the direction has little bearing on the journey. May it be an experience you can only describe as "infinitely more beyond all we dare to ask or imagine," (Ephesians 3:20, *Philips*).

Rather than looking forward, we so often consider the measure of our freedom by looking back. Rather than considering "how wide and long and deep and high is the love of Christ," we have become comfortable with the formulas and predictable confines of the law. We no longer know what it means to live in freedom.

In *Shawshank Redemption*, a graphic and pointed prison movie about the journey of two men's hearts through the trials of incarceration, one of the men describes what happens when you live within confinement too long. "At first, these walls, you hate them. They make you crazy,' he explains to the newest inmate. "After a while you get used to 'em, don't notice 'em anymore. Then comes the day you realize that you need them, and you don't know how to live without them."

With the death and resurrection of Jesus, God determined not only to rescue us, but also to remain and to share His heart with us, to walk with us. Grace. In spite of our weakness, in spite of what we deserve, God *... God determined* could not be stopped from reaching out toward us *not only to rescue* in kindness. Dying so that we might claim radical *us, but also to* liberty, He granted us undeserved freedom; He *remain and to* granted us grace. *share His heart*

Upon accepting our certificate of pardon, we *with us, to walk* are free! We are raised with Christ, a new creation. *with us.* No longer are we slaves to sin, old grids, and belief systems. No longer are we imprisoned to the confines of law, never living up to demanding standards and rules. The doors have been flung open and with a fresh wind blowing in our face, we walk out of our prison of sin and judgment. . . and without ever really learning how to *live*, most of us survive like fugitives.

While we understand that God's grace has granted us freedom from the penalty of sin, how many of us know what it means to live freely? Like the emancipated slave, we are easily immobilized by the lack of demands telling us which way to go. But we look down at the certificate of freedom in our hands. Grace. We too will hear and recognize the rustling of the Spirit say like the wind, "This is the way, walk in it."

Dare we trust grace alone? What does the rest of grace look like? What does it mean out on the streets? What does graceful living look like in the kitchen, while driving the kids to soccer, and in the midst of conducting business? Says Philip Yancey, "The world thirsts for grace in ways it does not even recognize."[1]

As I hum the timeless hymn, Amazing Grace, the much loved words come easily, "Amazing Grace how sweet the sound . . . I once was lost but now am found . . ." and then I come to the stanza, "How precious did that grace appear the hour I first believed." I confess these words lay heavy on my heart. Why? Because I ask myself, *Is grace as precious to me now as in that first hour?* I have no doubt that when I've been there, in heaven, ten thousand years, I'll still be singing praises of God's grace, but what am I singing about today? We need to know how to live in grace *here* and *now*—in every moment of every day. Saying we believe in grace is one thing; actually living it is another.

*Just as God's laws permeated Jewish life and defined God's character to His people, so His grace is meant to saturate our lives now.*

Just as God's laws permeated Jewish life and defined God's character to His people, so His grace is meant to saturate our lives now. Trace the roots of grace, or *charis* in Greek, and you will find a verb that means, "I rejoice, I am glad!" While Jesus lived with His people—eating, sleeping, fishing, celebrating, mourning in the day-to-day messes—He gave life's greatest gift—the ability to rejoice and be glad—He granted us grace.

Imagine a life of grace infused into our daily relationship with God, others, and ourselves! What can happen when we allow a theology of grace (what we believe about God's abundant favor) to become our biography of grace (the true story of our lives)? Grace does not belong in text. It is time to peel this "last, best word" off the pages of Scripture and allow its revolutionary power to mightily impact our life and the lives of those we touch each day.

Salvation by grace—God's pardon from sin—is not just a ticket for an event in the future. Something wonderful has happened to us that is meant to bring a transformation of miraculous proportions to our lives *now*. This too is a result of Christ's work on the Cross and His resurrection. "And God is able to make all grace abound to you, that always having all sufficiency in everything, you may have an abundance for every good deed" (2 Corinthians 9:8). As glorious as grace is for salvation, it is meant to be just as glorious in every day of our life!

## Grace as an expression of our life

As you live out the rest of your days on earth, how does God's kindness fit into your story? Have you ever stopped to ponder how God's extravagant, indulgent love impacted your day since you woke up?

◊   ◊   ◊

It was mid-July and the sun hung lazy and full in the sky until past dinnertime in South Dakota where I lived as a young boy. During the long, hot summer days, the pond behind our house was as warm as bath water; we ran barefoot and carefree, with sticky fingers where ice cream had dripped. And the circus would rumble into town.

Each year about this time, an endless stream of trucks with brightly colored cargo rolled in and set up, of all sacred places, on the baseball field. It was almost better than Christmas! For a couple of days the regular schedule of games and practices was disrupted while elephants plodded down the ramps carrying long poles to erect the big tents. Soon the aromas of cotton candy and popcorn would waft through the air to where my buddies and I stood perched outside the fence, taking it all in and anticipating what events might take place this year.

*As glorious as grace is for salvation, it is meant to be just as glorious in every day of our life!*

We had memorized from previous years the glorious, death-defying feats that would again take place on this very field. A dozen clowns smushed in a miniature car would all tumble out, wild-eyed jungle men juggling fire to the beating of drums (only the most courageous of which dared to swallow his fire), roaring tigers jumped through hoops, little white foo-foo dogs pranced in circles on their front paws before jumping into the arms of their big-bosomed trainer. It was all a child could ever hope for, although I secretly admit I always wished the ringmaster would put it all together in one spectacular grand finale where dozens of well endowed ladies would jump out of little cars juggling flaming poodles that were soon to be eaten by the tigers. But alas, each year I settled instead for the real finale, "The Flying Valentines."

I was never disappointed though. Each year more sensational than the last, the family of high trapeze artists called "The Flying Valentines" soared and flipped fearlessly through the air, leaping from tiny platforms atop high towers to grasp thin, swinging bars, their pink silhouettes sailing across the blue mid-western skies. I could hardly breathe. At any moment I was sure gravity would have its way and "The Flying Valentines" would be reduced to a crater somewhere near second base, nothing left but their pink tutus and tights imbedded in the dirt. But that never happened either. Fortunately for them, there was always the net.

The net. It would save a life at least once every performance. Inevitably a hand would slip from an ankle, or the timing would be off by a fraction of a second and a Valentine would spiral toward the earth and certain death, only to be gently caught and saved by the net. In the end, all the Valentines would free fall to the net in their exit of the performance, tumbling one by one toward it, never doubting its sound protection.

As memories of the circus play through my adult mind, I marvel at how similar the trapeze net is to grace. Sooner or later, either by accident or natural causes, when all our days are spent, we who are Christ's will exit this earth and be received by the net of grace into the eternal presence of God.

But is that everything we should expect of grace? Is it just for a safe exit? I don't mean to minimize the importance of life hereafter. Eternity is forever and I can never express my gratitude for the grace extended toward me that will eventually lead me "home." But what about grace now? What about these few years of breath we have left until the inevitable? Isn't there more to grace? The Bible certainly claims there is; in fact, it says that there is a lot more to grace.

Let's take another look at the art of trapeze. Juan Carlos Ortiz, a conference speaker, once recalled a circus attendee who had the privilege of talking to a performer after a show. He commented on how the net saved the highflier's life. The trapeze artist looked a bit humored. Still struck with awe the guest exclaimed, "That net saved your life!" In broken English, the artist expressed that this was indeed true, but then tried to explain the net's further purpose.

"Yes, the net saves us," he said in a heavy French accent, "but its most important purpose is to allow us to get better. With it stretching below we can try and fail without fear, becoming the very best we could ever be."

Perhaps a few daredevils might venture to the top rung of a seventy-foot ladder without a net, but how many would ever jump for the bar? Who would try a double-back flip with a full twist? This would be a bogus consideration rather than a studied art form. Yet when a trusted net is in place below, everything changes for the trapeze artist . . . and with the net of grace available right now, everything changes for us.

God's grace allows us to try and fail without fear while we stretch and grow. In this journey of learning to listen and know the voice of the Spirit within, I must become familiar with Him. I may not discern the call of His voice at times and if I didn't hear Him clearly or if I am deceived by an external voice, His grace gently breaks my fall so I can get back up and try again. "For a righteous man falls seven times, and rises again" (Proverbs 24:16). We don't need to be consumed with falling. With God's promise of his kindness I can fail and get back up. When I truly begin to grasp this—that Christ loves me unconditionally and will forever hold me, I can be bold and take more risks. I can move freely while listening for His voice calling me. And even if I fall, I am safe. I can get up again.

*God's grace allows us to try and fail without fear while we stretch and grow.*

This kind of freedom and fearlessness is rare in the Christian culture. A typical and all too true description of Believers finds us very near the ground, heads low, following the crowd. Tony Campolo once said, "Most of us are tiptoeing through life so we can reach death safely."[2]

Religion uses laws in an attempt to make us all look the same. But the grace of God enables us to live daring, free lives outside man-made lines as unique individuals. Remember the troubles the Pharisees had with Jesus? He was never where they anticipated Him to be; they would look for Him in the temple and He would be eating and hanging out "on the wrong side of the tracks." When He was supposed to be fasting, He was eating with tax collectors and prostitutes. He healed on the Sabbath when He was expected to rest. And all the while He was only doing what He had heard His Father say and seen His Father do (John 5:19, 26, 30; 14:10). Likewise, when we live in a grace relationship with God, we will be in line with His will, even though we can count on being out of line with the will of some religious leaders.

*Since keeping the law means depending on our efforts alone, abiding in grace will be something entirely different.*

For those exhausted by a heavy yoke of Christian traditions and self-standards, this is truly good news!

Growing in grace means you start your Christian life by grace, and it is by grace that you continue in it. Since keeping the law means depending on our efforts alone, abiding in grace will be something entirely different. Living in grace is simply learning to live as God intended—together.

**Together**

Law doesn't require much of a relationship, but grace certainly does. In fact, it is fully dependent on it. Take for instance a marriage. I can read numerous books on intimacy and come up with twenty-one hot tips on how to improve my relationship with my wife. I can really be serious about this too, making a comprehensive checklist of self-help guru advice, doing as each of the authors suggest. Yet, I may still never get to know my wife. If upon coming home in the evening I check in with my list rather than with Nancy, I'll fall short of knowing what she needs at that moment. The list becomes my focus, rather than Nancy. Growing in grace requires knowing one another and can never be based on a formula.

Just as I must spend time with my wife, we too must live moment-by-moment learning to listen as Jesus did, relying solely on His Father for direction. Jesus continually shocked those around Him with his unpredictable behavior. "I decide as I am bidden to decide," He said (John 5:30, *The Amplified Bible*). A life lived in faith with a full understanding of the net of grace allows for so much living, so much loving, so much "outside of the box," adventure that we've yet begun to discover our full potential! Who knows what grace might say?

## Risks of grace

Many Christians are afraid that if they really embrace grace and let go of the law there will be nothing to prevent them from sinning. In truth, the very opposite response occurs. Sin increases when one lives under law, but obedience flourishes under grace (see Romans 5:20-21). We can rest assured God will never ask us do anything that goes outside of Scripture, and it is highly important that any voice we hear is tested against biblical truth, but He may ask us to do something that goes outside the lines of our culture, tradition, or legalism (see Acts 4:19-20).

*Growing in grace requires knowing one another and can never be based on a formula.*

The bond that was broken between you and the law is not an imaginary one, and the marriage you now have with Christ is very real. After I delivered a message about the law, a pastor once asked me, "Isn't it okay to keep a little law, just a little guilt in our lives?" I understand what he is getting at. Life without secure fences can make us feel a little worried and uncertain.

Walking in the Spirit can be very unpredictable and frightening. Who knows where Jesus might lead you. "The wind blows where it wishes and you hear the sound of it, but do not know where it comes from and where it is going; so is everyone who is born of the Spirit" (John 3:8). Isn't it safer to be fenced in by at least a few religious rules? Without the law to keep us in line, what's to keep us from going wild? Without the constraints of a "little law and a little guilt," and a little self-performance, what will motivate us to stay on the straight and narrow? And from a pastor's perspective, if he can't use a "little law," how will he ever be able to lead and motivate and control those God has put in his care? There are good answers to all these concerns, but returning to the law is not one of them. Says Charles Spurgeon, "There cannot be a greater difference in the world between two things than there is between law and grace. And yet, strange to say, while the two are diametrically opposed and essentially different from each other, the human mind is so depraved, and the intellect, even when blessed by the Spirit, has become so turned aside from right judgment ... there is always a tendency in us to confound the two things. They are as opposite as light and darkness, and can no more agree than fire and water . . ."[3]

*Wondering if we shouldn't have a "little law" is like wondering if it's okay to have a "little affair" with an old girl friend.*

Wondering if we shouldn't have a "little law" is like wondering if it's okay to have a "little affair" with an old girl friend. Remember, we have died to law and that relationship is severed. Our new union is with Jesus, yet we somehow think that we can impress Jesus by committing adultery?! Friend, this would be no different than my choosing to go to bed with another woman in order to prove to my wife how worthy I am of her love. I don't know about your spouse, but mine wouldn't buy it! Nothing could be more ludicrous. On the contrary, such actions would destroy the beauty and intimate trust shared between us.

Our desire to perform "just a little" for Jesus is just as repulsive. Not only is it adultery, my self-imposed standards compromise the purity, purpose, and vitality of my new union with Jesus. Teaching Sunday school, leading the worship team, Wednesday Bible study, Thursday prayer meeting, Saturday outreach . . . will God be impressed with these actions in and of themselves? How ridiculous!

In Romans 7:3, Paul emphatically states, "If, while her husband [Christ] is living, she is joined to another man [law], she shall be called an adulteress."

I pray you will understand that your relationship with the law is over. Your life with Christ is forever. You have died to that which bound you and you have been joined to another, to the lover of your soul, and now, in Him, you can be free. This is all you've ever dreamed of; He is all you will ever want or need. A totally new adventure in grace awaits you as you walk with Jesus in the power of His Spirit.

## Yeast and legalism

After catching a glimpse of the extravagance and fearless freedom offered to us in a relationship of grace, we can begin to understand the strong language used against anything or anyone standing in its way. Jesus warns, "Watch out and beware of the leaven (yeast) of the Pharisees and Sadducees" (Matthew 16:6, parenthesis mine).

Remember, for the Jews, yeast was a metaphor for evil. Jesus' disciples knew that when yeast is mixed into a lump of dough its very nature is changed. Here Jesus is saying that when the yeast of the law (performance, legalism) is mixed in with His grace, it gradually but inevitably transforms and destroys its power of freedom.

Chuck Swindoll says legalism puts, "the emphasis on what we do for God, instead of what God does for us."[4]

The apostle Paul also warns against this attitude in his letter to the Galatians (see Galatians 5:9; see also 1 Corinthians 5:6-7). Christian teachers had followed Paul into Galatia, adding various religious requirements to the gospel of salvation. They did not deny salvation through faith in Christ, rather they added to it a few Jewish disciplines; supposedly to help the Gentile believers "mature" in their faith (Galatians 3:3).

*A totally new adventure in grace awaits you as you walk with Jesus in the power of His Spirit.*

Paul did not respond kindly to this! He says quite bluntly that basing our relationship with God on Christ's work and our own efforts actually destroys that relationship, making it of "no benefit" (Galatians

5:2). Martin Luther in his commentary on Galatians, says that to add any religious work to the gospel of grace seems to be a trivial matter, but does more damage than human reason can imagine.

"You foolish Galatians, who has bewitched you, before whose eyes Jesus Christ was publicly portrayed as crucified" (3:1). Emphatically Paul argues that the mature Christian life is not a mixture of grace and law, but grace alone. "Are you so foolish? After beginning with the Spirit, are you now trying to attain your goal by human effort?" (3:3, NIV).

"Bewitched" refers to "the evil eye," which was the primary mode of witchcraft in the Mediterranean world. The evil eye was a witch's spell that slowly sucked the life out of its victim (an apt description of legalism). Anyone who rejected life as God's gift and returned to working for it would surely lose that life. Paul doesn't care how talented or godly teachers appear, he wants to know whether they remain faithful to the gospel of grace. For Paul, adding anything to the finished work of Christ is not just off-center; it is evil and must be rejected (Galatians 5:7-12).

*Recognizing the heavy burdens and curses of any form of law, we must refuse to be taken captive by it again.*

The yeast of self-accepting performance poisons the Bread of Life. We see a similar metaphor in 2 Timothy 2:17, where the yeast of false teaching is likened to gangrene; left untreated, it will destroy the entire organism. Instead we are instructed, "Be diligent to present yourself approved to God as a workman who does not need to be ashamed, handling accurately the word of truth" (v. 15). Recognizing the heavy burdens and curses of any form of law, we must refuse to be taken captive by it again.

## Liberty worth fighting for

We must get used to the fact that the world's system is based on performance and law. If you are waiting for the world to give you grace, you will be waiting a long, long time. Unfortunately, your wait for grace may be just as lengthy and perhaps even deadlier from those from whom you might expect it—other Christians. In 2000 years people haven't changed much. The problem of legalism is as rampant today as it was in Paul and Timothy's time. In this case the words spoken by King Arthur in the movie, First Knight, ring true, "There is a peace that is only found on the other side of war."

Few things are worth warring over, but freedom in grace is one issue the apostle Paul would roll up his sleeves and fight for to the death. In fact, in Antioch, we find Paul in a heated confrontation with Peter (Cephas) where he is yelling, "Get it out! I say, you can't mix a little law in. A little arsenic will poison the whole body" (see Galatians 2) In what may be Chuck Swindoll's most profound work, *The Grace Awakening*, he emphatically states:

> I find it amazing that we as a nation will fight other nations for our national liberty, and that we as a people will, if necessary, fight one another for the freedom of those within our borders, but when it comes to the living out of our Christianity, we will give up our liberty without a fight. We'll go to the wall and square off against any enemy who threatens to take away our national freedom, but we'll not be nearly so passionate as Christians under grace to fight for our rightful liberty.[5]

Grace is Love in action. "We have come to know and have believed the love which God has for us (1 John 4:16a). We can be bold in this perfect love that promises, "there is no fear" (v.18). "Grace is not merely God's attitude toward us, but His activity on our behalf," preached America's evangelist of the 1930's, Charles Trumbull. "Grace does not mean that God stands off and smiles in our direction."[6]

Brennan Manning, a spiritual director in the school of grace explained, "God's love is based on nothing, and the fact that it is based on nothing makes us secure. Were it based on anything we do, and that 'anything' were to collapse, then God's love would crumble as well. But with the God of Jesus no such thing can possibly happen. People who realize this can live freely and to the fullest."[7]

Even though I often teach others about grace, it is amazing how quickly I fall under performance and fail to allow God to "grace" me. Receiving grace for myself flows only from hearing the Spirit say again and again, "My grace is sufficient for you too, Bill. Even in your failures, power is perfected in weakness" (2 Corinthians 12:9, my paraphrase).

Not only are we free in God's eyes, we are free from the judgments of others as well as our own! "There is therefore now no condemnation for those who are in Christ Jesus" (Romans 8:1). Yes, there is grace for me, and when I begin to be sensitive to His whisper, it changes the way I see myself and live my life. I have to remind myself of this constantly.

*Not only are we free in God's eyes, we are free from the judgments of others as well as our own!*

I can rest knowing the law is like a path on which I can walk, "to be my guide, my rule, my pattern, " says Spurgeon. "Law is the road which guides us, not the rod which drives us. . . The law is good and excellent, if it keeps its place" (1 Timothy 1:8). But it is God's Spirit that will teach us to walk this road in grace, making allowance for the faults of others and myself with humility, gentleness and patience (see Ephesians 4:1-3).

## Grace and others

"For you were called to freedom ... do not turn your freedom into an opportunity for the flesh, but through love serve one another" (Galatians 5:13). Is your marriage strained to its limits? Are your children selfish and nasty to one another? Is your boss unreasonably demanding? Grace, only grace, provides the answer. "This is my plea, that wherever I am I will live only to testify solemnly to the gospel of grace" (Acts 20:24). Paul understood that all of life (finances, lovemaking, parenting, etc.) must be seen through a grid of grace. By removing our old paradigm of performance, like taking off a catcher's mask, we can see life clearly. We must develop a new mind-set, one without all the frames of demands, constraints, and condemnation.

❁ ❁ ❁

It all started like most addictions, quite innocently really—just normal childhood curiosity and experimentation. I think he was introduced to it through some of his buddies after school; it seemed kind of cool to them and made them feel like they belonged. I didn't mind at first. I've been known to have a couple around the house too. Nothing serious, just a social thing for me, part of the athlete's subculture. But then my son, Jess, started hanging around other kids who were deep into it, and soon it became the center of all of his friendships.

Other parents didn't seem to think it was a big deal. Lots of boys were trying it. So I ignored it for a while but by the time I woke up to the situation, we had a serious problem on our hands. Baseball cards had infiltrated, then invaded, and ultimately taken up permanent occupation in my eleven-year-old's life.

My wife and I tried to distract Jess with other interests, but he wouldn't hear of them. I even attempted to persuade him into trying something more productive, like playing Nintendo or watching western movies with me. He resented my obvious interventions and soon my suggestions began to drive a wedge between us.

In time, his obsession dominated not only his social life, but his personal life as well. From morning till night baseball cards were all he could think about. Every dollar he earned, every cent of his allowance, went directly toward more and more cards, and cards that were more and more expensive.

In a few short months my son had hundreds of them, and he'd flip though them constantly. I grew worried about the possibility that his latest hobby was affecting his mind. I'd find him sitting alone in his room, mesmerized by the stacks of cards before him. I could pick out a random card of some player such as Ron Gant, and Jess could fire off all of his stats. Height? "6'o" Weight? "170 lbs." Batting average in, oh, let's say 1990? ".303." He could do this for more than a hundred players.

Being the concerned father, I tried hard to help him bring some balance into his life. "There is nothing intrinsically evil about baseball cards, son," I'd assure him, "but they do need to be enjoyed in moderation. Maybe you could devote a little time to memorizing Scripture too." Or I'd say, "Son, there is nothing wrong with spending some money on things you enjoy, but money is also to be invested for the future and given to those in need."

But none of my wise and loving correction seemed to work. With each mini-lecture, Jess would just look away and hang his head a little lower. And the wedge drove a little deeper between us.

The problem was obvious. Baseball cards were overtaking my son's life, and I had allowed them to destroy my relationship with him. As a counselor, I knew the cliché was true, "Love must be tough." When things are broken in a family, someone needs to emerge with the strength and the firm resolve to make changes, no matter how much it might hurt. So after much consideration and prayer, I finally did what should have been done months earlier. I stood tall, cleared my throat, took Jess firmly in my grasp ... and went out and bought some baseball cards.

We looked and sorted and talked and ended up buying rookie cards for some of baseball's best: Mark McGuire, Nolan Ryan, and Barry Bonds. We even bought the rookie card for Barry Sanders, one of football's heroes. I was, after all, trying to help him find some balance!

The transformation was immediate . . . not in Jess's life, but in mine. I have to admit; it was painful at first. I resented those idiotic cards, and it took an act of pure will to open my wallet as I did. But in the process, what really opened up was my heart. I started to see my son in new ways. For example, it turned out that his mind had, in fact, been affected by all those cards. The kid had developed an incredible memory, and I started to let him know that I thought that was amazing. When I got excited, he got excited, and he started to open up to me. Rather than cowering at my judgment, he began to sense a hint of freedom in my presence.

It took a while. After all, kids know what's going on, they're very perceptive. Every time I had lectured Jess about "balance," what he heard me say was, "You're doing it wrong again!" Why did he hear this? Because that is exactly how I felt. The real blessing is that kids aren't only perceptive; they're smart. When my actions and attitude showed my son that there now existed a net of grace in our relationship, Jess knew he was free to fly and fall and be all God had created him to be. As a result, we became awesome friends. And yes, we eventually did have numerous conversations about finances, scripture memory, and "balance;" but that was long after we found the great deal on the Nolan Ryan rookie card and made an even greater profit on it!

## In Summary

Perhaps Anne Lamott sums it up best in her book, *Traveling Mercies*:

"Grace is now; grace is relationship. It is unearned love—the love that goes before, that greets us on the way. It's the help you receive when you have no bright ideas left, when you are empty and desperate and have discovered that your best thinking and most charming charm have failed you. Grace is what takes you from that isolated place and puts you with others who are as startled and embarrassed and eventually grateful as you are to be there."[9]

You have been given a special invitation to a new way of living. May you come to see every life situation through the grid of grace. Learn to open your eyes in the morning with this prayer, "What is it, dear Father, that I get to be part of today? I awaken now to living in Your grace, a journey together, so unpredictable, I eagerly await its discovery."

"The wind blows wherever it wishes; you hear the sound it makes, but you do not know where it comes from or where it is going. It is the same way with everyone who is born of the Spirit."
—John 3:8, Today's *English Version*

❧ ❧ ❧

## Reflection ～～

What has walking in the Spirit meant to you in the past? How does understanding that God loves you apart from your performance (constantly living above the net of grace) affect the way you view walking in the Spirit now? Remember that freedom from the fear of failure should result because you know God loves you no matter what!

## God's Desire ～～

"But when He, the Spirit of truth, comes, He will guide you into all the truth; for He will not speak on His own initiative, but whatever He *hears*, he will *speak*; and He will disclose to you what is to come" —John 16:13 (emphasis mine).

"What actually took place is this: I tried keeping rules and working my head off to please God, and it didn't work. So I quit being a "law man" so that I could be God's man. Christ's life showed me how, and enabled me to do it. I identified myself completely with him. Indeed, I have been crucified with Christ. My ego is no longer central. It is no longer important that I appear righteous before you or have your good opinion, and I am no longer driven to impress God. Christ lives in me."
—Galatians 2:19-20, *The Message*

## Your Response ～～

*Father, help me to continually turn control of all my faculties and personhood over to You, so that I am empowered with the Holy Spirit in every moment of every day. I want to learn to live in oneness with Your Spirit—always listening for Your voice and relying on Your indwelling. Thank You that grace means I am loved by You always, completely and unconditionally, and that I am never ever in any state but in a state of grace.*

# ❖ 15 ❖

# *Being Transformed*

"And do not be conformed to this world, but be transformed
by the renewing of your mind, that you may prove what the will
of God is, that which is good and acceptable and perfect."
—Romans 12:2

H
ow could a person who has been given everything needed
for life and godliness continue to struggle?" Simply this,
says Bob George in his book *Growing in Grace*, "Even
though we were given everything we will ever need at our spiritual
birth, we still have a whole lifetime of growing in our understanding
of Christ and of the riches, power, and life that He has already given
us."[1] In becoming victorious we must "grow in grace." We must allow
the same impact of grace that sets our spirits free to fully liberate the
mind, will, and emotions of our *soul* as well.

The spirit has already been radically transformed by the
righteousness and holiness of God (Ephesians 4:24), but the soul is
slower in catching up. It must be renewed daily so we can experience
the "lining up" of our mind to match the truth that has already been

accomplished in our spirit. Until then, we remain dysfunctional or handicapped in other parts of our design.

We seem to have the idea that if we read (or hear) the Bible and pray, something magical happens in our behavior. There is some truth in this. Because behavior follows belief, however, the Bible gives us further instruction regarding transformation. The biblical principal of "renewing the mind" (Romans 12:1-2) is based on the fact that *what I believe* determines *what I do. Therefore, if I can change what I believe, I can choose to change how I behave.*

❡ ❡ ❡

One of the most rewarding privileges I have in working with people is seeing the victory and joy a person experiences when he or she begins to replace lies with God's truths, and is set free. This is exactly what had taken place with a client we'll call Jenny.

Jenny is one of the neatest ladies I've known. Several years ago while taking one of our renewal courses, Jenny delighted in seeing many areas in her life turn from defeat and weariness to triumph and rest. Since then she's eagerly anticipated what each day will bring while walking hand-in-hand with God, expressing a fresh message of grace to all those around her.

In spite of life's trials and challenges, she continues to demonstrate what it means to live an abundant life. Jenny has been able to embrace life unhindered because she is convinced of her worth and purpose. You can therefore imagine the depth of Jenny's discouragement when an issue developed in her life, one that she couldn't seem to overcome. To make matters worse she was frustrated that this particular bone of contention was taking up so much of her energy when there were so many other valuable issues to focus on.

During the past few months Jenny had been filled with dread as she dragged herself out of bed to face another day, and her once bright countenance seemed to be shadowed much of the time. Even though she willed herself to continue doing most of what she'd been doing, the vibrancy that typified her life was missing. What happened?

Like most of us, Jenny didn't realize she was getting "life" from something besides God until it was threatened. Having always been athletic and a lover of the outdoors, Jenny's weight and body image had never been much of a concern. Her weight rarely fluctuated and she'd been able to stay petite and shapely... until her 48th birthday. In the past two years, Jenny had suffered health problems, which had hindered her ability to engage in her usual activities. But as the New Year approached, Jenny's health improved and she knew it was time to get back into her regular exercise and eating routine. She anxiously looked forward to a brand new start.

Beginning a new dance aerobic program in January, she was faithful to her new routine. But after two weeks of dedication, rather than losing pounds, she put on two more. Determined not to be discouraged she pressed on, committed to losing the unwanted weight. A couple more weeks passed and when she got on the scale she'd gained even more! Jenny resolved to take an even tighter grasp on her eating and work out even harder. After a couple months, the results still seemed so hopeless that she was ready to give up.

When it came time to exchange winter clothes for summer ones, everything was too tight. Dark thoughts ran through her mind that said, *I'm just an ugly, fat slob* and, *I have no discipline or character*! She began to question her husband's motive for giving compliments and it was difficult to receive his hugs, fearing he would be repulsed with her new, slightly chubby areas.

Jenny finally found the courage to discuss her situation with me. She already knew biblical truths well enough to recognize that she had obviously been receiving feelings of significance and value from being a certain weight and size, and she knew the way she was attempting to deal with her self-image wasn't in line with God's Word. Her focus was on improving her willpower so she could get back to the weight and size she'd been before. At this point her only conclusion was, *"I'm doing all the right things, but it doesn't work."* In other words, *"I'm a failure."*

Never minimize the impact of a counterfeit source of life experienced by another person. The seriousness of Jenny's situation wasn't based on the number of pounds she wanted or needed to lose. It was much more serious than that. Whether a person feels worthless and rejected because of three pounds or 300 pounds, if there's little peace and joy in his or her life, an overhaul is needed!

## What? Why? How?

"And you shall know the truth, and the truth shall make you free." —John 8:32

You will find this chapter to be very practical. This is the place where you will determine to act in cooperation with the Holy Spirit regarding how you want to live. Jesus came "to bind up the broken hearted to proclaim freedom for the captives." (Isaiah 61:1). He is "the Way." He is *the way* of change, *the way* out of bondage into freedom, *the way* out depression into joy, *the way* out of anxiety into peace, and *the way* out of frustration into contentment. With His grace we have the courage to continue.

We've been given permission to rest assured in grace without condemnation. As a result, the chains have been loosened so we can move, grow, and break out of old patterns of unhealthy thinking and living. It is here that we will find healing for our thoughts and freedom from obsessions. With the guidance of the Holy Spirit, we can encounter the lie of performance-based acceptance and replace it through a step-by-step process with the truth of God's grace. In an earlier chapter we talked about the difference between seeking *zoe* life our own way, and seeking it God's way. Even though the spirit is willing, our flesh (which includes our mind) is still weak and is in need of training so it can openly receive and communicate what the Holy Spirit wants to share. Too many times we hear abstract messages about growing in God. So here I want to address, with answers directly from Scripture, these three questions: *What* exactly needs to happen? Why must this take place? And finally, how lasting transformation and change can be yours?

## "What?"

*The mind needs to be renewed.*

Lasting and liberating change takes place only when we follow God's lead in remodeling our thinking. All the words on these pages and all the truths revealed, in and of themselves, will not make a difference in our actions and our relationships with those around us without the process of renewing our minds. God states very clearly in His Word the way of lasting change: "be transformed by the renewing of your mind" (Romans 12:2). Scripture tells us that *"renewing the mind"* is the process of changing a person's belief and, therefore, his or her behavior. The word *"renew"* means "to make qualitatively new; a renovation that makes a person different than how he or she was in the past."

According to Matthew Henry, "The mind is the acting ruling part of us; so that the renewing of the mind is the renewing of the whole man, for out of it are the issues of life, as stated in Proverbs 4:23."[2] Every philosophy, regardless of its origin, is geared toward reaching the mind. Likewise, God has provided us His authoritative Word not only to breathe supernatural life into our Spirits, but also to transform our minds with all we need for a free and abundant life.

Though our "re-creation" completely transformed our spirit in Christ, our mind still needs to be renewed to the truth of who we are. Renewing the mind is the path to "making right again" a person's beliefs, and, therefore, his or her behavior. The word "transformation" comes from the Greek word *metamorphoo*, as does the word "metamorphous." We usually think of the metamorphosis of a caterpillar into a butterfly. Through the work of the Cross, God made us new creations. Now we must spend the rest of our lives lining up our beliefs with that reality, in other words, being transformed.

Even though our spirits are holy, our thinking is still defiled (my friend Pat calls this "stinking thinking"). We can't go for long without being really miserable because our souls will be out of sync until our minds are aligned with our spirits. How did our thinking become like it is? While our belief systems are being formed throughout life, they can, and most likely are, being corrupted by Satan's lies and the world's pain. These corrupt belief systems are referred to as *"strongholds"* or *"fortresses"* in the Bible. Untrustworthy fortresses or beliefs are built with blocks of thought and prevent us from having an accurate picture of God, others, ourselves, and the circumstances surrounding us.

## "Why?"

So our thinking and behavior reflects what is true.

We renew our minds so that our thinking and our behavior reflect the truth about who God is and who we are as His new creation. By keeping the mirror of God in front of us, we are reminded of our true nature and of whose we are.

"And do not be conformed to this world, but be transformed by the renewing of your mind, that you may prove what the will of God is, that which is good and acceptable and perfect" (Romans 12:2).

Do you yearn to know what is good and perfect for you, your spouse, and children? Do you want your family and loved ones to ultimately succeed in all they do? Daily renewing our minds and walking in our new identity is the description of God's plan for us for living an exceptional Christian life until He returns. We must willfully choose to participate in a fresh way of thinking, taking "every thought captive to the obedience of Christ," and "destroying every lofty thing raised up against the knowledge of God" (2 Corinthians 10:5).

*The enemy occupied our minds during our pre-Christ years and spent that time building walls and fortresses out of lies.*

The enemy occupied our minds during our pre-Christ years and spent that time building walls and fortresses out of lies. Even though Christ defeated our foe, the enemy is reluctant to give up occupied territory. He would like to deceive us into believing our mind is territory that still belongs to him. But Jesus doesn't come as a news reporter, presenting fair and objective information, leaving us to draw our own conclusions. Jesus comes bringing divine authority to combat the evil lies and to take back what is rightfully ours. The people who encountered Jesus on earth were increasingly awestruck with the authority He demonstrated over the wind, the sea, demons, and disease. Our confidence in this battle is in that same Lord!

## "How?"

*By removing the false and putting on the truth.*

Before beginning the renewal of our minds we must realize that the source for change is in the person of the Holy Spirit (as opposed to our own positive thinking or increased willpower). The indwelling Spirit will show us *what* needs to be changed, *when* it is to be renewed, as well as providing the *power* to do so. What is your part in the renewing process? Having faith in God's Word and being willing to "set your mind on the things above" (Colossians 3:2). As with grace, we must never forget the Christian life is not just a group of principles to follow, but rather a moment-by-moment relationship with our God.

As we read God's Word and meditate on it, we begin to see where our thinking or behavior does not line up with God's. We must then take off the false thought and replace it with God's thought. Many times false beliefs about ourselves result from a particular circumstance or a series of circumstances rather than who He says we are. For example, you may believe that you're a person with no self-control, but God says that, as a Christian, you have the Holy Spirit within, and one of the fruits of the Spirit is self-control.

Even more importantly, Scripture realigns our beliefs about God Himself. Perhaps we have believed Him to be a vengeful, uncaring God, but He tells us in His Word that He is merciful and reaches out to us all day long. We cannot know these truths without going to His Word. God communicates to our mind primarily through the Scriptures.

We choose with our will to put our trust in God even when we don't fully understand His plan for us. With the power of the Holy Spirit enlightening us to the truth

**God communicates to our mind primarily through the Scriptures.**

of His Word, we will be led daily through a renewing process. As we begin to perceive inconsistencies in our thoughts and behavior, we can then remove (or put off) those thoughts and replace (or put on) the truth of God's word.

◊ ◊ ◊

In the southwest corner of modern day Turkey, nearly forgotten and well off the beaten path, lie the ruins of a great city. Today you can walk and climb freely in Sardis, its marble squares overgrown with trees, moss, and brush. Huge pillars from once grand buildings now lie scattered in the streets like a child's set of building blocks. Still, it is a beautiful place—green, cool, and quiet except for the chirping of birds and a few locals playing soccer in the old market area, stopping only to casually offer tourists souvenirs.

It's all very peaceful now, but check your history books or ask the boy selling postcards and he will point to the ruins of a fortress atop a high cliff and tell you tales of the ancient city, with its legends and lore of both glory and bone-chilling destruction.

The city of Sardis was once a bustling center of commerce, culture, and communication. On the floor of a broad, lush valley, she was watched and protected by her mighty fortress high above. Accessible only by a winding narrow road leading to a single gate, the fortress was shielded not only by thick rock walls, but also sheer cliffs on three of her sides. The expansive view from on high allowed several days warning of any attacking army or opposing force, giving plenty of time to gather the valley's inhabitants into the city's protective walls. Once safe inside, the people could easily withstand any onslaught from the outside.

Over the centuries, the attacks would come. Yet generation after generation of Sardisians rested in safety, sleeping soundly behind the wall and under the watchful eye of the city's fortress... until one spring moonless night, when a small band of enemies made their way up the crags and cracks in the cliffs.

Leaving the city below undisturbed, silently they made their way toward the summit—the citadel. Under cover of darkness and the slumbering city, they scaled her wall, and disappeared into the shadows inside the mighty fortress above the city. Unaware and unconcerned, the people slept. In the days ahead, the infiltrators would blend in, all the while subtly taking siege. At night, they began taking their turn watching the gates.

The night the grand fortress fell, blood flowed in the streets and fires lit the sky. Brute force was unnecessary, however. The gate to the city was simply opened from the inside by the adversaries, allowing the army to enter with full force. The attack was swift, merciless, and definitive. It was a brutal evening. Ah, but the battle was not lost that night; Sardis had fallen prey to the cancerous infiltrators long before. The invasion really began on that dark, unsuspected night when they slept, and the enemy crept in unnoticed.

In the book of Revelation, Jesus issued a stern warning to the young church in Sardis, referring, no doubt, to this embarrassing and deadly chapter of their city's history. "Wake up, and strengthen the things that remain! . . . If therefore you will not wake up, I will come like a thief, and you will not know what hour I will come upon you" (Revelation 3:2-3).

We are warned numerous times throughout Scripture of dangerous enemies seeking our destruction. "Be of sober spirit, be on the alert! Your adversary, the devil, prowls about like a roaring lion, seeking someone to devour" (1 Peter 5:8). Our enemy is not an army of angry men we can see. "For our struggle is not against flesh and blood, but against the rulers, against the powers, against the world forces of this darkness, against the spiritual forces of wickedness in the heavenly places" (Ephesians 6:12). The enemy's weapons are not like other weapons; they fight with lies, temptation, deception, and accusations.

Rest assured, the place of battle is not made of stone walls and thick wooden gates. Spiritual battles take place in the fortresses and the strongholds of our minds, which may appear impenetrable from the outside, but in reality have been silently, strategically invaded by the enemy.

## Battle Plan for Taking Every Thought Captive

Let there be no doubt: a battle is being waged for your mind. Just as sure as evil intruders scaled the fortress walls of Sardis and invading attackers stormed through castle gates, you have an enemy bent on your destruction. Corrupt fortresses must be captured and brought down so that God's truth concerning our lives can be built.

*Spiritual battles take place in the fortresses and the strongholds of our minds, which may appear impenetrable from the outside, but in reality have been silently, strategically invaded by the enemy.*

Are you wondering why you are still sinning or not having much victory over an area of your life? The Bible says that our old reasoning, thought patterns, and habits must be destroyed. The vernacular used in 2 Corinthians 10:3-4 is similar to the battle language of first century warfare. "For though we walk in the flesh, we do not war according to the flesh, for the weapons of our warfare are not of the flesh, but divinely powerful for the destruction of fortresses." These words were well understood in an era where fortresses and strongholds were constructed at strategic points along the city wall and manned by soldiers of military brilliance. These military experts had a bird's-eye view of the battle. Knowing exactly what to watch for, they shouted orders to the fighting men as to where to attack, where to stand their ground, and where to defend.

If an enemy force had taken over the rule of a city, such as in Sardis, the king would have to strategically take back his people's territory. In order to recapture a city, the king's army must do three things: break through the wall, invade the strongholds, and take back the castle's command and communications centers. This is the same battle tactic we are to use in renewing our minds. God has made a way for you of taking back your city, and He promises deliverance!

God gave us His battle plan in Second Corinthians, "We are destroying *speculations* and *every lofty thing* raised up against the knowledge of God, and we are taking every thought captive to the obedience of Christ" (2 Corinthians 10:5). "Speculations" are otherwise known as our reasoning, thought patterns, and habits formed by Satan's influence; while "lofty things" are those things which are natural, human, and non-biblical. The Spirit of God breaks through the wall of speculation and conquers the lofty things, enabling us to obliterate wrong thinking. When a thought doesn't line up with *the knowledge of God*," we must capture it and bring it to Christ. Our whole way of thinking must be retrained in Him. This recapturing of our mind is an ongoing process.

*Our whole way of thinking must be retrained in Him.*

Even though Jenny had conquered many old fortresses previously, she was confronted again with a new attack. Let's walk through the steps she made with the Holy Spirit to oust the enemy and take back what was rightfully hers.

**Step 1: Identify any behaviors, thoughts, or actions that do not line up with God's Word.**

When I say Jenny had lost her joy, I mean she was not living in the fullness of who God defined her to be. She was familiar with the Scripture verses that say do not be anxious or discouraged (Philippians 4:6; Matthew 6:33). Therefore, when she became consumed and miserable with herself, *her behavior and attitudes raised a red flag* indicating that this area obviously needed a change.

Then she asked the Holy Spirit to guide her through the process of renewing her mind in this area. Being sensitive to the Holy Spirit, Jenny asked for the Holy Spirit's help by praying, "Search me, oh, God, and know my heart; try me and know my anxious thoughts" (Psalms 139:23).

## Step 2: Identify the beliefs about circumstances, yourself, and about God that are behind the behaviors, thoughts, or actions.

We must ask ourselves, *What does this behavior or attitude reveal about what I truly believe?* Most likely finding the answer will require the help of another person not as close to the issue. This is why Jenny came to see me.

A. *Belief about circumstance:* Jenny couldn't lose weight. Her belief about this circumstance was that she needed to have discipline to stay thin in order to feel good about herself and be acceptable to others. Her self-image was the issue, even though the scale had became the focus.

B. *Belief about herself:* Jenny believed that to be beautiful and desirable she must be thin. She also believed the deception that if she had enough willpower, she *would* lose weight. So she concluded that she must have a weak willpower and discipline, and her upbringing had taught her that a person with no discipline was a disgrace. Because she was not seeing her desired weight loss she concluded, *I'm failing; I'm not acceptable.*

C. *Belief about God:* Jenny questioned God's response to her. She wondered why she had to experience the health problems that contributed to weight gain in the first place. She found it hard to believe that God could possibly love someone so undisciplined. She figured He wanted her to "get a grip," so she prayed for self-control.

*. . . we must take off the old lie before putting on the truth.*

After the corrupt fortress is identified, it must be dissembled and the rubble cleared before a new one is erected. Many times Believers diagnose problem spots and attempt to learn new material without first getting rid of old reasoning or broken thought patterns. If I'm sweaty and smelly after playing a competitive game of racket ball, I can't just throw on a new shirt over my gym clothes. I need to shower, take off my old clothes, and put on new ones. Similarly we must take off the old lie before putting on the truth.

## Step 3: Put off the lie and put on the truth.

We must admit and come to terms with the lie, bringing it to the light by confessing it to someone trustworthy. (See Ephesians 5:13 & 14; Proverbs 18:24.) "Putting off the lie" involves brutal honesty. Through counsel, Jenny realized that her self-loathing was inconsistent with her new nature as God's child. After spending time in contemplation and prayer she began to realize that she'd been deceived. She was then able to tangibly put off this lie by writing the following:

> Father, through past experiences and feelings, I have come to believe that I have to be a certain weight in order to be okay with myself. I've come to believe that I have no willpower and not only am I unattractive but also I'm not even a good Christian if I can't gain control over this situation. I've even come to believe that You truly aren't interested in me as a loving Father would be. I acknowledge this is a lie and I choose to put off this lie as instructed in Psalm 119:29.

"Putting on the truth" involves professing the truth of God's Word and "setting" our mind on it (Philippians 4:8). We cannot renew our mind without Scripture. We easily forget that it is alive and powerful, making even demons shudder (James 2:19). The power of His Word actually knocks people to the ground (John 18:6)! Whether written or spoken, God's Word is essential to our healing, for it is "living and active and sharper than any two-edged, sword and piercing as far as the division of soul and spirit" (Hebrews 4:12).

After studying the fruits of the Spirit again (Galatians 5:22-23), Jenny realized anew that her self-control and adequacy comes only from God (2 Corinthians 3: 5-6). Also, "seeing that His divine power has granted to us everything pertaining to life and godliness, through the true knowledge of Him who called us by His own glory and excellence" (2 Peter 1:3), she discovered she actually has all the willpower she needs.

She gained renewed confidence and strength that God is absolutely for her and has created His best for her. Furthermore, she is reminded that her body doesn't belong to her, but to God and so she knows her acceptance should not be based on a standard that she has determined. Now she is free to do anything to be healthy and a good steward of her body—but without being imprisoned by it. She purposes to believe that she is acceptable and loved by God regardless of her weight.

Jenny's prayer for "putting on the truth" sounded something like this:

> Father, Your word is true and in it You say, "Do not be anxious then, saying, 'What shall we eat?' or 'What shall we drink?' or 'With what shall we clothe ourselves?' " . . . for your heavenly Father knows that you need all these things" (Matthew 6: 25, 32). You say value is not tied to my appearance but rather to my birthright as Your child and that I am adequate (2 Corinthians 3) and perfectly suited with willpower—I've been granted everything pertaining to life (2 Peter 1:3). I trust that You have my best interest in mind.

*This final step in renewing the mind requires making choices in accordance with the true belief you have just put on.*

Just saying "no" or suppressing our thoughts is not enough. We also need to redirect our thinking to a new course, through exercises such as the one above, to exchange false thoughts with truth. I guarantee the results will be lasting and nothing short of amazing!

### Step 4: Make new choices.

This final step in renewing the mind requires making choices in accordance with the true belief you have just put on. We must be aware that our feelings and reasoning may not (and most likely won't!) line up with the truth we have just put on, but they will in time (Genesis 4:7). Furthermore, we must be very careful to avoid "self-effort Christianity" in this and every area of our walk, knowing that self-effort will only doom us to failure (Philippians 4:13; Colossians 2:23). Just as our negative behavior was the result of wrong thinking, positive behavior will be the result of right thinking.

My friend, George Sanchez, in a booklet entitled *Changing*

*Your Thought Patterns*, uses an illustration that conveys step four of renewing the mind beautifully.

When rain falls on a hill, the water finds the path of least resistance to move down the hill. After many rains, the waters carve deeper and deeper paths down the hill. If we compare these paths to our thought patterns we realize that "the longer we think along a given line, the stronger that thought pattern becomes. Every time we react in a certain way, we reinforce that thought pattern." If we wanted to change the course of water down a hill, we could build a dam, and provide a new course for the water, no longer allowing it to follow the old paths. We can, similarly, build a dam in our minds. When a thought comes to our minds that we know does not line up with God's truth, we can build a dam, not allowing ourselves to think in that way. But we must go further than that. We need to provide a new course for our thinking, a course that follows the mind of God.[3]

Paul writes to the Ephesians about damming up old hurtful patterns and changing the course for a new way of living so that life is brought to others as well. "He who has been stealing must steal no longer, *but must work, doing something useful* with his own hands, that he may have something to share with those in need" (Ephesians 4:28, emphasis mine). Paul also wrote to his friend Timothy to "... flee from youthful lusts and *pursue* righteousness, faith, love and peace with those who call on the Lord from a pure heart" (2 Timothy 2:22, emphasis mine).

Sanchez continues:

How does a thief stop being a thief? It's not enough just to stop stealing. Saying "no" to a destructive habit is not enough. In order to change, the thief is told to get a job and earn money honestly. Then he is to give to others in need so that perhaps they won't be tempted to steal. Now the process is complete. The negative habit has been dealt with by an act of the will, which chooses to stop it.[4]

Likewise there could be any number of behaviors Jenny could do to dam up the hurtful pattern and change the course of her new belief.

First, she might need to clear her closet of her size four jeans and stash the bathroom scales. Next she must focus on celebrating her health with her husband, accepting his compliments, undressing with the lights on (dim is okay), going to the beach, and doing fun activities even though she doesn't feel altogether comfortable. By choosing to take the focus off herself and concentrate on others, she can rest in God's opinion of her.

From the world's perspective, she may never make the grade but then again, sizes and shapes come and go with whatever is in fashion. Truth never changes, but perspective does. The neighbors and the media may always be critical, but victory comes when Jenny can act in a way that God's Word says is true. Her body doesn't belong to the world; it belongs to her husband and to God (see Romans 14:7-8; 1 Corinthians 7:4).

We must consider this process of recapturing strongholds for any destructive mind-set and behavior. The same steps apply for every life situation. What should a porn addict do? What about the woman obsessed with a clean house? "In reference to your former manner of life, you lay aside the old self . . . be renewed in the spirit of your mind, and put on the new self " (Ephesians 4:22-24).

The battle for our mind will continue until the day we are face-to-face with our King. As we retake certain areas, Satan will undoubtedly step up efforts to maintain control of other areas, and may very well attempt to take new ground. In these situations, he may not make an obvious frontal attack. He may very well take on the role of a traitor, one who pretends to be an authority and a friend of the King to hide his intentions as a thief—one who steals, kills, and destroys.

In folklore we often find traitors to the crown. In stories such as the tale of the Prince and the Pauper, the common folk saw the heart of the evil captain and assumed that to be the heart of the King. In the shadows of the castle, they existed under the silent suffering of oppression until the day the son of the king came and took up his sword against the evil.

In the legend of Robin Hood on the other hand, the citizens

of Nottingham never took the evil sheriff to be an authentic representative of good King Richard. From the beginning, Friar Tuck, Little John, the commoners, and, of course, Robin Hood, rejected the sheriff's "authority" and resisted his tactics and lies. Why? *They knew their king.* They knew what he was like. They knew the heart of their leader, and those who know the heart of a good king will never submit to the insurrection of a traitor to the crown.

## In Summary

"He brought me up out of the pit of destruction, out of the miry clay; and He set my feet upon a rock, making my footsteps firm." —Psalm 40:2

God has taken back His city and we are now free to know Him personally without inhibition or doubt. The enemy will surely come again, but the stronger our walls and citadels of truth, the less likely the enemy will be able to infiltrate our city. *As habitual and troublesome as corrupt strongholds prove to be, the strongholds of truth are just as mighty and clearly more so!*

Ultimately, change will happen when we move from wrong beliefs about God to right beliefs about Him. New thinking is a part of the process of experientially moving from our old identity to having an accurate image of ourselves and a right perception of our circumstances, while discovering the true image of God. Only then can we become in our thoughts, beliefs, and behavior what we already are in the inner man.

Satan's schemes will take on many forms, but those who have a personal relationship with the King and know His heart will be able to recognize the lies and the tactics of the traitor. God offers so much more than a life filled with battles against evil and lies. He yearns for us to live in harmony and unity with Him, the Creator of all things, the perfect Father we never had.

Let us press on to know Him.

◊ ◊ ◊

No matter what issues you might be facing, the cycle of transformation is usually the same. The cycle begins with a behavior that you want changed in your outward life (Living Being) and then progresses through your Thinking, Believing and Worshiping Being and back again to your Living Being. The diagram illustrates what this process might look like for a workaholic. What could this look like for issues you are facing?

## The Cycle of True Transformation
FIG.4

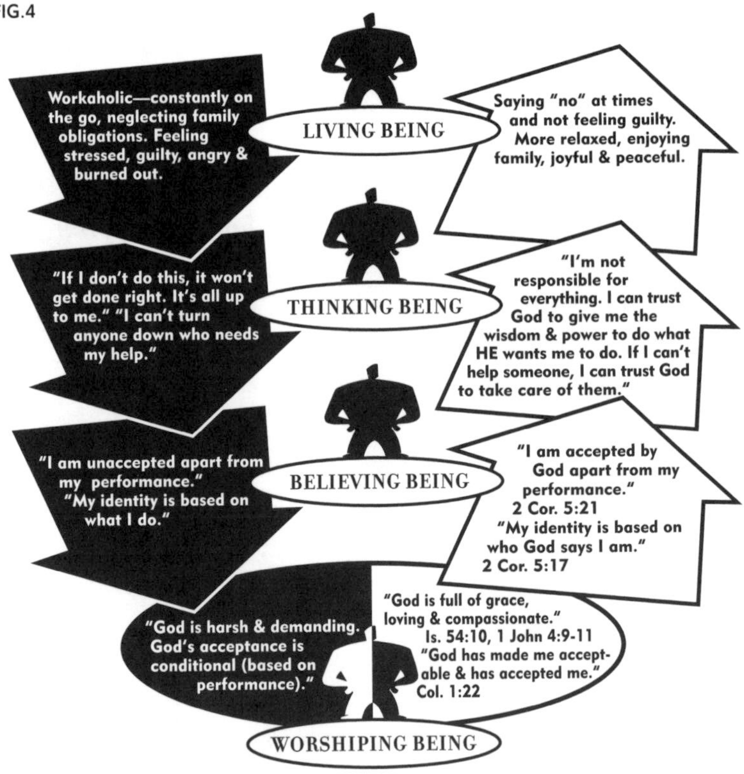

## Reflection ~~

• In what ways have you allowed the world or church to conform you to its image?

• What situations or circumstances can make you feel threatened, such as Jenny did was by her weight? This can be a good indicator of a stronghold in your life that needs renewing.

• Meditate on Ephesians 4:17-25.

• In relationship to the above, make a list of thoughts and beliefs you need to put off. Next to each one, write the thought or belief on which you need to meditate. Find an applicable Scripture and begin to "put it on."

## God's Desire ~~

"And we also thank God continually for this, that when you received the message of God from us, you welcomed it not as the word of men but as what it truly is, the Word of God, which is effectually at work in you who believe—exercising its superhuman power in those who adhere to and trust in and rely on it."
—1 Thessalonians 2:13, *Amplified Version*

"And do not be conformed to this world, but be transformed by the renewing of your mind, that you may prove what the will of God is, that which is good and acceptable and perfect."
—Romans 12:2

## Your Response ~~

*Father, please bring the above Scriptures to mind when I am accosted by lies throughout the day. Thank You for promising to provide all the strength and power necessary for the process of renewing my mind. Help me to relinquish to you the responsibility for bringing these areas to the surface. Make me faithful to continue through the process, even when it is painful and wearisome.*

# PART III

*Beyond Belief*

"Only the penitent man will pass."
"Only in the footsteps of God will he proceed."
"Only in the leap from the lions head will he prove his worth."

With little to guide him other than his wits and these words of cryptic wisdom offered in an ancient book, Indiana Jones presses on to his final destination. In blind faith he must take the final precarious steps in the direction of his prize.

Heralded as the greatest adventure film in history, Indiana Jones, the Last Crusade ranks among Hollywood's all-time best. With the combined talents of filmmakers George Lucas and Stephen Spielberg, and the acting of Harrison Ford and Sean Connery, it remains one of my favorites.

The film centers around one quest— the search for the relic cup used by Christ to serve the first communion, the "Holy Grail." An action-packed journey ensues. As the quest nears its end, Jones finds himself in a cave facing three deadly challenges before he can lay claim to the archeological find of tremendous and unsurpassed value. The way is littered with the time-bleached skeletons of many who have tried and failed. Danger lurks and the suspense mounts. The stakes are raised as Indiana's father lay dying from a gunshot wound, in desperate need of the Holy Grail's healing power.

Jones ducks to miss whirling, blood-stained blades. Slipping and almost plunging into a bottomless chasm, he recovers and takes a courageous step of faith into oblivion. And ... and . . . he makes it! He has arrived! The challenges and obstacles keeping him from the prize have been overcome. A warm, golden glow radiates from one last passageway. The prize is at hand. The grail awaits.

Wouldn't it be odd if Indiana Jones stopped right there? What if he sat down to rest and consider all the pain that's been wrought during his pursuit? What if he was content with pondering all the things he'd learned to get to this point without ever taking the final steps to seize the cup?

Our quest in this book has been a bit like Indiana Jones' quest for the Holy Grail. Guided by the ancient Book, we have come a long way. We've navigated the principles of mental maps and the authority of Scripture. We now know how our beliefs hold the key to understanding our behavior. The matrix of His plan for us outside of the confines of traditional Christian tradition has been revealed. We've recognized the law and put it in a proper context of grace. Catching our Creator's reflection we've begun to understand our true identity and how to live life with a renewed mind. But what if we stopped here so close to our treasure?

We stand in awe and wonder at the works of God. We proclaim His majestic greatness. But do we know Him? I don't mean know about Him, but know Him. Did you know that of all the things in the heart of God, one of His deepest longings is for us to know Him?

# ❧ 16 ❧

# The Ultimate Pursuit

"Then you will call upon Me and come and pray to Me,
and I will listen to you. And you will seek Me and find Me, when
you search for Me with all your heart.
And I will be found by you."
—Jeremiah 29:12-14

It is every parent's nightmare. Something that only happens to someone else, a person you don't know, an unfamiliar face on the evening news. But this time it happened to one of my best friends and his family. Dan and Lornell were doing some routine shopping at the mall when, suddenly, life became anything but routine.

At first it was just a nuisance. "Where did that little squirt run off to now?" A hasty glance is made down the next aisle. Nothing. The next aisle, and the next. Nothing. After running and scanning several aisles in each direction, the terrifying reality hits: "He's not here!"

At this point, all other emotion gives way to immediate panic and terror. Dropping everything and abandoning all tasks that, just seconds ago, were the most important things on their mind, and while all the other shoppers go on about their business, Dan and Lornell begin a frantic search.

Ten minutes pass. Still nothing. Security is paged.

"Don't worry, sir, this kind of thing happens all the time," came the response. But this isn't like all the other times, and as minutes pass, the assurances of the security guards pass as well. The guards make emergency calls to every store in the mall. The speaker system crackles with mall-wide announcements. "Would anyone who has seen a small, blond boy wearing blue overalls and red tennis shoes please contact mall security immediately." Nothing. The city police are called in to do parking lot searches, but by now forty-five minutes have passed. The child could easily be out of the state .

Though their options are limited, they mobilize absolutely every available resource. *There is no cost too high, no action too extreme.* Their precious little boy is too valuable to live without ... unimaginable. Dan calls his business; his employees immediately prepare to close the store and come to the mall to join in the search. There are fleeting thoughts of needing to raise ransom money. . .

◊ ◊ ◊

Let me ask you this: to what lengths would you go to find the most precious person in the world to you? Would your search give testimony of your love for him or her? What could be more focused than looking for a lost child? No matter what my highest priority in life, if my child were to be missing, I would abandon everything to search for him. All else immediately pales in significance. I could not remain still; I would be moved to action; I would search until he was found.

When Israel was lost in captivity, far from their home, God declared the plans He had for them were for a future with hope. "Then you will call upon Me and come and pray to Me and I will listen to you, and you will seek Me and find Me when you search for Me with your whole heart, and I will be found by you" (Jeremiah.

29:12-14). He can be found by you too, when you search for Him with your whole heart.

How passionate is your search for God? I'm not concerned about how you feel right now, I'm wondering how desperate you are. Your search for God may not seem as *urgent* as a parent's search for a lost child, but isn't it in actuality even more so? If in fact, you need Him like no other, if indeed you can find no lasting fulfillment outside of your Source of Life, are you willing to make the pursuit your utmost priority, strategically unleashing your every resource to find Him?

*. . . if indeed you can find no lasting fulfillment outside of your Source of Life, are you willing to make the pursuit your utmost priority, . . .*

(My friend's child was found, by the way. After an excruciating hour, a passerby noticed two little red tennis shoes and a pair of blue overalls under a rack of clothes in a nearby store. Sure enough, there was a little, blond boy in them, and moments later he was delivered safe and sound to his parents.)

## Filling the Void

I must agree with J. I. Packer, "The world becomes a strange, mad, painful place, and life in it a disappointing and unpleasant business, for those who do not know God."[1] This is the most essential truth about our existence. All we have accomplished prior to this chapter is to bring you here, to bring you home to the central theme of your entire existence. The purpose of life is to live in a love relationship with our God, for He says, "I don't want your sacrifices, I want your love; I don't want your offerings—I want you to know me" (Hosea 6:6, *Living Bible*).

"When God repeats something in Scripture, I am sure it's to make a point," says Tim Hansel. "For example, in the book of Ezekiel, over sixty times it says, 'I want you to know Me.'"[2]

If God is deserving of my life-long pursuit and the center of all meaning and fulfillment and joy, I must keep my purpose in clear sight. For example, as soon as I am finished writing today, I will head home to finish packing because my wife and I are flying out at 6:00 A.M. tomorrow to visit our middle son. When I leave here, my purpose will be to get to my house. That purpose will determine every turn I make.

The reverse is true also; if we don't know the reason of our existence, every decision is going to stem from guesswork and confusion. Only when I know my purpose do I have clear direction, and I can single-mindedly make choices that will lead me toward my destination.

*Only when I know my purpose do I have clear direction, and I can single-mindedly make choices that will lead me toward my destination.*

Our natural logic tells us to trust only what our eyes can see and to set our goals on what we can physically accomplish such as acquiring knowledge, power, or riches. All the while God wants us to trust and accept His offer—*to know Him, the Source* of all knowledge, power, and riches! "Let him who boasts boast of this, that he understands and knows Me, that I am the Lord who exercises lovingkindness, justice, and righteousness on earth; for I delight in these things,' declares the Lord (Jeremiah 9:24).

Knowing our purpose in life is the essential truth of life. Why? Because when we are fulfilling what we are created to be, we will reflect the image of God accurately and in doing so will experience the contentment God fully intended us to have. I don't mean I always *feel* warm and cozy with Him because sometimes I feel like God moved to Denver without leaving a forwarding address! At times I feel like I call out to Him only to hear the hollow sounds of "FATHER ... Father ... father," echoing back to me even though I know, in my mind at least, that this is not true. My Father promises that he will never desert me or forsake me (see Hebrews 13:5).

I was sitting in an audience listening to one of my favorite speakers, J. I. Packer, when I was captured by a profound phrase he used. I'll never forget these words: "What makes life worthwhile is having a big enough objective, something which catches our imagination and lays hold of our allegiance; and this the Christian has, in a way that no other man has. For what higher, and more exalted, and more compelling goal can there be than to know God?"[3]

How can we know eternal pleasures? *Begin to know God, and enjoy Him right now.* All through the book of Jeremiah and in so many other parts of the Bible we clearly see that God delights in us knowing Him, so why do we settle for having a relationship with God through someone else? We go to a conference or a church service and listen to a speaker talk about our Father and go home thinking we had a relationship with Him that day; when all we really got is someone else's story about his or her relationship with Him. Hearing this information can be good and make us more aware of God, but until we spend time with Him for ourselves, we simply don't nurture our own personal relationship.

*Intimacy with God, as in all close relationships, requires time spent in His presence.*

"Two ways of knowing exist," says Michael Philips in *A God to Call Father.* "The first is information you possess. You say you know facts and data concerning multiplication tables, the discovery of America, and lots of other matters. The first kind of knowing is learned. The second kind of knowing comes through interaction and cannot be taught."[4] Knowing God involves so much more than information. He longs for us to know Him deeply. Intimacy with God, as in all close relationships, requires time spent in His presence.

❁   ❁   ❁

Junior high is a lot like the '6os: one big psychedelic blur. I just happened to be in junior high in the '6os, and my memory is pretty foggy too, but I still have images of my mother in pink-and-orange polka dot dresses and her hair in a beehive on her head.

Everybody was trying to "make love, not war," but try as we did, love relationships just seemed to get more and more mixed up. The Beatles told us, "All you need is love," and then they broke up. We sang the Beach Boys' new hit, "I Get Around," but then itchy rashes started showing up. For a young kid on the edge of puberty, love looked a bit precarious. We junior highers were content with just trying to figure out guy/girl relationships.

Fortunately for us, there was "the relationship strategy." It was 1966 and all across the nation connections were being developed between twelve and thirteen year olds through intermediaries, which is a fancy way of saying we had "go-betweens." The strategy was simple: If a guy liked a girl, he'd get some other guy to ask some other girl if the girl liked the guy. If the girl liked the guy, she would tell the other girl who would tell the other guy who would then tell the guy that the girl liked him. That's just the way it worked, plain and simple. In fact, I'm guessing our strategy may be in use yet today.

Our game plan was so cool! It allowed for the *illusion* of relationship, the *emotion* of relationship, the *suspense* of relationship, and even the public *appearance* of relationship without any of the *risk* of relationship. The idea was to stay busy and distant enough that you never really had to share real thoughts or expose your *true* heart to another, even though we could not have articulated this process at the time.

Such were junior high love stories in the '60s. Sadly, so are many of the love relationships between Christians and their Creator. Busy, distant, and public. We read good books written by others explaining what God might want to tell us. We listen to sermons from pulpits and radios imparting knowledge about God. In groups, we talk about Him, discuss His character, and even offer our prayers—all the while far more concerned about what those around us think of our words than He does.

*We are designed to worship God, but as a result of the Fall, we were left without the means to do so—our spirit is born dead to the ways of God.*

## Incurably Religious

Man is incurably religious. Whether we study ancient or contemporary civilizations, no matter how primitive or complex the people group, they display fear and/or desire to appease or worship a higher being (see 1 Kings 12:28; Deuteronomy 4:19, 9:16; Ezekiel 32:4). Humanity has always sought after Deity. Have you wondered why? We are designed to worship God, but as a result of the Fall, we were left without the means to do so—our spirit is born dead to the ways of God. Nevertheless, this aching void in the spirit for worship continues to exist.

Because of this desire for worship, we are compelled to do something to fill our aching void. The Deceiver, taking full advantage of this God-given desire, leads man to turn worship inward toward self, and outward toward creatures rather than the Creator (see Isaiah 57:10-13; Jeremiah 2:27-28; John 4:20-24; Romans 1:22-23; 1 Corinthians 2:14; Galatians 4:8-9).

One evening over dinner, my counseling instructor and dear friend, Jim Craddock, made a bold statement that has remained with me. He said, "Satan knew that if he could distort man's view of God by destroying their relationship, mankind would create gods in man's image and essentially worship themselves." Romans 1:25 states this very clearly. "For they exchanged the truth of God for a lie and worshiped and served the creature rather than the Creator, who is blessed forever." We see this very thing played out in our cities, neighborhoods, and our homes, but this wasn't the Deceiver's only ploy.

Another primary tactic the enemy uses to keep us off balance is deceiving us into doubting God's favor. We have this, "He-loves-me; He-loves-me-not view of God," says Steve Frye.[5] Why is God's love so hard to receive? We were created to participate in a perfect relationship. But not only did Adam and Eve step away from that relationship; every day since, Satan has made it his priority to twist our understanding of one simple word—Grace—the one simple word at which the devil curses and angels stand in awe.

Grace is poison to the one who robs, steals, and destroys. It is grace that opens us to the love of God. Therefore, we can be sure the Deceiver continues to war against us with the same strategy he used against Eve. He persuaded her to disobey God by painting a false picture of Him, casting Him as a miserly father who held back the best for Himself. Satan did this by casting doubt on God's word, His character, and His motive of immeasurable compassion and grace

(Genesis 2-3). In the garden the father/child image was terribly disfigured.

## Distorted Father Image

Ultimately Satan not only set out to misrepresent the image of God as our supreme being, but also as our Father who came to the garden looking for his children. "I will be a father to you, and you will be sons and daughters to Me" our Creator said (2 Corinthians 6:18). The common perception of a distant, angry God leaves one's soul ravaged and empty. We have been robbed! Satan has attempted to steal our identity as God's children. We've been blinded from knowing and experiencing our central purpose in life—our intimate father/child relationship.

*We've been blinded from knowing and experiencing our central purpose in life—our intimate father/child relationship.*

We have the desire to worship, but we've been left on our own to create an image of God as Father. The only way we know to do this is by the association of our earthly examples of "father," or the lack thereof. Just as we do in our search for life, we piece the puzzle of our father/child relationship together as best we can. Without realizing that our perception of this relationship is so robbed and distorted, we create God's image from the only tangible symbols we know: religious leaders, authority figures, and our own dads.

Do you worry that your search for God is lacking? Do you wonder, *Is something wrong with me because I don't have a burning desire or desperation for Him? Am I really a Christian?* Perhaps, you aren't completely certain about who you are searching for. Our self-image in relation to God is established when we are young children. Our images of trust and worth are shaped and developed by those more powerful than us. We're not able to be objective and filter out truth or untruth as children; we are left vulnerable, able only to receive what comes our way. Once this self-image is set, we begin to interpret data from all our experiences, and they in turn form and support our beliefs about God and ourselves.

The concept of "God as Father" carries with it such heavy emotion (consciously or unconsciously) because the name "Father" is loaded with heavy meaning in relation to our most vulnerable years of childhood. The symbol of "Father" stirs vivid memories, pleasant or unpleasant, in the "child" heart within each of us. Is it any wonder then that our childhood greatly influences how we interpret or view life situations in relation to God and His care for us?

Following are a sample of scenarios that can cause us to have a negative and false picture of God:

- Divorce
- Death of loved ones
- Alcoholic homes
- Workaholic parents
- Verbal, physical, and sexual abuse
- Absent father

Sadly the primary victim of these life circumstances is the child. Every child is created for relationship and, therefore, is ultra-sensitive to his or her interactions with those in authority. From one's limited ego-centered perspective, beliefs about life are formed early. When a situation turns out poorly, a child will usually determine, *I must be the cause of this.*

I once met with a client who as a child of severe poverty during the Depression, was given away by her parents. As her counseling progressed, it became apparent that never once did she consider her childhood abandonment as a painful choice made by her parents. Instead she was left to wonder all those years, *What was wrong with me? Why did they give me up and not my brother or sisters?* This experience caused her to doubt God's faithfulness and to live with the fear that He would most likely abandon her too.

Throughout life each of us has come to accept a concept of "father" in light of either our earthly fathers or other significant authority figures such as mothers, coaches, teachers, spiritual leaders. We must realize, however, that no matter how consistent these perceptions of our earthly authority figures may be, they are terribly inaccurate in regard to our heavenly Father, to whom we often transfer our perceptions. Even the best of fathers cannot accurately portray our heavenly Father because they are limited, and God is not.

*Even the best of fathers cannot accurately portray our heavenly Father because they are limited, and God is not.*

I'll never forget the day I went to confession as a young boy. Religiously I quoted my rehearsed confession of sin, "Bless me Father for I have sinned. It has been nine weeks since my last confession. I lied six times, fought with my brothers four times, stole three times ... " Immediately the priest leaned toward the confessional window and blurted, "TELL ME YOUR SINS!"

Shaken, I quickly repeated my memorized list of wrongs. Again came the response, "Tell me your sins!" When I hesitated, the door burst open and the priest grabbed me by the arm. Banging me up against the wall, he continued yelling at me demanding I tell him my sins. In the midst of the confusion, my mother came to my rescue.

I wasn't aware that the day before my confession some valuables had been stolen from the church and when I confessed to stealing, the priest reverted to his own method to find out if I was the culprit. Though I can chuckle now about the whole scenario, during my childhood, my perception of the priest's spiritual authority was transferred to God. As a result, God seemed to me strict, harsh, and not at all personable.

## Transferring Fathers

Rather than our earthly fathers being a miniature model of God's lovingkindness, we tend to reverse the reflection and anticipate that God is like our parents, teachers, coaches, or our spiritual leaders. You can imagine what this means for those whose authority figures have abandoned children, shown lack of emotion or commitment, or brought trauma to the family. The child is actually put in double jeopardy. Not only is the parent or guardian no longer trustworthy, but also the child feels deep alienation from God. The pain is multiplied when a child cannot anticipate comfort from God.

Interestingly, even those with healthy fathers can find themselves shortchanged. They can easily become convinced that human love is all there is to be expected from God, who is in fact infinite in His measures of love. Even if a parent is incredibly tender and patient, he or she is still limited to human capacity with its subtle agendas. Considering all, I have never met anyone whose parents did not leave some distorted image of God.

*Rather than our earthly fathers being a miniature model of God's lovingkindness, we tend to reverse the reflection and anticipate that God is like our parents, teachers, coaches, or our spiritual leaders.*

My dad is now a wonderful Christian man, but when I was a child he struggled with alcohol. Still, I never doubted his love. My dad was a faithful provider and, unlike many dads, never lacked showing love and commitment. In fact, he never missed an event such as ballgames or performances. But there were some events I wished he'd have missed. I couldn't trust him at times. When he'd been drinking, he would show up and embarrass me. And sometimes his capacity to be my protector was neutralized by the alcohol he hated. When he drank too much, it left me feeling vulnerable and exposed.

As I grew into my role of a Christian husband and father, I found myself becoming more and more uneasy when I had to travel, which was often in my early baseball career. But I couldn't understand where the anxiety came from. I wasn't afraid to fly, so that wasn't its source. As I examined my thoughts more closely, I discovered my apprehension came as a result of my fear for the safety of Nancy and my boys while I was away. Fervently I prayed, asking that I might be able to trust in God's provision and safety. Still the overwhelming emotions of fear gripped me.

One night I finally allowed myself to hear God's whisper, *Bill, do you think I'm unreliable when it comes to protecting your wife and kids? I* was stunned, but realized He was exactly correct— I had transferred my image of my dad onto God. I was then lead to Psalm 127:2 where His truth was made known to me. "Unless the Lord guards this city, the watchman keeps awake in vain." Then He whispered quietly into my spirit, "Bill, what can pass through the shield of My love?"

*You mean, Lord, if I were to stand at the door of my house with a machine gun in hand, my family would not be safe unless you are the One watching over them?* I prayed. Upon renewing my mind and taking hold of this belief, I could rest, assured that God was faithful and that nothing could happen to Nancy and the boys without first passing through His sovereign protection of love.

I still have tendencies of overprotecting and over-teaching my children which I know will, in turn, give them a distorted view of God as their Father. I'm continually correcting and instructing them, and they are left to wonder if they will ever get it right or measure up. It doesn't help to carry regrets about the past; instead I know that just as I don't hold my father's past weaknesses as an excuse from knowing God, my sons will have to look past my faults to see an accurate view of their heavenly Father.

*You may have images of God that need to be completely destroyed because they are so misrepresentative of God.*

## Destroying God

It's imperative to recognize that we may have an accurate view of God in some instances, yet in other aspects, our perception can be grossly misrepresented. We simply cannot develop a warm, trusting relationship with One whose image has been distorted. You may have images of God that need to be completely destroyed because they are so misrepresentative of God.

This realization hit me full force after a counseling session. After hearing a young woman's story, I literally could not speak. I walked out of my office feeling absolute devastation. What I heard maddened me; I felt crazy with grief. This beautiful girl had been sexually abused by her dad until she was thirteen, the year she finally sought escape by running away from home. Hoping she had found a place of refuge, she was taken in by a pastor ... who proceeded to degrade and sexually molest her. Need I say she hated men, especially those in any position of authority? Her picture of God was so distorted by the time she came to see me that we needed to completely destroy the image she had of Him before her healing could begin.

Before we can address the pressing questions such as, "Where was God during all this?" and "How could He allow this to happen?", we must completely tear down false beliefs about Him and then rebuild a true picture of God. Only after the false god is destroyed can the loving Father, our God of compassion, take His rightful place.

*I find the reason we often struggle so terribly in our circumstances is that we don't know or truly believe who God is in the midst of them.*

I find the reason we often struggle so terribly in our circumstances is that we don't know or truly believe who God is in the midst of them. God promised to reveal Himself to those who seek. Those who know Him by name will put their trust in Him (see Psalm 9:10).

Do you long to know God? In the days when the Bible was written, a person's character was revealed in his name. God has many names by which He is known in Scripture: Creator, Master, All Sufficient One, The Lord my Shepherd. Each of the names of God declares His presence, His character, and His action on our behalf in specific situations. For example: *Jehovah Jireh*, shows God as our provider; *Jehovah Nissi*, is our protection and banner; *Jehovah Shalom*, is our peace that reaches beyond understanding. Here we are not simply describing God with His different names. It is critical that you understand that everything in *your* life will be defined by your knowledge of His character and attributes.

The Eternal, Creator, King of Kings, and Lord of Lords who rules over all heaven and earth; God, mighty in power, wants your love—wants you to know Him. When His children choose to follow the Father of Lies, still His love never ceases. His heart remembers them and longs for a relationship with them. Why? "Can a woman forget her nursing child, and have no compassion on the son of her womb? Even these may forget, but I will not forget you," He said (Isaiah 49:15). God is our Father and He waits for us.

## Coming Home

"I know nothing which can so comfort the soul; so calm the swelling billows of sorrow and grief; so speak peace to the winds of trial, as a devout musing upon the subject of the Godhead."[6]
—C. H. Spurgeon

Not only are we born with an innate desire to know and worship God, but also the vulnerable child within each of us yearns to be held secure. In all the people I've counseled, we've found at the center of their being, a deep longing to be childlike and held by someone they can trust. Because each of us is meant to be God's child, we each have a child's desire to crawl up into His lap and be safe and secure. This is why the New Covenant, our new inheritance matters so much. No longer sinful descendents of Adam, we are rightful heirs to the throne of God. We are now God's chosen children. His words speak to us with the same tenderness spoken generations ago to our forefathers.

To grasp the depth of God will take us all eternity. I can hope only to awaken this inborn desire to know Him. You will primarily come to know your Father as He reveals Himself to you through His Word. The heavens also and all creation declare the glory of the Lord, and He will go to great lengths to show Himself to you (see Psalm 19).

Are you too busy? Jesus redirected the one who was "bothered and worried about so many things." He said that "few things are necessary, really only one ...." Then He commended the one that left the dishes in the sink, the checkbook unbalanced, and the television off. He praised the one who chose instead to rest at His feet, saying she "has chosen the good part, which shall not be taken away from her" (Luke 10:40-41).

"As the deer pants for the water brooks, so my soul pants for

Thee, O God. My soul thirsts for God, for the living God ..."
—Psalm 42:1-2

I pray that your eyes will be opened and your image of God will become true—that of a loving, compassionate, tender, and generous parent (see Romans 8:15 and 2 Corinthians 6:18). Unlike the limitations of our earthly fathers, which so influence our beliefs about our heavenly Father, we are free to relate to God in new undistorted ways upon realizing His nature and desire for us. God's character is the pinnacle of our desire for freedom and the central message of this book. Here we find God passionately drawing us to Himself in a safe and peaceful and exciting embrace.

*God's character is the pinnacle of our desire for freedom and the central message of this book.*

❁ ❁ ❁

Some years ago at a social function, one of England's leading actors was asked to recite for the pleasure of his fellow guests. He consented and asked if there was anything special that his audience would like to hear. After a moment's pause, an aged minister arose and said. "Could you, sir, recite the Twenty-third Psalm?"

A strange look passed over the great actor's face. He paused for a moment and said, "I will upon one condition—after I have recited it, you, my friend, will do the same."

Impressively, the great actor began the Psalm. His voice and his intonation were perfect. He held his audience spellbound, and as he finished, a great burst of applause broke from the guests.

Then as it died away, the aged minister arose and began to recite. His voice was not remarkable; his intonation was not faultless. When he finished, no sound of applause broke the silence, but there was not a dry eye in the room, and many heads and hearts were bowed in reverential awe!

The great actor rose to his feet. His voice shook with uncontrollable emotion as he laid his hand upon the shoulder of the aged minister and said to the audience, "I have reached your eyes and ears, my friends. This man has reached your hearts. The difference is just this: I know the Twenty-third Psalm, but this man knows the Shepherd."[7]

## Reflection ⌒

Examine your own relationship with God. Do you live your relationship with Him primarily through other people? Perhaps more through a pastor, books, or radio teachers rather than through personal, one-on-one time with Him?

What false assumptions have you made about God as a result of your interaction with, or observations about, your parents and other authority figures? Write a Scripture reference that states the truth about God, then meditate on this truth so that you will be "transformed by the renewing of your mind" (Romans 12:1-2).

## God's Desire ⌒

"So let us know, let us press on to know the LORD. His going forth is as certain as the dawn; And He will come to us like the rain, Like the spring rain watering the earth . . . For I delight in loyalty rather than sacrifice, and in the knowledge of God rather than burnt offerings".
—Hosea 6:3,6

"And I will give them a heart to know Me, for I am the Lord; and they will be My people, and I will be their God, for they will return to Me with their whole heart".
—Jeremiah 24:7

"Jesus said to him, 'Have I been so long with you, and yet you have not come to know Me, Philip? He who has seen Me has seen the Father'".
—John 14:9

## Your Response ⌒

*Father, you have been with me with each step I have taken, even when I have walked away from You in self-will and pride. In Your faithfulness,*

*You are always there, with outstretched arms and love in Your eyes, waiting eagerly and patiently to love me. Please open my eyes so I will not miss the marvelous and personal ways You are caring for me, blessing me, and guiding me as my faithful Father.*

# ∜ 17 ∜

# Daddy!

"For you have not received a spirit of slavery leading
to fear again, but you have received a spirit of adoption
as sons by which we cry out, 'Abba! Father!'"
— Romans 8:15

One of my favorite stories is the one where Jesus and His disciples are in a small boat being tossed and torn by a wild and dark sea. Surging waters beat at the sides of the vessel, and fierce winds shred its sails. I imagine the fear of the men as the waves and gusts threaten the lives of all on board.

While the panicked crew fights against the merciless powers of nature, it dawns on one of them to look for Jesus. Where is He? Soundly sleeping, snuggled down in the body of the boat like a child in the back seat of a car during a slow, arduous road trip through a blizzard. Let the storm do its worst; Jesus is resting, fast asleep in the arms of His Abba (see Luke 8).

A. W. Tozer once said, "It is better to apprehend one truth of God's being, a full truth, a live truth, and apprehend it all the way to its core and then to live in the reality of that discovery, than to know ten thousand facts about God and not live in them."[1]

We have covered a tremendous amount of information so far in this book. Sometimes as I've been writing, I wonder if I've come to grasp even one fraction of one truth all the way to its core. What we are dealing with is so deep, so incredible, I feel humbled by it all and I realize how little I really know about myself and God. I can easily become overwhelmed, but I am reminded by the New Testament writer who said,

"Continue in the things you have learned and become convinced of [them], knowing from whom you have learned them" (2 Timothy 3:14, emphasis mine). Though I feel like a child in the truths of God, these words hold me so I don't wander far. I am convinced in moments of doubt because I have come to trust Jesus, from whom I have learned them. We can't possibly begin to mine the depths of who God is in the brief space of this chapter, so allow me to focus on the culmination of all God's names, the name that was reserved until His Son could reveal it to us Himself, the name "Abba."

**Daddy**

The word *ABBA* is the Hebrew word most like our affectionate name, "daddy." Ultimately this name of God is by far the most intimate and most tender, yet it captures His other characteristics too. Jesus showed us the Father both while sleeping like a child, and then by standing in the midst of that howling storm and commanding it to cease in the authority given by his Abba, "Peace, be still," He said. (Mark 4:39, KJV) Throughout the many trials and tests during His life here on earth, Jesus rested assured in the presence of His Father whose names include: *Jehovah Jireh, Jehovah Nissi, Jehovah Shalom*. These timeless characteristics of God all culminated into one name: Jesus. He knew his "daddy" would *provide*, *protect*, and bring *peace*." Furthermore, the Son lived in the consciousness that He was infinitely and unconditionally loved by Abba. And then, He invited us to share that heritage. How unfathomable it is to consider the intimacy shared within the Godhead! Yet, here we find Jesus inviting us in so we might share and live in that love! "That they may all be one; even as Thou, Father, art in Me, and I in Thee, that they also may be in Us … " (John 17:21).

## Becoming Childlike

For some, calling God "daddy" feels unfamiliar and awkward. For those with deeply disappointing or hurtful father/child relationships, it may seem out of the question. For most of us, however, the name "daddy" somehow just doesn't seem formal enough for God. Besides that, we feel a little silly using a word that seems too childlike.

In the generation and culture in which I grew up, you didn't hear the guys sitting around drinking Cokes and saying, "Well, my daddy always said … " Never! We might say, "My dad, or my 'ol man" (in as deep a voice as we could muster), but daddy was a name reserved for the little kids. Most cultures tend to teach their children to become more and more independent as they mature, moving them away from a "daddy" relationship to a more distant one. This mentality carries over into our spiritual upbringing as well. Because we've learned to approach God as adults, we're thrown a "curve ball" when we're asked to be like children in our relationship with Him.

*Because we've learned to approach God as adults, we're thrown a "curve ball" when we're asked to be like children in our relationship with Him.*

I often wonder what the Jews did when Jesus first prayed addressing God as "daddy" in public. The Jews wouldn't dare to even *write* the name of God in whole. Respected religious leaders, using great care and after a ceremonial cleansing, would still only write a few letters of God's name because it was considered so holy. Jesus' use of the name "Abba," insinuating the most childlike and intimate of relationships, must have astounded those in His presence.

Even though Jesus was God and never ceased to be Deity, when He took on flesh, He became a true man and lived as one of us. Jesus showed us how to re-enter the sweet father/child relationship we so quickly outgrew. Jesus lived as man was originally intended, living in fearless childlike dependence on a trustworthy Father. By age twelve He spoke to God saying, "Abba," and this is the mode of living that He proclaimed. Every act the Son of God displayed, whether sleeping on a windswept boat or in the dark hours of Gethsemane, He relinquished all, trusting only as small children do.

*Jesus lived as man was originally intended, living in fearless childlike dependence on a trustworthy Father.*

I have fond memories of my boys when they were little. Even while driving in the midst of a howling snowstorm they would "konk out." They knew that not only would their daddy get them home safely, but also I'd carry them up to their own beds where they would awaken in the morning. I pondered the beauty of their innocent faces, their relaxed trust and ultimate rest. In those moments I know I experienced a portion of Abba's heart ... and it made my own feel like it might burst! How He longs for us to rest so completely in Him with the trust of a childlike heart!

### Developing a childlike heart

"Unless you . . . become like children, you shall not enter the kingdom of heaven," said Jesus (Matthew 18:3). Those who, like a child, remain teachable and open to change stand in stark contrast to the rest of us adults who quickly become strangers to surprise. Just like the subtle shift from running and jumping into daddy's lap, we are continually nudged into becoming adults. Though maturity is good and necessary, with it we lose the childlike freedom of our hearts and we take on adult hearts. In learning to become independent from our parents, we instill the same mentality with God: we equate freedom with independence rather than the carefree trust of a child asleep in her daddy's arms.

Why did God tell us to have a child's heart? Without such freedom, we'll never be able to experience the rest He offers as Abba. If, in fact, we are created for this child/father relationship, we can't fully know God unless our hearts remain open, inquisitive, and teachable without preconceived ideas and judgments. We must not be ashamed to ask, "Why?" Unashamed, we can admit that we don't have the answer.

## Contrast between childlike and adult thinking

| CHILD HEART | ADULT HEART |
| --- | --- |
| Dependent | Independent |
| Teachable | Expert, professional |
| Always asking why | Don't question me |
| Always expecting to learn | We know everything |
| Not ashamed to say, "I don't know" | Ashamed of not knowing so will pretend to know |
| No preconceived ideas —sees only what is there | This is the way it's always been |
| Reckless confidence in Father's love | Trusts in own devices for safety |
| Loves surprises | A stranger to surprise |
| Open to change | Can't see things as they are; already decided the way it should be |
| Believes in unconditional love | Believes everything must be earned |

Malcolm Smith summarizes this comparison between the adult heart and the childlike heart when he said, "The adult attitude toward God is a closed arrogant, self-sufficient mind. This mind cannot see the way things really are because it has already decided the way they must be—it is closed to the delight and wonder of discovering something new."[2] This is what renewing the mind is all about—taking off our independent, adult-like thinking and replacing it with wide-eyed wonder.

Which column above best describes Jesus? "WWJD" (What Would Jesus Do?), the popular slogan among kids and teens, has indeed been instrumental in making young people aware of their actions, calling to mind whether their actions line up with those of Jesus. Though I don't deny that the handy reminder may have made a difference for some, I think we may need to take a closer look. Perhaps we should not be asking, "What Would Jesus Do?" as if there is some specific script that we are supposed to follow in every specific situation. Rather what did Jesus do all the time? He stayed intimately connected with the Father, He listened to His leading, and then He acted. I think we easily confuse the word "mimic" (an attempt to copy actions) with the word "model" (a similarity in character and movement *after being with a parent or respected one.)*

Jesus never ceased to be God, even when He became man. The book of Philippians, chapter two, says that Jesus did not count equality with God a thing to be grasped, but He emptied himself and took on a human form so that we might identify with Him and understand Him. When the Word says that He emptied himself it means that He stepped away from His throne, set aside His crown, and entered our atmosphere taking on our limited flesh, *so that He, of His own choice, could show us how to live as men and women were meant to live, in complete dependence on our Father.*

*. . . we are to learn from Him and experience the uninhibited joy of His childlike vulnerability and total reliance on Abba.*

Still Jesus didn't perform for us like an actor on a stage; He asked us to follow Him, to abide with Him, and to enter in. Our challenge to be "imitators" of Christ is not to simply do the things that Jesus did, but rather we are to learn from Him and experience the uninhibited joy of His childlike vulnerability and total reliance on Abba. What must we do? We are to be reformed so we might model Jesus' dependence on God, not merely His acts! WWJD? Jesus walks and talks with His Father every minute of the day so that He might show us the Father.

### Modeling our Father

One day I traveled back to the University of Wyoming where I was supposed to meet a college buddy of mine whom I hadn't seen in several years. He was coaching at the time and invited me to come to the auditorium where the state wrestling meet was being held; I'd find him there. I opened the doors to the stadium, and my heart sank. All of a sudden reality hit me. I could spend hours looking for him in there!

I looked down across a sea of people. There was nothing to do but take the plunge. Pushing my way through hoards of sweaty people, I started across the gigantic gym. In the midst of so many bodies jammed together, I couldn't see more than three or four people at a time. Just as my eyes were glazing over and I was about to give up, a little boy who was ambling along the less crowded sidelines caught my eye.

Hey, I knew that walk! It was just like my friend's sort of off-balance swagger. Rushing to get close behind him, I followed the little guy all the way around the gym and through the mob. Sure enough, he plopped down on the bleacher right next to my friend, Tom.

Now I'm pretty certain Tom didn't take time to teach his son how to walk like he did. I know some physical traits are genetic, but who can deny the subtle shaping that takes place simply by spending time together? I saw this displayed right before my eyes that day in a crowded stadium.

Many similarities between parents and their children do not result automatically from inborn traits but rather develop gradually over the years as children spend time with their parents. I always marvel at how some adopted children resemble and even sound like their parents. The same will be true for me; the more I spend time with Abba, the more I will be like Him.

Jesus modeled the Christian life for us this way. He knew Abba so intimately that He put Himself completely in the Father's hands, and relied fully on Him. We read all throughout the New Testament of Jesus attesting to the fact that He did nothing on His own initiative, said nothing of His own, doing and saying only what the Father did and said (see John 5:19, 30; 14). He came as a model for us so we could see that our Father can be trusted in this way. Religion is for adults, but kinship is for children. When we become childlike, we will become like our daddy, our Abba.

## In Our Father's Embrace

"We cry out Abba! Father!"— Romans 8:15

EMBRACING HIS SAFETY

A few times in my life God has opened for me a small window of understanding into what the Abba Father relationship is all about, using an earthly picture to give me a glimpse of an incredible spiritual reality. I don't know how to explain this, but it's as though He paints a picture of an earthly event, with me in it, then uses it to teach me something much, much deeper and more significant than the frame I am currently in.

Such an event was portrayed for me one day when my son, Nic, was twelve years old. He had just gone through a couple of rough baseball seasons, spending most of his time in the dugout while recovering from a bone cyst that had formed in his upper arm. But that was all behind him now and he was reveling in the much-loved sport again. On this particular day he was pitching a game that would determine first place in the Canyon Lake Little League.

Nic was throwing well and as the innings passed it looked like the game "was in the bag." My son wound up for a fastball ... and at the apex of the throw, right when his hand passed his head, there was a sickening, bone-shattering snap that drew gasps from the crowd, and dropped my child into the dirt in an agonizing heap. I can still hear it as if it were yesterday, "Daaaaaddyyyy!"

The echoing cry of "Daaaaaddyyyy!" is still etched in my mind. In that moment I was awakened to an instinct I'd never before known. Never had I been stirred into action more immediately, more directly, or with more determination. I had to get to my child. Nothing between us could keep us apart: the score, rules, bleachers, fence, people ... no obstacle could hold me back. My child was in desperate need of his dad, and his father was in desperate need to reach his child.

It is a portrait I'll never forget. But as significant as that earthly moment, it was a mere shadow of an even more profound spiritual reality. For across the expanse of eternity, our heavenly Father responds to our desperate cry as well. No matter what has gotten us to our point of desperation—circumstances, innocence, ignorance, poor choices, or rebellion, none of it matters. The One who knows us intimately runs to those who call to Him in need. We can rest in His safety.

After his arm had been set and everything had settled down for us at the hospital, we had some time to talk. I asked Nic, "Son, what made you call out?"

"Dad, I knew you'd know what to do," came his quiet, yet confident reply. All stubbornness had been set aside and his utter dependence allowed me to cover him, protect him, and give him my best care. What if Nic had pulled away in anger or had hidden his pain to avoid embarrassment or weakness?

## EMBRACING HIS DISCIPLINE

Nic's injury, as it would turn out, was a blessing. Revealing a dangerous weakness in his bone, his injury led to special treatment and it was allowed to heal properly. God's ways are so far beyond our understanding that it is often hard to accept the paths He has for us. Sometimes we simply need direction, and sometimes we must be broken so we might grow straight and strong again.

I've only recently seen the parallel between Nic's story and my own. A broken arm made Nic call out for me, his dad; a destroyed shoulder brought me to my knees, calling out for help and for meaning and healing from my heavenly Dad.

Both in my life and Nic's, Abba used baseball fields to bring us to the point where all we would call out was, "Daaaaaddyyyy!" The One who writes the symphony of our lives also orchestrates events to bring us to an end of ourselves. Left on our own, we would be headed for destruction and death.

God's discipline is always done out of astounding, unfathomable love for training and correction, but never out of punishment. Not only does He bring His correction, but also discipline, protecting us from more serious injury. And this goes for all His children, whom He loves. No one is exempt. We are broken so we might grow stronger.

If we can understand that all discipline is born out of God's love for our benefit, we can accept His discipline rather than rebel and fight. We can trust that His purpose is to keep us from falling into greater pain. He loves us so much He will use anything to keep us safe and to help us grow.

"My son, do not regard lightly the discipline of the Lord, nor faint when you are reproved by Him; for those whom the Lord loves He disciplines...All discipline for the moment seems not to be joyful, but sorrowful; yet to those who have been trained by it, afterwards it yields the peaceful fruit of righteousness" (Hebrews 12:5,6,11).

## Reckless trust

When our youngest son, Kyle, was just four years old, we lived in a home that had a split foyer. Whenever I would come through the door, I would immediately hear the pitter patter of little feet (they were so chubby we called them "marshmallow pads") followed by the appearance of Kyle who would take a flying leap from the top of the stairs into my arms!

I had to be ready for this, and no matter what I had in my hands, I'd have to drop it immediately to catch him! Without ever giving it a thought, my son absolutely trusted I would catch him—until the day a good friend of mine, Jim Mortimer, came home with me and went in the door first!

Sadly, Kyle's reckless trust was shaken that day and though he'd still come running, he'd hesitate for a moment to assess whether he could trust me to catch him. We are like this in our relationship with God. We can only trust Him when we believe He is faithful and trustworthy. When I challenge you to a life of reckless trust, I don't mean living a sinful life, but rather living a life like a child, without fear, willing to risk all because you know for certain Your Father's arm are wide open to receive you.

Do you trust God in all areas of life? Can you leap into His arms without hesitation in those tough areas like finances? Money represents the power of choice. Dare we relinquish control even over our bank accounts? If we are to truly come to know Abba as *Jehovah Jirah*, the One who provides, we must be willing to release all our resources into His hands.

I must confess that I tend to feel more comfortable when God has His money in my bank account than when He has that same money in His account! Still I must ask why? A secure child doesn't worry about how much money is in his own bank account, or his parent's for that matter. What other areas need to be placed into the hands of our daddy? Do you struggle or fear the uncertainty of the future? Do you worry about your husband or children's safety?

*I must confess that I tend to feel more comfortable when God has His money in my bank account than when He has that same money in His account!*

When I read of the sufferings of the early church, of their imprisonment and beatings, and their undying zeal to go out again and again to preach the gospel, I come to the conclusion that they must have known something in their entirety that we've only touched. I get a glimpse of the power, the unwavering faith in Christ they knew so fully, and I must confess, I'm not there yet. Still, I speak with authority, because I've tasted it; I've touched it. I know it's real, even though I've not yet arrived. Even though I'm so young in this journey, I carry this burning flicker. Oh, how I desire that you too will catch the burning flame of the message of our Father's infinite compassion.

The life of the Messiah was marked by rejection, loneliness, misunderstanding, and danger, yet nowhere is Jesus ever recorded as showing fear; only absolute trust. After willingly giving Himself over, He stood before Pilate and said "You would have no authority over Me, unless it had been given you from above" (John 19:11).

Jesus never doubted if He'd done enough to deserve His Father's acceptance. When trouble came He didn't wonder if God was angry.

Jesus showed us that faith is not a struggle, but rather the child's response of utter confidence in Abba. Reckless trust in His Abba's unconditional love carried our Lord through agonizing hours of the Passion Week and to His death and resurrection. With confidence He was able to say, "An hour ... has already come, for you to be scattered, each to his own home, and to leave Me alone; and yet I am not alone, because the Father [Abba] is with Me" (John 16:32). "This childlike trust gave Jesus confidence in the blackest hour of His impending suffering," says Malcolm Smith.[3]

**In Summary**

How do we get to the place where we are able to trust God in such a way that we throw ourselves recklessly into His arms? Just like a little child, our core identity is formed at home, in an abiding relationship with Christ. Jesus says simply, "Make your home in me, as I make mine in you" (John 15:4 JB). Brennan Manning, author of *The Ragamuffin Gospel*, writes, "Home is not a heavenly mansion in the afterlife but a safe place right in the midst of our anxious world."[4]

Max Lucado, in *The Great House of God*, said it this way:

". . . .Home is that sacred space—external or internal—where we don't have to be afraid, where we are confident of hospitality and love... It would have been enough if God had just cleansed your own name, but He does more. He gives you His name. It would be enough if God had just set you free, but He does more. He takes you home. You were intended to live in your Father's house. Any place less than His is insufficient. Any place far from His is dangerous. Only the home built for your heart can protect your heart. And your Father wants you to dwell in Him.[5]

# Reflection ～

A childlike spirit is God's desire for us and it is the only path to experiencing the rest He offers us as our Abba Father. Examine the lists contrasting the Child Spirit and the Adult Spirit to determine if you have fallen prey to a life dominated by Adult thinking.

How would relating to God as an unconditionally loving and perfect Father enable you to move from Adult thinking to a Childlike mind-set?

# God's Desire ～

"The sheep that are My own hear and are listening to My voice, and I know them and they follow me, and I give them eternal life, and they shall never lose it or perish throughout the ages—to all eternity they shall never by any means be destroyed. And no one is able to snatch them out of My hand. My Father, Who has given them to Me, is greater and mightier than all else; and no one is able to snatch them out of the Father's hand. I and the Father are One."
—John 10: 27-30 *The Amplified Bible*

# Your Response ～

*Father, I realize that I don't know You as You really are. Because of this I don't know the kind of intimacy that You desire with me. I want to know You as fully as possible. That can only happen if You help me remove the lies that have blinded me to Your true character. Please, open my eyes to see You in all your glory, majesty, love, grace and goodness.*

# ❧ 18 ❧

# Obedience Unleashed

"Give us love, sweetest of all gifts...Give us in
our hearts pure love, born of your love to us, that we
may love others as you love us."
—Ken Gire[1]

Walking with Abba is an exciting adventure each day because we never know where He will lead us in the next moment. This is what the Father/child relationship is intended to be, reckless child-like trust so we can be free from preoccupation with ourselves! Once I am convinced that I am okay, because God says so, I no longer need to worry about striving to be righteousness. With a sigh of relief, I can now live in quiet assurance. I am free to love others.

❦ ❦ ❦

It's been told that a well-loved evangelist, famous in his day, was on his way to a coliseum to do a crusade. While in route to his destination he was seated near the back of the train in the company of a weathered old man whose presence was made known by a lingering cloud of body odor and stale alcohol. Seemingly unfazed by one another's company, the travelers rode quietly side-by-side.

The drunk, who seemed unaware of anyone other than himself, took a nip periodically from the bottle concealed in a brown bag. But all at once the inebriated beggar stopped his bottle midway, looked over at the other passenger and offered him a drink. The evangelist responded politely with, "No thank you, sir."

This same scenario happened several times more until finally the conductor of the train came back to notify the evangelist, by name, of the train's arrival. "Reverend Trumbull, we are nearing the coliseum."

When the evangelist's name was announced, the bum flinched visibly, and was embarrassed by what he'd done. Stammering, he tried to slur an apology. "I'm. . .I'm so-rry, rev-rund. I bet you think I'm a no good drun-ken sinner!" Hanging his head, he awaited the inevitable chastisement. But as the famous preacher gathered his belongings he answered in a tender voice, "No, on the contrary. I think you're a very generous man."

As the story goes, not long after his ride with the evangelist, the drunken man made a decision to follow Christ and went on to live wholly dedicated to serving God; his life forever changed by the grace extended to him one day at the back of a train.

❦   ❦   ❦

Because Abba loves and accepts us so completely, we no longer need to follow certain practices or to go to others for validation. This brings us exhilarating freedom to focus on God's desire to love others through us. The moment our eyes open in the morning, we can wait with eager anticipation for God's voice to instruct us on how together we will love that day.

If God's part in the New Covenant could be summed up in one word, it would be GRACE. Our part summed up in one word would be LOVE . . . and true love results in an open-hearted response of overflowing gratitude and awe which looks very much like acts of love. In other words, OBEDIENCE.

Could this be what Jesus meant when He said, "If you love Me, you will keep My commandments" (John 14:15)?

Keeping God's commandments is no drill. Jesus was so certain of His Father's love, and abided so completely in that love, that keeping the Father's commands came naturally. Doing nothing apart from God was His normal mode of operation. This is the way He lived, long before ever asking us to do likewise.

"Truly, truly I say to you, the Son can do nothing of Himself, unless it is something He sees the Father doing; for whatever the Father does, these things the Son also does in like manner." (John 5:19)

Here Jesus is saying that He, even the very Son of God, would do nothing apart from our Father. His desire was to be only a vessel, allowing God to live through Him.

But He didn't stop there. He tells us that it is good that He went away, so that the Holy Spirit can come and indwell each one of us, so we too can be assured of the love of God (John 16:7). The lessons He learned from His Father, we learn from Him. So we too will be able to be vessels through which He lives and acts. Paul assures us, "we have this treasure in earthen vessels, that the surpassing greatness of the power may be of God and not from ourselves" (2 Corinthians 4:7).

*And when He is living with us and through us, this is what it means, "to abide."*

This, my friend, is *zoe* life in its entirety. Christ is the only one able to live this life! The one and only one, but He chooses to live it through us! And when He is living with us and through us, this is what it means, "to abide."

### The Abiding Life

The night before Jesus was betrayed, He knew He must instill some final comfort and wisdom to His closest and dearest disciples. This night would be the last time they would see Him before His crucifixion. In the few short hours that lay ahead, what would He tell them? What words of lasting power and significance would He choose to impart from His Father? What could He do or say to communicate eternal love? How would He adequately instruct them to live in His absence?

If I were in His shoes, sitting across from my sons at the foot of my bed, knowing I would die in the night, I can scarcely imagine the deep emotion and sense of urgency that would overtake me. Tears would run down my cheeks as I looked into each of my sons' expectant eyes. What does a father say in a moment like this?

Jesus took His disciples for a walk that night through a nearby vineyard. While strolling through the rows of well-tended vines, He wanted them to taste and touch, to engage every one of their senses so they would never forget the words He was about to share from His Father. This is what He said, "I am the vine, you are the branches; he who abides in Me, and I in him, he bears much fruit; for apart from Me you can do nothing" (John 15:5).

Showing the tender and protective heart of God for His children, Christ shares the innermost secrets of His Father. Jesus must make certain His followers understand clearly that He is the *only* person capable of living the Christian life and always will be. His Father didn't want any of His children to come under the weight of having to perform to certain standards or be crushed under the condemnation of others. He knew without a doubt that we would be dismal failures if we tried this on our own, just as the early Christians would have been, had they not waited for the Holy Spirit to come upon them.

*Jesus knew how desperately we would fail if we attempted to live like Him without abiding in Him.*

In the early part of Acts, Jesus told His disciples they would be His witnesses and would do even greater things than they had seen Him do. "But," He warned, "Do not attempt to do this on your own! Go up to your room, and for 'heaven's sake,' don't come out until the Spirit comes upon you. If you attempt to do this on your own, you'll blow it!" *Jesus knew how desperately we would fail if we attempted to live like Him without abiding in Him.*

Abiding in Christ means "to remain, dwell in, or make your home in." This is the highest form of obedience we could ever attain. Basically, obedience means that if you are in Christ, stay where you are! Remain where you were meant to live . . . in Him. The branch stays connected to the vine, daily drawing life from it. Abiding is this intimate sharing of *zoe* life from the Vine and expressing love as our natural response. Brennan Manning, teaches this lesson well, reminding us:

> Just as a mother does not think in terms of law and obligation when, in the middle of the night, she runs to the bedside of her crying child, but rather responds naturally to her maternal being. . .When through the Spirit we live in Christ Jesus, life is doing what comes supernaturally. Our new being over flows into action as the natural expression of our real self.[2]

The abiding life means, "We love, because He first loved us" (1 John 4:19).

## What Obedience is Not

Obedience is often misunderstood because it is easily confused with "doing" rather than "being"—the essence of abiding with Christ. To clear away some common misconceptions, let's briefly consider what obedience is not.

OBEDIENCE IS NOT FORMULIZING.

*Obedience focuses on God, hearing His voice and obeying His will.*

Have you ever focused so hard on one object that everything else gets blurry? Perhaps you are focusing on a particular discipline: "I will not eat that cake. . . I will not eat that cake!" And all the while God is trying to tell you to go hug your child. But because you are so focused on not consuming extra calories, The Holy Spirit's voice is drowned out by your own will to not eat, all the while missing the opportunity of extending His love to your child. Like this example, formulas focus on a set of dictates and performing according to them. Obedience focuses on

God, hearing His voice and obeying His will.

We've seen grace expressed, but the danger now lies in making what we do an established form. Take for instance, the story of the evangelist on the train. Our tendency is to model his exact example in responding to a drunk, rather than listening to the Holy Spirit prompt us in responding uniquely to our own given situation. Churches tend to clone model ministries and we tend to copy respected leaders. We may miss the point of grace entirely if we make a predictable equation out of saying, "No thank you" to an offer from a drunk when God may actually be whispering, "Invite him home for supper." What if He gently prompted you to accept the man's kind offer to take a sip?!

*It is a profound irony that the Son of God visited this planet and one of the chief complaints against Him was that He was not religious enough.*

I believe that when God tells me to do something out of the ordinary, even if it's an act that borders on the radical, as long as it does not clearly violate His Word, I can boldly go for it. If for some reason I misunderstood, His grace will catch me and I can continue on without fear. By doing so, I'll just keep getting better and better at hearing my Lord, and be more and more thankful for his marvelous grace!

## OBEDIENCE IS NOT FOLLOWING MAN-MADE TRADITIONS.

Obedience does not always follow the traditions of men. If we keep our focus on serving God first and foremost, we will be in line with His desires even if, at times, we are not in line with the wishes of some Christians. Says, the author of *Holy Sweat*, Tim Hansel, "The religious accused Jesus of being a drunkard, a glutton and having tacky taste in friends . . . It is a profound irony that the Son of God visited this planet and one of the chief complaints against Him was that He was not religious enough."[3]

## OBEDIENCE IS NOT SINLESS PERFECTION.

Though we have been cleansed of our sin and indwelt by God, we still have the capacity to walk in the flesh and sin. The Bible would not tell us to stop presenting our bodies to sin as instruments of unrighteousness, if doing so was not possible (see Romans 6:12-13). But because Christ has set us free from the bondage of sin, we are given the choice of *posse cari*, choosing not to sin. And what about the command to be perfect (Matthew 5:48)? "Perfection," taught St. Therese, "consists simply of doing [God's] will and being just what [He] wants us to be."[4]

## OBEDIENCE IS NOT PASSIVITY

Abiding is not sitting and doing nothing. I assure you, God is very active and if you are allowing Him to live through you, you will be bold in knowing which actions to take. God invites, but never forces us to participate with Him.

"But by the grace of God I am what I am, and His grace toward me did not prove vain; but I labored even more than all of them, *yet not I, but by the grace of God with me*" (1 Corinthians 15:10, italics mine).

## OBEDIENCE DOES NOT NEGATE INDIVIDUAL PERSONALITY.

Lastly, we must know that when God raised us to newness of life, we maintained our personal uniqueness. Our heart is knit together with His, but it is still our heart. The Scriptures say each of us is a one-of-a-kind masterpiece painted by the Master Painter, Himself (Psalm 139).

*Lastly, we must know that when God raised us to newness of life, we maintained our personal uniqueness.*

Imagine for a moment, a long string of Christmas lights in various colors. We know the source of each bulb is a white light, but each light is encased in a different colored shell. Just like the string of bulbs, which are all lit with the same white light, (representing the Light of Christ), we are all clothed in an array of colored casings and will express Christ in a way that is uniquely ours.

A good friend of mine, Steve Balsley recently shared how God comforted him and his family after the loss of a loved one, "You know, in real life Jesus just doesn't look like He does in His pictures. Today He looked like Todd, encouraging me through him. Yesterday he looked just like Terri, giving my wife a hug."

"You are our letter, written in our hearts. . .written not with ink but with the Spirit of the living God, not on tablets of stone, but on tablets of human hearts (2 Corinthians 3:2-3).

"If we know that each of us is absolutely unique, then our encounters with God will likewise be unique. No one will ever have the same relationship with God that you do. No one,"[5] says Tim Hansel. We are one of a kind, a letter from Christ, written by the Spirit of the living God to the world.

> *Obedience is not the pious attitudes, actions or motives we may have believed it to be, but rather it is simply expressing our love which has been given to us by Him*

## What Obedience Is

Obedience is not the pious attitudes, actions or motives we may have believed it to be, *but rather it is simply expressing our love which has been given to us by Him.* If we truly have the Spirit of Christ within, we will yearn to do right . . . even when we feel selfish, needy, and tired. The abiding life is one where we relinquish our own motives and goals and enjoy the stroll with the One we love. Obeying God is often considered a duty, but how mistaken that is. If we respond and walk according to the path God has laid before us, we will be focused on a much greater cause than our own limited agendas and self-centered desires. In other words, obedience means . . . *to listen.*

Says Hansel,

"The ultimate call is not that we are committed to a task, but to a Person. There's a time to roll up your sleeves, but that time must also be matched with a time to be still, to listen—which is the core of obedience. In fact, the word obedience comes from the root oboedire, which means,'to listen.'"[6]

To listen means we are willing to open ourselves up to developing a deep and lasting friendship established in trust. The degree to which we are willing to listen, is directly related to the vitality and delight of our friendship with Him.

## Strolling in the Spirit (Listening)

Obedience means we are walking in step with God. We are familiar with the concept of "walking in the Spirit," which brings to mind brisk action, much like an aerobic walk like the idea of strolling. Unlike simply following or keeping a quick pace on a busy street, strolling brings to mind patches of afternoon sun sprinkling down through the leaves of trees lining a winding path where lovers meander—*with no set goal in mind other than being together.* Likewise strolling in the Spirit means spending time with a very good Friend.

There's a mountain behind our counseling center and sometimes, when a buddy of mine stops by, we grab the next available time slot, ditch the office and head for the hills. Sometimes I talk; sometimes I listen to what he's got to say. But much of the time, we just walk with each other soaking in all that's going on around us and between us, all the while being continually aware of each other's presence.

"Look at those clouds," my friend might say. "Wow!" I respond. "And God made them just for us." Or I might say, "Check out the eagle!" To which my friend might respond, "Yes, and He made her just for us." But often, we just walk together and that is enough.

*Talking some, listening some, but always continually being aware of Christ's presence wherever I go, whatever I do.*

I think this is what walking in the Spirit is like. Talking some, listening some, but always *continually being aware of Christ's presence wherever I go, whatever I do.* This idea is somewhat new for me so I try to practice the presence of God by ditching my busy schedule and taking walks with Him like I do my other friends.

"Wow, look at that beautiful deer bounding through the field!" I might say. "Yes," God responds. "And I made him just for you." Or I might say, "Check out that beautiful woman lying by the pool!" To which Abba responds, "Indeed, my son, but I made her for someone else."

This kind of "walking in the Spirit" is quite different from the "quiet time" approach where we make little compartments in our life and then anticipate that God will remain in a select few of these compartments but not others. Isn't it common for us to say things like "I need to spend time with God," or "I'm so far away from the Lord right now," or even "I need to pray more?" This paradigm doesn't fit at all with the Biblical fact that *Christ has, in reality, already taken up a permanent, permeating residence at the very core of our life!*

*Even more so, when I'm walking in the Spirit, engaged in a moment-by-moment strolling dialog with the Spirit, it seems unnatural to sin.*

I'm very much in favor of focused, one-on-one time with Christ. I look at my "quiet time" with God like I look at a special date with my wife. Give me a Bible, a quiet room and an hour, and I feel you've given me a small piece of heaven. Nevertheless, if we think we leave Jesus behind in the morning when we close our Bible and say "Amen," we're missing out on the profound, powerful, and practical walk with Abba. I believe this is what the Lord meant when He instructed us to "pray without ceasing" (1 Thessalonians 5:17). "Lo, I am with you always . . ." (Matthew 28:10). "Walk with Me," He quietly invites.

There is a powerful and practical side affect of this approach to walking in the Spirit. The majority of our struggles or demons are battled when we feel alone and discouraged. If I was spending the day with someone I really love and respect, I seriously doubt that I would be inclined to shoplift, surf for internet porn, drink too much, or even gossip. It just wouldn't be the natural thing to do in the presence of someone I love and respect. Even more so, when I'm walking in the Spirit, engaged in a moment-by-moment strolling dialog with the Spirit, it seems unnatural to sin. It just doesn't fit. The more we become aware that He is with us, the less inclined we are to act independently of Him and sin. The Bible doesn't say to quit walking in the flesh so that you can walk in the Spirit. Paul wrote, "But I say, walk by the Spirit, and you will not carry out the desires of the flesh" (Galatians 5:16).

## Focusing on a Greater Cause

Fred has a problem with drinking too much alcohol. Though he's been counseled numerous times to stop drinking and to memorize the verse that says not to be drunk with wine but be filled with the Holy Spirit, he still sometimes stops at the liquor store and drinks in excess.

Suppose Fred is traveling on the freeway home, toying with the idea of making another stop at the liquor store. Just before the exit, he gets a call on his cell phone saying that his son has been in a car accident and has been taken to the emergency room. What is Fred most likely going to do? Because *his focus is now on something greater*, he doesn't even consider stopping at the liquor store. Instead he thinks of nothing but getting to his son. He is drawn by something (in this case someone) more powerful in his life than drink.

So is it when we focus on God who is in us. Ephesians 1:19 says there is a power of surpassing greatness at work towards those who believe. This is one manner in which God calls us to obedience. Focus is changed by a greater cause and *our good works are the result of His life in us*. Our efforts are not the condition, or the secret, or the cause of His life in us.

## Desire not a Duty

While teaching I am often asked the question, "Doesn't acting in obedience put us right back into performance mode, yoking us back to the law?" To which, I must answer with another question. "Do we obey out of duty or desire?" Which would you prefer, your spouse to come home because it is expected of him or because he can't wait to see you?

*It may sound strange, but I really began to enjoy the Bible when I realized that I didn't have to read it.*

It may sound strange, but I really began to enjoy the Bible when I realized that I didn't have to read it. Is there a law that requires we read the Bible a certain amount of time each day? No! Then why read it? Because we love God and have a desire to fellowship with Him in His Word, and because we believe He is the source of true wisdom for living. When I was a legalist, *I was bound and determined* to read the Bible because I felt I must. Now I am free to read it because it is what I want, and even when I don't feel like it, I know it is still wise for me to do so!

God doesn't love you more because you obey, but it is what you were created for. This is one of the purposes for which He removed your sins; so that His Spirit can indwell you! All the commandments— all true obedience is summed up in the phrase, "Love one another" (1 John 4). That's what we were made for!

*When we allow Him to perform the Father's wishes through us, our joy will be full.*

When we allow Him to perform the Father's wishes through us, our joy will be full. I forget this sometimes myself. For example, Satan comes to me and says, "Now here you are, giving your wife Nancy a back rub, isn't that nice of you . . . say, when was the last time she rubbed your back?"

At first I think, "I'm not going to listen to that, I'm fulfilled . . . well, now that you mention it, about two weeks!" All of a sudden my focus shifts from loving my wife to dwelling on what Nancy has not done for me, and pretty soon I'm miserable. I even begin to focus on how I can get her to do things for me, and when she doesn't, I'm discontent. I started out fulfilled and satisfied and now, after dwelling on the lie, I'm unhappy and focused on myself.

John Piper addresses this common scenario in his book, *The Dangerous Duty of Delight*, and says this about marriage, "If you live for your private pleasure at the expense of your spouse, you are living against yourself and destroying your joy. But if you devote yourself with all your heart to the holy joy of your spouse, you will always be living for your joy and making a marriage after the image of Christ."[8]

I'm learning . . . slowly . . . about responding in delight rather than simply fulfilling or expecting duty. Besides, I already have what Satan is offering; he is trying to convince me that I don't; just as Eve and Adam already had what the deceiver was offering them. They didn't need anything more, they were already content and fulfilled.

Satan is forever offering us nothing! There is nothing The Father of Lies likes better than to have a child of God believe his or her Father is holding out!

## Dangerous Desires?

Many Christians believe that God does not want them to realize their desires, and are easily convinced that our longings are sinful and selfish. But the psalmist prayed that God would give us the desires of our hearts (Psalm 37:4). Wasn't it our Maker who instilled the desire (not to be confused with temptation) in the first place? Do you love poetry? Numbers? Music? Nature? Dance? Children? We are often deceived into believing that the greatest virtue is unselfishness rather than love. C.S. Lewis says in his sermon, *The Weight of Glory*, "The idea of unselfishness carries with it the suggestion not primarily of securing good things for others, but of going without them ourselves, as if our abstinence and not their happiness was the important point."[9]

We can certainly be obedient and still have dreams come true. In fact, our delight is encouraged especially when it is uplifting to others. Our fulfillment is actually considered praise when it glorifies God. Making personal sacrifice does not necessarily mean that we are meeting the needs of others or expressing God's love. "Of this I am certain," said Albert Schweitzer, "The only ones among you who will be truly happy are those who have sought and found how to serve."[10] Ask God to reveal how together you can live and serve in your fullest potential!

## Producing Fruit

"By this is my Father glorified, that you bear much fruit, and so prove to be My disciples." —John 15: 8

We can't discuss obedience without bringing up the loaded discussion about fruit. We can't deny God's Word where it says He is glorified when our lives not only bear fruit a little, but much fruit. Now be careful, this is a heavy grid for the majority of us. The

Bible candidly says that in order to prove our devotion as disciples, we must bear fruit. The tendency is to become "fruit factories," and in their spare time, Christians preoccupy themselves with judging others' fruit! How can this possibly be separated from performance?

The key is found in defining spiritual fruit. How do you define the fruit that brings glory to our Father? Having someone come to Christ or memorizing verses, or going to church? Indeed these actions are fruit for the Kingdom, but in light of our new understanding of obedience, spiritual produce has a much broader definition.

*Christian fruit, likewise, is the outward expression of the inward nature of Christ— this is the glory of God!*

Fruit is described as the outward expression of the inward nature. If you see apples on a tree, you know that the inward nature of the tree is, in fact, apple. If the inward nature of a tree is apple, we can be sure it will not bear oranges. Christian fruit, likewise, is the outward expression of the inward nature of Christ—this is the glory of God! Remember, "The fruit of the Spirit is love, joy, peace, patience kindness, goodness, faithfulness, gentleness and self control; against such things there is no law" (Galatians 5:22-23).

Therefore, we can anticipate our fruit to be the fruits of the Spirit in action. Bearing fruit might be to love your child by holding him on your lap and reading him a story. It might mean spending the evening with an elderly aunt instead of going to church Wednesday night.

But again, the key is this: *We can only bear fruit by abiding in Jesus.* (John 15:5) When we do, He works through us, He bears the fruit, and that proves we are His disciples.

## What About Disobedience

If I were to claim that I value a friendship with you, and yet it became obvious that your opinion matters little to me, and if I rarely honor anything you desire or ask, it would be hard to deny our relationship was not nearly as meaningful as I might claim.

Similarly, if we find ourselves fighting against what God asks of us and what He says is best, we must honestly assess why.

To choose our own way above God's is a form of self-worship. By doing things my own way, I am stating to myself and the world that I know better than God does. The opposite is also true. When I obey, I am declaring He knows best and my life is then a high form of praise to Him—a life of worship.

**When I obey, I am declaring He knows best and my life is then a high form of praise to Him—a life of worship.**

God is good and when we are obedient to His will, we experience our oneness with *zoe* life. Being submissive to His perfect and loving ways means we have to trust Him. He alone brings abundance and reward, whereas rebellion against His desires guarantees nothing but trouble.

Let's say, for instance, there is a sticker on the lid to your car's gas tank that says "diesel fuel only" but you decide to try unleaded anyway. You are certainly *free* to pick which kind of fuel to use, but your choice carries heavy *consequences*. Says Chuck Swindoll in *The Grace Awakening*, "I'm free to choose righteousness or disobedience. If I choose the latter I will have to take the consequences: mental anguish, a guilty conscience, hurting and offending others... and bringing reproach to the name of Christ."[11]

When Christ came, He freed us, leaving us with a decision. We can submit to Him as our Master, or we can go back and opt for sin to master us. *When we trust our own decisions more than those of Abba, we are literally giving power to the sin we wish to be free from* (see Ecclesiastes 8:11, Romans 1:24, 1 Corinthians 15:56). Do you trust that God knows best for you each day? Obedience is the test.

❧ ❧ ❧

If you're worried that my attitude toward obedience may be too lax, and that living the abiding life may not accomplish enough for the kingdom, you may be surprised to learn that a person expressing love through grace will out perform anyone under law. I've seen it time after time. For example, giving a tithe of ten percent is often regarded as a law. But how much more generous would we be if we listened to God's prompting to meet the needs of others, regardless of the amount, in whatever capacity He was nudging us?

This kind of dependence on God, this kind of listening and obedience requires faith. "Faith comes along when we realize that we cannot do it on our own,"[12] said Joseph Garlington. Faith is our mode of operation. To live in faith is to be so focused on the object of our relationship, Jesus, and where He is leading that we forget all about our feet. In any act of obedience, love is our motivation and the Holy Spirit our power. "If you learn that you never have to perform in order to continue in His love then you will have an awakening desire to perform as never before to please him,"[13] says H.R. Roush, author of *Jesus Loves Me*.

What is our main purpose in life? It can be summed up in two parts. The first is to be in relationship with God; to know and love Him. The second part of our purpose is to declare God, by bearing His image, so the rest of the world will know what He is like and can come to love Him too. In order to do this we must return to the original design; living in union with our Creator so that our whole being; body, soul, and spirit, be kept blameless (see 1 Thessalonians 5:23). Digging into one of the clearest and yet most mysterious truths of the Bible, we find the supernatural reality that *"it is no longer I who live, but Christ who lives in me"* (Galatians 2:20).

❦ ❦ ❦

Perhaps Eden isn't so far away. Living a life of grace is that moment-by-moment strolling dialog with God: listening, speaking, moving, pausing, laughing, resting. Yes, much like a dance. As you may remember, my wife Nancy loves to dance, and as you hear her story you'll know why:

"When I was a little girl I was one of the lucky ones who had grandparents living nearby. I would get to go and stay with my grandma and grandpa for a week or two at a time. Their house was filled with treasures and privileges different from the ones at home. One of these special treats was when Grandpa and Grandma took me along to the dance that took place every Saturday in the little neighboring town of Whitewood. This was the big event of the week and we all dressed in our finest. My grandpa wore a suit and tie. He smelled like Old Spice and his shoes shone like the sun.

"Sipping on red punch and munching a cookie, I would eagerly a wait my turn to dance with Grandpa. When it was finally time, he'd take me in his arms and set my little feet on his big shiny shoes and we would dance. Oh how we would dance! We twirled and we whirled in perfect time to the music. I would throw my head back and feel as if I was flying! My Grandfather danced with the refined movement and ease known only by those who've danced for more than forty years. Together, we were poetry in motion.

"While snuggling under the blankets back at my grandparents' house after a glorious evening, I'd sometimes wonder how I might look if my grandfather had been invisible. *On-lookers would have seen a young girl waltzing around the room with sweeping style and grace, uninhibited and free.* Dozing off, I couldn't imagine dancing without Grandfather. As long as I was in his arms, I'd never have to worry about performing the moves right. In his arms, I too was a grand dancer."

Isn't this where we yearn to be, dancing freely in our grand Father's arms? Isn't this what the world needs to see, us standing on the feet of Jesus, making visible the invisible, God loving through us? Isn't this what our friends and family need to hear, Him speaking though our words, and our actions communicating the whole gospel of His grace? Though He is bodily invisible to the world's eyes, when we're dancing in the arms of Abba, we can be seen living the carefree life we were meant to live. It is then that He is glorified. It is then that the world will want to know the One who leads us.

## In Summary

Obedience is our love expressed, pouring forth from the Source of abundant joy. Now we can forget about self and love one another. This is the commandment in which all others are fulfilled. We have the love of Christ to lead us. If we allow Him to live through us, saturating our souls with His truth and unleashing His presence through our spirit, He will propel us far beyond daily struggles with sin and merely getting by. Moreover, we will express love in ways never before imagined.

"These things I have spoken to you, that My joy may be in you, and that your joy may be made full."

—John 15:11

# Reflection ~~

Take an hour this week to stroll with God through His creation. Try it! Carve out a good chunk of time and really go for a walk with Him. As your eye is caught by things especially meaningful to you, remember to attribute that as a gift of love from His heart to yours.

If you were to practice being continually aware of God's presence every moment as you go through the day, what effect would this have on your attitude and behavior?

# God's Desire ~~

"And we have come to know and have believed the love which God has for us. God is love, and the one who abides in love abides in God, and God abides in him. By this, love is perfected with us, that we may have confidence in the day of judgment; because as He is, so also are we in this world. There is no fear in love; but perfect love casts out fear, because fear involves punishment, and the one who fears is not perfected in love."
—I John 4:16-18

"For the grace of God has appeared, bringing salvation to all men, instructing us to deny ungodliness and worldly desires and to live sensibly, righteously and godly in the present age, looking for the blessed hope and the appearing of the glory of our great God and Savior, Christ Jesus; who gave Himself for us, that He might redeem us from every lawless deed and purify for Himself a people for his own possession, zealous for good deeds."
—Titus 2:11-14

# Your Response ~~

*Father, please show me when my motivation for obedience is coming from duty rather than from desire. Help me to realize that when I am acting out of duty, I am cutting myself off from the power of Your Spirit and am, once again, trying to earn Your love. Use me, in any way You see fit, as I continually rest in You, to bring the sweet fragrance of Your love to each person You place in my path today. Through Your power and love alone will my brief life count for eternity. So I choose, by Your grace, to remain in You, to make my home in You forever.*

"I have loved you with an everlasting love; therefore, I have
drawn you with lovingkindness
Again I will build you, and you shall be rebuilt...
Again you shall take up your tambourines,
And go forth to the dances of the merrymakers."
—Jeremiah 31:3-4

# ⚜ 19 ⚜

# Final Thought

"Within our hearts is a longing—A profound cry
of the soul for something our theologies can only point us to,
but never replace; intimacy with God."
—Ken Gire[1]

Spiros Zodiates, a well-respected Greek scholar, defined *zoe* as "a noble word expressing all of the highest and best which Christ is and which He gives to the saints. The *highest blessedness* of the creature."[2] When Christ raises us to newness of life, as described in the book of Romans chapter six, we are raised to a life in which we are intimately united with Him.

The highest and best of who He is, Christ gave to us! Dare we begin to grasp this truth? Abiding with Him means to enter that blessed intimate union—a union before shared between only the Father, Son, and Holy Spirit!

Says Jean Eudes,

"He belongs to you, but more than that, he longs to be in you, living and ruling in you as the head lives and rules in the body. He wants his breath to be in your breath, his heart in your heart, and his soul in your soul, so that you may indeed "Glorify God and bear him in your body, that the life of Jesus may be made manifest in you."[3]

To live fully and abundantly in *zoe* means to dance free of our grids, free of the expectations of exhausting Christian traditions, and free from the rigorous labor of self-effort. Free falling into Abba's arms with the new found freedom of a little child . . . this is as good as it gets. Troubles will come, but even in those times, God will hold you and lift you up in His love. How little we know, yet like a child, how much we can trust! I pray you will be moved to escape the noise—audible, mental, relational, and emotional noise—that bombards your soul. May your heart be opened with fresh sensitivity to Abba and the enjoyment that awaits you as you stroll through life with Him.

Dare to be caught up in the melodies of grace and freedom.

*There is something about a baseball field. It's hard to put my finger on just what that something is, but as far back as I can remember, I wanted to be nowhere else. Was it the smell of fresh cut grass in the early morning? Was it the freshly oiled leather in my glove, or the feel of a baseball's stitching on my fingertips?*

Do you yearn for those carefree days . . . daring to dream . . . dance . . . to live again? Do you hear Abba say, "You are Mine. I AM yours. I AM the Life you so desperately seek. Won't you join Me?"

REFERENCES

## Introduction
[1] Hannah Whitall Smith, *The God of all Comfort* (Chicago: Moody Press, 1956), 7.
[2] Ken Gire, *Windows of the Soul* (Grand Rapids, MI: Zondervan Publishing House, 1996), 99-100.

## Chapter 2
[1] Preston Gillham, *E-grace*, "Abusive Husband," #79.
[2] John Eldridge, *The Journey of Desire* (Nashville, TN: Thomas Nelson, 2000), 2.
[3] Rachel Naomi Remen, *Kitchen Table Wisdom*, 8.
[4] Phillip, Yancey, *Reaching for the Invisible God* (Grand Rapids, MI: Zondervan), 52.
[5] Hannah Whitall Smith, *The God of All Comfort* (Chicago: Moody Press, 1956), 9.
[6] Steve McVey, *The Divine Invitation* (Eugene, OR: Harvest House Publishers, 2002), 132. (McVey is quoting Tony Campolo.)
[7] Derived from Hannah Whitall Smith.
[8] Steve McVey, *Grace Walk* (Eugene, OR: Harvest House Publishers, 2002), 17.
[9] Lee LeFebre, *Control Freaks* (Self-published pamphlet).
[10] Ibid.
[11] Charles Trumble, *Victory in Christ* (Fort Washington, PA: CLC Publications, 2002), 9.
[12] Phillip Yancey, *Reaching for the Invisible God* (Grand Rapids, MI: Zondervan Publishing House) ,18.

## Chapter 3
[1] Doug Herman, *What Good is God* (Grand Rapids, MI: Baker Books, 2002), 129-131.
[2] Henri J.M. Nouwen, *The Way of the Heart* (New York: Ballantine Books, 1981), 29.

## Chapter 4

[1] Gene Edwards, *Divine Romance* (Wheaton, IL: Tyndale House, 1993) xi, xii, xiii, 5.

[2] John Eldridge, *The Journey of Desire* (Nashville, TN: Thomas Nelson), 92

[3] *The NIV Worship Bible*, (Grand Rapids, MI: The Corinthian Group, Inc.), 1.

## Chapter 5

[1] Jeff VanVonderen, Good News for the Chemically Dependent and Those Who Love Them (Minneapolis MN: Bethany House Publishers, 1991)

[2] Union Life Ministries, The Mystery of the Gospel (Grand Rapids, MI: Dickenson Press Inc.).

[3] Robert McGee, The Search for Significance (Nashville, TN: Word Publishing, 1998), 21

## Chapter 6

[1] Ravi Zaccharius, from www.blueletterbible.com.

[2] Ibid.

[3] Jan David Hettingta, *Follow Me, Experience the Loving Leadership of Jesus* (Colorado Springs, CO: NavPress, 1996), 17.

[4] C.S. Lewis, Source Unknown.

[5] Jim Craddock, *Be Transformed* (Oklahoma City, OK: Scope Ministries International, 1998), vii.

[6] Here I have bracketed practical applications following each promise of the Scripture provided by Wayne Barber.

[7] A.W. Tozer, *The Pursuit of Man* (Camp Hill, PA: Christian Publications, 1978), 648.

[8] Hettingta, 24.

[9] Ibid, 9.

[10] Martin Luther, Source Unknown.

[11] Charles R. Swindoll, *Grace Awakening* (Word Publishing, 1990), 136.

[12] Richard Foster, *Celebration of Discipline; The Path to Spiritual Growth* (San Francisco: Harper, 1988), 15-16.

[13] Dietrich Bonhoeffer, *The Way to Freedom* (New York: Harper & Row, 1966), 59.

[14] St. Ambrose, *The NIV Worship Bible* (Dana Point, CA: The Corinthian Group, 2000), 6.

## Chapter 8

[1] Ken Blue, *Healing Spiritual Abuse; How to Break Free from Bad Church Experiences* (Downers Grove, IL: InterVarsity Press, 1993),10.

[2] Jerry MacGregor, *1001 Surprising Things You Should Know About the Bible* (Grand Rapids, MI: Baker Books, 2002), 14. According to MacGregor, not only is the Bible the world's best-selling book, it's the most shoplifted book!

[3] Adapted from Steve McVey, *Grace Walk* (Eugene, OR: Harvest House Publishers, 1995), 85.

[4] Jerry MacGregor & Marie Prys, *1001 Surprising Things You Should Know About the Bible* (Grand Rapids, MI: Baker Books, 2002), 16.

[5] Both the Jewish Bible and Christian Old Testament contain the same thirty-nine books, although they are arranged and numbered in a slightly different order. In Jewish traditions the Bible is call the *Tanakh*, an acronym of the Hebrew words *Torah* (for "law" or "teaching"), *Nevi'im* ("the Prophets"), and *Kethuvim* ("the Writings").


[6] In first century Judaism, there were as many different sects and branches of beliefs as there are denominations today! One of the primary characteristics of the Pharisees was their devotion to the ancient "traditions of Israel or the Fathers"—*non-biblical* oral laws (known as Halakah) and customs "believed" to have been passed down from generation to generation. . . all the way back to Mt. Sinai.

The prevailing Pharasaic worldview at the time of Jesus was that every Israelite was secured a place in the world-to-come. This was based upon a status of "righteousness." In other words, righteousness was believed to be attributed to all who are members of the Covenant YHWH God had made with Israel.

In other words, the sages of Paul's day believed that God chose Israel not of His own Sovereign choice, but because she deserved to be chosen! And further, that God offered Torah to all the nations, but only Israel was willing to receive it. Therefore, a "works of righteousness" of the Fathers was credited to the Covenant Nation without faith nor a biblical focus on the Promised One to come.

Paul, however, discovered in Torah that a "renewed" covenant in

301

Jeremiah would be received and embraced by "faith" bringing with it the enablement to live out the ways of God . . .since "righteousness" was credited to anyone on the basis of the atonement of Messiah, the finished work of redemption.

[7] Spiros Zodhiates, TH.d., ed. *Lexicon to the Old and New Testaments, Hebrew Greek Key Study Bible* (AMG Publishers, Chattanooga, TN 37422, U.S.A.1997), 1791.

[8] Steve McVey, *Grace Walk* (Eugene, OR: Harvest House, 1995), 115.

[9] Blue, 52.

[10] Ibid, 59.


## Chapter 9

[1] Bill Gillham, *Lifetime Guarantee* (Eugene OR: Harvest House, 1993), 51.


## Chapter 10

[1] Dr. Paul Brand & Phillip Yancey, *Fearfully & Wonderfully Made* (Grand Rapids, MI: Zondervan Publishing House, 1981), unnumbered page.

[2] Lewis Thomas as quoted in *The Medusa and the Snail*. Dr. Paul Brand & Philip Yancey, *Fearfully & Wonderfully Made* (Grand Rapids, MI: Zondervan Publishing House, 1981), 25.

[3] Hansel, Tim, *Holy Sweat* (Dallas TX: Word Publishing), 113.

[4] Ibid.

[5] Andrew Murray, as quoted by Jim Craddock, *Pneumenetics* (Oklahoma City, OK: Scope Ministries).

[6] Penn-Lewis, as quoted by Jim Craddock, *Pneumenetics* (Oklahoma City, OK: Scope Ministries).

[7] Philip Yancey, *Reaching for the Invisible God* (Grand Rapids, MI: Zondervan Publishing House), 106.

[8] Bob George, Growing In Grace (Eugene OR: Harvest House, 1991), 12.


## Chapter 11

[1] A. W. Tozer, *The Divine Conquest* (Camp Hill, PA: Christian Publications, 1992), 36-7.

[2] Preston Gillham, Lifetime Guarantee Ministries, *E-Grace*, Article #54.

[3] Gillham, Article #66 & 67.

[4] Gillham, Article #21.

[5] Dick Flaten, *Marvelous Exchange* (Dallas TX: Exchanged Life Ministries), 20.

[6] Max Lucado, *A Gentle Thunder* (Dallas TX: Word Publishing), 86-7.

[7] Charles Trumbull, *Victory in Christ* (Fort Washington, PA: CLC Publications, Pocket Companion Edition, 1991), 26.

**Chapter 12**

[1] Charles Trumble, *Victory in Christ* (Fort Washington, PA: CLC Publications, Pocket Companion Edition, 1991).

[2] James M. Boice, *Romans, Volume 2: the Reign of Grace*, Romans 5:1-8:39 (Grand Rapids: Baker Book House), 670.

[3] D. Martyn Lloyd-Jones, *Romans, The New Man: An Exposition of Chapter 6* (Grand Rapids: Zondervan Publishing House, 1973), 84.

[4] Jerry MacGregor & Marie Prys, *1001 Surprising Things You Should Know About the Bible* (Grand Rapids, MI: Baker Books, 2002), 49.

[5] Lloyd-Jones, 83.

**Chapter 13**

[1] Philip Yancey, *What's So Amazing About Grace* (Grand Rapids, MI: Zondervan Publishing House, 1997), 13.

[2] Steve McVey, *A Divine Invitation* (Eugene, OR: Harvest House Publishers, 2002), 132.

[3] Rev C.H. Spurgeon, *The Allegories of Sarah and Hagar*, (Sermon No. 69, Delivered on Sabbath Morning, March 2, 1856, at New Park Street Chapel, Southwark.
Blue Letter Bible.org)

[4] Chuck Swindoll, *The Grace Awakening* (Dallas TX: Word Publishing, 1990), 19.

[5] Ibid.

[6] Charles Trumbull, *Victory in Christ* (Fort Washington, PA: CLC Publications, pocket companion edition, 1991), 56.

[7] Brennan Manning, *Reflections for Ragamuffins* (Harper San Francisco, 1998), 1

[8] Rev C.H. Spurgeon, *The Allegories of Sarah and Hagar* (Sermon No. 69, Delivered on Sabbath Morning, March 2, 1856, at New Park Street Chapel, Southwark. Blue Letter Bible.org)

[9] Anne Lamott, *Traveling Mercies; Some Thoughts on Faith* (New York: Anchor Books, 1999), 139.

**Chapter 14**
[1] Bob George, *Growing in Grace* (Eugene, OR: Harvest House Publishers, 1991), 12.
[2] Matthew Henry, *A Commentary of the Whole Bible* (Old Tappon, NJ: Flemming H. Revell Company), 457.
[3] George Sanchez, *Changing Your Thought Patterns*, (Booklet from I.A.B.C.), 6.
[4] Ibid, 8.

**Chapter 15**
[1] J.I. Packer, *Knowing God* (Downers Grove, IL: InterVarsity Press, 1973), 14-15.
[2] Tim Hansel, *Holy Sweat* (Dallas TX: Word Publishing, 1987), 30.
[3] J. I. Packer
[4] Phillips, Michael, *A God to Call Father* (Wheaton, IL: Tyndale House Publishers, Inc, 1994), 53-54.
[5] Steve Frye, *I AM; The Unveiling of God* (Sisters, OR: Multnomah Publishers, 2000), 34.
[6] J. I. Packer, 14.
[7] Source unknown.

**Chapter 16**
[1] A.W. Tozer, quote from an old sermon transferred from reel-to reel by Gordon Donaldson onto cassette tape.
[2] Malcolm Smith, from personal tape series.
[3] Ibid.
[4] Manning, Brennan, *Reflections for Ragamuffins* (San Francisco CA: Harper, 1998), 33.
[5] Max Lucado, *The Great House of God*.

**Chapter 17**
[1] St. Anselm, *The NIV Worship Bible* (Dana Point, CA: The Corinthian Group, Inc 1984), 1573.

[2] Manning, Brennan, *Reflections for Ragamuffins* (San Francisco CA: Harper, 1998), 235.

[3] Tim Hansel, *Holy Sweat* (Dallas: Word Publishing, 1987), 61.

[4] Kathy Bence, *Under Her Wings* (Nashville TN, Upper Room Books, 2001), 106.

[5] Tim Hansel, *Holy Sweat* (Dallas: Word Publishing, 1987), 37.

[6] Hansel, 151.

[7] Charles Trumbull, *Victory in Christ* (Fort Washington, PA: CLC Publications, 2002), 30.

[8] John Piper, *The Dangerous Duty of Delight* (Sisters, OR: Multnomah, 2001), 64.

[9] C. S. Lewis, *The Weight of Glory and Other Addresses* (Grand Rapids, MI: Eerdmans, 1965), 1-2.

[10] Hansel, 159.

[11] Charles Swindoll, *The Grace Awakening* (Dallas: Word Publishing, 1990), 139.

[12] Joseph Garlinton, *NIV Worship Bible* (Dana Point, CA: The Corinthian Group, Inc., 1984), 1565.

[13] H. R. Roush, *Jesus Loves Me*, Available at www.jesuslovesme.com.

## Chapter 18

[1] Ken Gire, *Windows of the Soul* (Grand Rapids, MI: Zondervan Publishing House, 1996), book jacket.

[2] Spiros Zodiates, *Hebrew-Greek Key Study Bible, New American Standard* (Chattanooga, TN: AMG Publishers, 1997), 1838.

[3] Jean Eudes, *The NIV Worship Bible* (Dana Point, CA: The Corinthian Group, Inc., 1984), 1533.

# ABOUT THE AUTHOR

**Bill Ewing** founded Christian Life Ministries in 1981. Since then, he and his staff have reached out to thousands of hurting, broken and frustrated lives with a fresh and thoroughly biblical approach for living life that offers true freedom, healing, hope, and peace.

Bill was Co-founder of the International Association of Biblical Counselors (IABC) and is an Associate Member of the Association of Exchanged Life Ministries. He is ordained through the Evangelical Church Alliance and holds a double major in Criminal Law and Psychology from the University of Wyoming.

He is an accomplished athlete, particularly in baseball where he was a College All American, held the National Home Run Record and was a record setting professional player in the California Angels farm system until a shoulder injury ended his career in 1979.

He and his wife, Nancy, live in the Black Hills of South Dakota. They have three grown sons.

For more information on Bill Ewing's counseling and speaking services, contact Bill at www.reallifepress.com or at:

Christian Life Ministries(CLM), P.O. Box 9272, Rapid City, SD 57709

Call 605-341-5305 or visit them at www.clmweb.org.

# ABOUT THE COLLABORATING WRITERS

**Donna Wallace** has written nine books and has several more on the way. She has taught and studied on university campuses for thirteen years, has been a founder of two postmodern churches and is a licensed Minister of Education with a Masters degree in Theological Studies. She loves speaking, writing, and guiding retreats in the areas of Intimacy and Identity Development.

To find out more about Donna's speaking and writing ministry, visit her website at **www.mereimages.org**.

**Todd Hillard** has been a pastor and a missionary with the Evangelical Free Church of America since 1987. He has a B.S. in Psychology from the University of Utah and a M.A. in English Linguistics from the University of Arizona. He is the founder of "Real Life Press," which is dedicated to the production of quality publications for the body, soul, and spirit.

Besides writing, he specializes in speaking to teens and adults on the topics of grace, identity, temptation and sexuality. Contact him at todd@reallifepress.com.

# OTHER MATERIALS FROM BILL EWING AND CHRISTIAN LIFE MINISTRIES:

## Playing and Coaching Winning Baseball and Softball

AS A RECORD SETTING PROFESSIONAL BASEBALL PLAYER with the California Angels farm system, Bill Ewing's love for the sport serves as the foundation of this wonderful three part training video, designed for coaches, parents and players.

In part 1, Bill draws on decades of experience as a player and coach to outline a powerful structure for practice sessions that increases productivity, confidence, teamwork, and fun!

In part 2, he instructs in the basics of the sport and critical skill development. Rich in special tips and drills, this section gives clear and complete guidelines for increasing the abilities of any player.

Finally, in part 3, Bill talks from the heart about developing a personal coaching philosophy. Drawn from many of the principles found in Rest Assured, Bill will help you build up your team, players, and parents in a healthy, encouraging athletic environment.

*Playing and Coaching Winning Baseball and Softball* is now available on VHS tape and DVD for $24.99 through Real Life Press.

See www.reallifepress.com for details!

# Rest Assured Training Course

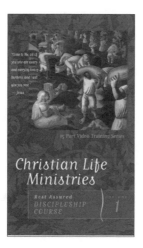

THE PRINCIPLES DISCUSSED IN Rest Assured ARE DRAWN FROM Christian Life Ministry's Lay Ministry Training Course. The LMT course has been attended by hundreds of pastors, parents and students of all ages. They consistently find that the truths taught in this class are effective tools in ministering to their families and churches, as well as leading to unique spiritual growth in their own personal lives.

This expanded course is available for small group Bible studies, Sunday School classes, and counselor training. The complete course material includes videos or DVDs of the 15 sessions, extensive class handouts, and one set of supplementary audiotapes, booklets and books.

Available only through:
Christian Life Ministries
P.O. Box 9272, Rapid City, SD 57709
Call 605-341-5305 or visit them at www.clmweb.org.

ADDITIONAL COPIES OF

# REST ASSURED

CAN BE PURCHASED THROUGH:

**Real Life Press**

purchase online at
**www.reallifepress.com**

Be sure to visit our website for special internet prices, volume discounts, and information on upcoming books, study guides and projects.